Sentaro, Japan's Sam Patch

Cook, Castaway, Christian

F. Calvin Parker

iUniverse, Inc.
New York   Bloomington

Sentaro, Japan's Sam Patch
Cook, Castaway, Christian

iUniverse books may be ordered through booksellers or by contacting:

iUniverse
1663 Liberty Drive
Bloomington, IN 47403
www.iuniverse.com
1-800-Authors (1-800-288-4677)

Because of the dynamic nature of the Internet, any Web addresses or links contained in this book may have changed since publication and may no longer be valid.

ISBN: 978-1-4401-9838-0 (sc)
ISBN: 978-1-4401-9839-7 (ebk)

Printed in the United States of America

iUniverse rev. date: 1/15/2010

Contents

Illustrations

Note on Japanese Terms

In this book Japanese personal names are written in the Japanese order, with the surname first. References to Japanese authors of works in English preserve the original (usually Western) order.

Consonants in Japanese terms are generally pronounced as in English, except that the doubling of a consonant indicates a protraction of its sound. Vowels and diphthongs are pronounced approximately as follows:

a as in f*a*ther
e as in r*e*d
i as in mach*i*ne
o as in h*o*me
u as in r*u*le
ai as in *ai*sle
ei as in *ei*ght

A macron over an *ō* or *ū* indicates that the pronunciation is prolonged. In the main text the macrons are omitted from well-known place names (Tōkyō, Kyōto, Ōsaka, Kōbe, Hokkaidō, Honshū, Kyūshū), and common nouns that have entered the English language, such as shogun (*shōgun*).

Acknowledgments

As the subject of a book-length biography, Japan's Sam Patch is a formidable challenge because his life is relatively obscure. Some of his years are quite well documented, but others have to be reconstructed from parsimonious data. Teasing out valid scraps of information from the scattered, often unreliable, sources has been fun but also frustrating. Had it not been for the help and encouragement of many friends, I could not have finished this work.

Chief among these enablers is Kawashima Daijirō, whose input was indispensable when I wrote *Jonathan Goble of Japan: Marine, Missionary, Maverick* (1990). Through the years, Kawashima has shared with me the Japanese-language materials he uncovered not only on Goble but also on Sam Patch, Goble's protégé. I have relied heavily on the sagacious judgments expressed in both his personal letters and his publications.

Miyachi Yasunobu, a Baptist pastor, zealously pursued the life of Sam Patch (Sentarō) as the first Japanese Baptist. He published his findings in many issues of a paper titled *Shu no ashiato* (The Lord's footprints). Miyachi introduced me to *Dotō o koeta otokotachi* (Men who overcame the raging sea), an important study of Sentarō and his fellow sea drifters. The book's chief author, Inoue Tomoyoshi, kindly donated a copy for my use.

Chikamori Haruyoshi, longtime president of the Joseph Heco Society in Japan, visited me when I lived in Tokyo and often sent me long letters and relevant publications in response to my questions. His two biographies of Heco have also proved helpful.

Ogasa Yoshinori, a reporter for the *Chūgoku shimbun,* Hiroshima's leading newspaper, called on me when he was visiting the United States in pursuit of Sam Patch's trail. We picked one another's brains, and I drove him to Margaret Ballagh's old home in Virginia to investigate traditions about Sam's alleged visit there. After returning to Japan, Ogasa wrote up his findings in a series of forty-four articles and kindly sent me copies.

Katherine Plummer gave me a copy of her highly readable work, *The Shogun's Reluctant Ambassadors: Sea Drifters,* after we met at a conference in Tokyo. One of her major sources was Haruna Akira, on whose *Hyōryū:*

Josefu Hiko to nakamatachi (Drifting: Joseph Heco and his companions) I too have drawn heavily with deep appreciation for the author.

Marilyn Reppun of the Hawaiian Mission Children's Society Library in Honolulu and Charlene Dahlquist of the Lyman House Memorial Museum in Hilo facilitated my research into Sam's visits to Hawaii.

Closer to home, the late Herbert A. Wisbey Jr., who collected a trove of local material on Goble and his protégé in New York State, aided and encouraged me on numerous occasions. Ruth Simmons, curator of the W. E. Griffis Collection at Rutgers University, went out of her way repeatedly to meet my needs. Staff personnel at many other libraries have likewise shown outstanding courtesy in rendering assistance. I think especially of personnel in the Yokohama Archives of History, the Shizuoka Prefectural Library, and the Japanese collections at Cornell University and Duke University. To all I am deeply grateful.

Finally, I wish to thank David and Betty Swain for reading the nearly final manuscript. Their comments were most valuable. I also thank Lauren Ann Finley and Andrew Parker for two illustrations drawn for this book, and my wife Harriett for her proofreading and encouragement. I alone am responsible for the errors and deficiencies that remain.

This work is a revision of *The Japanese Sam Patch: Saga of a Servant* (Notre Dame, IN: Cross Cultural Publications, 2001). The publisher ceased operations in 2005.

Note on citations: I have often reduced the number of reference notes in a paragraph by grouping two or more citations in one note. Quotations are cited first, in the order of their appearance.

Introduction

IN the northwest corner of Charlotte Cemetery, Rochester, New York, there stands a three-foot-high granite stone with a bronze plaque inscribed as follows:

> The Grave of
> SAM PATCH
> Who Leaped to His Death
> Over the Upper Falls and Into
> The Genesee River
> At Rochester, N. Y.
> Friday, November 13th, 1829
> His Remains Were Found
> In the Lower Genesee River
> March 17th, 1830
> And Interred in This
> CEMETERY[1]

This Sam Patch was an agile cotton spinner who for two or three years entertained the public with spectacular leaps from dizzy heights. He jumped from topmasts and yardarms, from bridges and cliffs and makeshift perches. He even conquered Niagara Falls. His feats attracted ever-growing crowds, making him a national celebrity and generating such nervous strain that one spectator bit off the end of his thumb. Andrew Jackson, who named his frisky horse Sam Patch, was in the first year of his presidency when the great daredevil made his Friday-the-thirteenth leap over the High Falls into the swirling Genesee River and into the rich folklore of his country.

Even though Sam's body was eventually found and duly buried, as the bronze plaque affirms, rumors of his survival had a life of their own. All too often his fans had shouted "He's dead!" only to see him reappear. There were Sam Patch sightings not unlike the more recent Elvis Presley sightings. Wild stories were fabricated, fantastic legends were born. The death-defying showman, it was rumored, had jumped from London Bridge and dined with the British queen. Another story had it that a New England sea captain had found him in the China Sea. Nurtured by credulity and embellishment, these and other fanciful tales persisted through the years.

More than two decades had passed when, in one of those peculiar twists of history, a New England sea captain did find a Sam Patch in the China Sea. Commodore Matthew C. Perry, a native of Rhode Island, arrived at Shanghai in 1853 to lead a naval expedition to Japan. Awaiting him aboard the war steamer *Susquehanna* was a plucked-from-the-ocean sailor who had been added to the ship's roster under the name of Sam Patch.[2] This Sam

Book cover illustration, 1870

was one of seventeen Japanese mariners rescued from the storm-battered junk *Eiriki-maru,* taken to San Francisco, then consigned to the Perry expedition for repatriation. The U.S. government had noted the castaways' potential usefulness as negotiating chips for persuading Japan to end its centuries-old isolation from the outside world. But when Perry transferred his commandant's flag to the *Susquehanna* for the dangerous foray into forbidden Japanese waters, Sam Patch was the only one of the seventeen castaways still under U.S. naval jurisdiction. Indeed, he was the sole Japanese to accompany the expedition that concluded an historic treaty of friendship between the United States and Japan.

Sam's potential for strengthening Perry's hand in the negotiations, never substantial, went unexploited. The commodore's tact, firmness, and firepower spelled success. What Sam contributed to that colorful drama was an entertaining sideshow. He groveled before pompous officials who wanted him back in Japan, but as Perry's *Narrative of the Expedition* says, "all the eloquence and persuasiveness of the Japanese were insufficient to induce him to leave the ship."[3] The lowly seaman made a mockery of those two-sworded dignitaries who might have whacked off his head had the American flag not been waving over their own heads.

Thus Japan's Sam Patch was catapulted into the history books of two leading countries of the world. His sobriquet, a Western household name, contributed to his prominence and, because of the peculiar customs regarding names in Japan, enhanced his pedigree.

From Sentarō to Sam Patch

Like their Western counterparts, Japanese writers and artists made generous use of pseudonyms. Benjamin Franklin used more than fifty; Hokusai used at least thirty. But in Japan it was conventional for men in the upper ranks of society to use a string of personal names regardless of literary or artistic bent. The custom filtered down to commoners like Sam, who under a snobbish feudal law were not permitted to have a family name except in special cases. In part compensation for this deprivation, commoners could and did use a plethora of personal names, nicknames, and aliases. One of Sam's shipmates, for instance, was variously known as Bunta, Yotarō, and Rishichi. Obviously, one's names could be totally dissimilar.[4]

Sam's names included Sentarō, Santarō, Sempachi, Kurasuke, Kurajirō, Kurazō, Unosuke, and perhaps Matō. The bestowal of Sam Patch on the sailor-cook went beyond all these by including a surname, something he would never have gained in feudal Japan. The Western sobriquet also became an unmistakable badge of identity amid the daze of multiple Japanese names. His gravestone bears one name only, which is written with two kanji (Chinese ideographs) and pronounced Sampachi.

American sailors habitually christened a foreign crewmate with a familiar name rather than cope with one they could not pronounce. But in this case, why did they choose Sam Patch instead of something like the later "Joe Jap"? The sailors on the *Susquehanna* who scaled its masts when the boilers were shut down must have known about America's famous "Jumping Sam," himself a one-time sailor. Some may have heard about a vessel of the U.S. Revenue Service named *Sam Patch*.[5] When a shy little man from Japan was thrust into their midst, something about this exotic being brought their own folk hero to mind. No doubt the sailors noticed the ease with which the waif, though not a stuntman, jumped about the ship and threaded his way through the rigging. But more important, his unpronounceable name or names sounded a little like Sam Patch.

Clara Arthur Mason, a Baptist missionary in Tokyo who cared for Sam during his final days, identified that name as *shimpai*. This is a common word meaning worry or anxiety. Sam would mumble *"shimpai, shimpai"* whenever he felt uneasy, and especially when kidded about the fate that likely awaited him in Japan. "The sailors thinking it might be his name," Mason explained, "Americanized this word, Shimpai, into Sam Patch and by this name he went until his death."[6] Whether she heard this explanation directly from her dying houseguest is unclear.

Edward Warren Clark, a science teacher who employed Sam as cook, gave a different explanation after quizzing him about his past. "It was while on board the *Mississippi*," Clark wrote, "that the sailors—who could not pronounce his Jap name—dubbed him with the title of 'Sam Patch,' as the nearest equivalent to his real name which they could think of."[7] The "real name" familiar to Clark was Sentarō or Santarō. He probably did not know that a sketch based on a daguerreotype taken of Sam in San Francisco prior to the Perry expedition bore the caption "Simpatch" (equivalent to Sempachi). This name is much closer to "Sam Patch," pronounced Sampachi in Japanese. So Clark's explanation is more plausible than Mason's. But contrary to Clark, the Japanese landsman was called Sam Patch in the deck log of the *Susquehanna* before he ever laid eyes on the *Mississippi*. Perhaps Sam himself confused the two ships or forgot when he first began to hear the name.

The *Mississippi* brought Sam to New York, where he returned to civilian life under the patronage of Jonathan Goble, a shipmate discharged from the marines. A pious Baptist with a flawed character, Goble regarded Sam as a potential asset to his future missionary work in Japan. As Goble's protégé, Sam gained a smattering of English education in Hamilton, New York, but resisted efforts to convert him to the Christian faith. Three years passed before he submitted to an icy-creek baptism and emerged as the first known Japanese Baptist. In 1860, despite mistreatment at the hands of his patron, Sam accompanied Jonathan and Eliza Goble to Japan as helper and cook.

The Gobles, devoid of adequate financial support from America, turned Sam over to Robbins and Elizabeth Brown, Dutch Reformed Church missionaries with the resources to support him. The Browns released Sam to their younger colleagues James and Margaret Ballagh, who became so dependent on their "faithful but inefficient servant" that they brought him along when Margaret, neurotic and pregnant, required medical treatment in America.[8] Sam later worked as cook for E. Warren Clark, as noted above, and part-time coachman for Nakamura Masanao, a renowned literary scholar. When Sam died of beriberi in 1874, Clark and Nakamura buried him in Nakamura's family plot at Hondenji, a Buddhist temple in Tokyo.

Small but Significant

Clark testified that the box into which Sam's lifeless body was stuffed was "scarcely three feet square." He was a small man indeed. In 1950, a full century after the castaway's rescue, the average height of Japanese males was only five feet four inches (163 centimeters). This represented a sharp increase of nearly three inches over the average stature of military recruits in 1900, an increase credited to improvements in diet and medical care. Since these improvements date mainly from the opening of Western settlements, William Elliot Griffis was probably correct when he wrote in *The Mikado's Empire* (1876) that the average height of Japanese men was five feet.[9]

Sam must have been shorter still. F. C. Pollay of Pulteney, New York, a sailor who returned home with Sam on the *Mississippi*, noted that the Japanese were "what we call a small people," then cited Sam Patch as "a fair sample of the average Jap." But he wrote these words fifty years after the two were together, when his recollection might have been skewed. Another of Sam's acquaintances wrote that the Japanese "are generally much larger than he is." This assessment is more reliable because it was current, not a memory of the distant past.[10]

If Sam's body was diminutive, so was his mind. "They tried to make a minister of him," Clara Mason wrote, "but he was a man of small intellectual ability, and preferred manual labor." To Warren Clark he was a man of "humble capacity." "Sam had great opportunities in the world," Clark observed, "but he didn't have any brains to start on." William Griffis, who visited Clark and Sam in Shizuoka and shared his house with them in Tokyo, commented that Sam's head had "never been ballasted with over two-thirds the average quantum of wit."[11]

Indeed, when Sam fell into American hands he was illiterate, never having attended school. And when he reentered his country with the Gobles nearly a decade later, he could read and write but little English despite several years of classroom instruction. It was a time in Japan "when a scrappy knowledge of English might be turned to very good account," wrote the Quaker statesman Nitobe Inazō. But "Sam lacked Yankee pluck," Nitobe observed, "and he lived and died a poor house-servant."[12]

By way of contrast, Sam's junk mate Hikozō, christened Joseph Heco in the Roman Catholic Church, acquired American citizenship and played so significant a role in Japan that a Joseph Heco Society flourishes today. No such scholarly attention has come to Sam Patch. But even one of mediocre talent and lackluster career becomes interesting when that person copes with a strange culture, communicates in a foreign tongue, converts to a feared religion, toils for an alien taskmaster, and bears the taunts of his own kind. All these Sam did.

The timing adds to the significance of Sam's experiences. He came to a California engulfed in the gold rush, lived in New York State when the whole country was about to explode over slavery, visited a Hawaii resisting American influence, and returned to Japan with a religious faith then proscribed by law. For five years, apparently, he was the only Japanese Protestant in the country.

Again, sailors and cooks and coachmen become worthy of notice if they work for or are associated with well-known people, whose lives they often illuminate. As noted already, Sam's life is intertwined with the lives of Heco and Perry; the Gobles, Browns, and Ballaghs; Clark, Griffis, and Nakamura. He served them in the same way a stage assistant dressed in black serves Kabuki actors. His nimble movements in the shadows help them do well in the limelight. In their prominence lies his own claim to fame.

Sentarō (Sam Patch)

Sam Patch has gained sufficient notice to be the victim of misinformation. Frederick Wells Williams wrongly assumed that he had sailed to Japan on the *Morrison* long before joining the Perry expedition. Another scholar, Harry Emerson Wildes, helped perpetuate this confusion. Perry's *Narrative of the Expedition* is misleading in a different way. It strongly implies, and some writers have subsequently affirmed, that Sam accompanied the expedition by his own free choice. His Japanese shipmates testified rather that he was held hostage and taken against his will.[13]

Several Japanese writers declare that Sam assisted Jonathan Goble with his translation of Matthew's Gospel, the oldest extant Bible portion published in Japan. A stone tablet at Sam's grave adds that he "devoted himself fully to its completion." In fact, Sam had no part in the translation except for teaching Goble some Japanese many years earlier. More astonishing, a biography of Sam was published in a series on heroes of the Christian faith. The series was aimed at young readers fifth grade and up.

Among others featured are the social worker Sawada Miki, the Bible teacher and essayist Uchimura Kanzō, and the Salvation Army leader Yamamuro Gumpei. Adding Sam to the ranks of these spiritual giants required considerable manipulation and embellishment of the facts. Unfortunately, it is not obvious to nonspecialists that the book is hagiographic and laced with imaginative details—even a fabricated account of Sam's wedding. Indeed, the life of this modest castaway-turned-Christian has been distorted by tales no less fanciful than those told of the original Sam Patch.[14]

More recently, Sam was pressed into service as guide to students exploring a website featuring the Black Ship Scroll. This scroll by anonymous Japanese artists is a colorful depiction of Commodore Perry's visit to the port of Shimoda. The figure captioned "Japanese interpreter Matō" may have been Sam Patch (see page 68). Sam has also gained attention as the likely subject of one of the oldest extant photographs of a Japanese, which bears a striking resemblance to the sketch of Sam based on the San Francisco daguerreotype (see pages 31 and 33).[15]

Finally, there is something cathartic and refreshing about the life of a faithful servant who was meek and reserved, the virtual opposite of his flamboyant namesake. The American Sam Patch liked to shout, "There is no mistake in Sam Patch!" He would have made a curtain call at Genesee Falls had he emerged from the foam. In contrast, the Japanese Sam Patch was no show-off, no publicity hound, no braggart. True, Warren Clark once noted that Sam could amuse others with his "droll style and strange stories," but that was about the extent of his showmanship.[16] Perhaps this book will help him step out of the shadows and unzip his black disguise.

Chapter 1

Gods and Demons at Sea

From this ship [a Southern Barbarian trading vessel] for the first time emerged an unnamable creature, somewhat similar in shape to a human being, but looking rather more like a long-nosed goblin or the giant demon Mikoshi Nyūdō.
— Unknown author of *Kirishitan Monogatari*[1]

IKUCHIJIMA—a five-syllable name that trips up foreigners but rolls easily off a Japanese tongue—is one of the myriad islands and islets that dot the picturesque Inland Sea. A tourist favorite, Ikuchijima offers a charming blend of old and new attractions dispersed over twelve square miles of lush terrain. The island's crown jewel is Kōsanji, a Buddhist temple constructed in the twentieth century but so classical in splendor that it is called the Nikkō of Western Japan. Hordes of pilgrims and sightseers come by ferry or over the mammoth new bridges that link Ikuchijima with Shikoku and the mainland of Honshu. The once-secluded island where Sam Patch was born about 1831, the second year of the Tempō era, has been caught up in the stunning development of greater Japan.[2]

Sam disappeared at sea in 1850 and was presumed dead by relatives and friends. He eventually made his way back to Japan, but there is no record he ever again set foot on Ikuchijima. Japanese school children are well acquainted with the legend of Urashima Tarō, who spent a happy three years in the sea-god's palace and then returned to his home village. He barely recognized the place, because unbeknownst to him, not three years but three hundred years had passed since he left. If Sam were to emulate the folktale hero and reappear phantom-like today, he would be equally bewildered. Sam would find that Ikuchijima, little changed in two millennia of history before his shipwreck, has since undergone a staggering transformation.

Even so, Sam would not be utterly lost. There are ancient landmarks that would catch his eye at once. The temple Kōmyōbō dates from the eighth century, and the three-tiered pagoda of Kōjōji from the fifteenth.

Also intact is Sam's family temple, Kōfukuji, where he and the other neighborhood children likely played hide-and-seek, hop-scotch, and blindman's buff in the temple grounds. Some of the houses and mud walls are also centuries old. Mandarin orange trees flourish now as then, though in fewer groves. And on a clear day Shikoku and Honshu are still visible from the peak of Kannon Mountain. With a little imagination, a resurrected Sam Patch could blot out the newfangled bridges from the marvelous view he enjoyed as a youth.

Sam's native village was Fukuda, adjacent to and now a part of Setoda. In ancient times Setoda was a sheltered pirate base. With the development of water commerce in the Edo period (1603–1868), it became a prosperous fishing and shipping port as well as a breeding ground for hardy seamen like Sam Patch, proud heirs to the daring of the pirates. Setoda's population at the time of Sam's birth was about 1,750, or six hundred households.[3]

Little is known of Sam's family. The death register in Kōfukuji reveals that his father's name was Kumazō. Probably a fisherman and part-time farmer, Kumazō had no family name to bequeath his only son. As noted in the Introduction, the lower classes—peasants, artisans, merchants—had to make do without surnames, which were restricted to priests, nobles, and samurai. Exceptions were sometimes made for meritorious achievement, as in the case of Manjirō, who like Sam was a fisherman's son and a castaway who had been taken to America. After his return to Japan in 1851, Manjirō was raised to samurai status and granted the surname Nakahama in recognition of his valued expertise on the outside world. Thanks to his fate at sea, Manjirō was helpfully informed about shipbuilding, whaling, and peculiar Western customs such as reading while seated on the commode.[4]

Although Sam Patch never earned a Japanese surname, he did accumulate a plethora of personal names. The first was his "child name," customarily given within a week of birth. Probably this was Sentarō. His Japanese shipmates called him Sentarō, as did Americans who knew him well. It is the primary name used of him by Japanese writers today. This book uses the name from this point in his life story until he acquires his American nickname.

At times Sentarō was also called by the variant Santarō, an appellation that means "stupid" or "fool." Stupid he was, in the sense of unlearned. Sentarō's ignorance of kanji is evidence that he lacked formal schooling. He grew up at a time when, by rough estimates, no more than 45 percent of the male population and 15 percent of the female could read and write. Although commoners studied in thousands of popular schools called *terakoya*, and in exceptional cases were admitted to official domain schools, the majority of children, even boys, never sat in a classroom.[5]

Sentarō shared in the religious worldview of his rural community, which cherished folklore and honored Buddhist and Shinto deities alike. He reveled in the dances and music of the *bon* festivals honoring the dead and probably took part in the traditional shrine ceremonies for boys in their third and fifth years. No doubt he revered the Jizō statues that abounded on Ikuchijima. These were replicas of the compassionate bodhisattva who could protect seamen as well as children. Sentarō's family temple was affiliated with Rinzai, one of the two major sects of Zen Buddhism, but it is unlikely that this connection had a significant bearing on Sentarō's life. Registration at a temple had been legally required of all citizens since the seventeenth century, when this system, called *terauke,* was adopted to help identify and exterminate Christians.

Before reaching his teens Sentarō was hit with a series of tragic losses that inevitably left their scars. His maternal grandfather Jūemon died in Tempō 12 (1841). His mother, identified in the temple register only as Kumazō's wife, died the following year, and his father the year after that. The orphaned child was probably cared for by a relative, perhaps his uncle Tasaburō. No record survives of his early teens, but he probably took part in the customary *gempuku* or coming-of-age ceremony at about the age of fifteen. He would have received gifts of adult clothing, which for the lower classes included a loincloth, and a "current name" that may have incorporated the name of his sponsor. This name might have been Kurazō, by which Sentarō identified himself to Japanese officials during the Perry expedition. Two variations found in other references to Sentarō are Kurajirō and Kurasuke. In all three names *kura* means storehouse and implies a wish to rise above poverty and be a person of means.

Life on the *Eiriki-maru*

In 1850, Sentarō took his first step in that upward direction when he was employed as cook on the newly built *Eiriki-maru* (literally, "prosperity-power ship"). Owned by Matsuya Yasaburō, a sake brewer in the district of Nada on Osaka Bay, the *Eiriki-maru* was a *taru kaisen*, a "barrel circuit ship" designed to carry barrels (*taru*) of sake from Osaka to Edo. Osaka was the nation's commercial center, its storehouse and "kitchen." Edo, later named Tokyo, was the nation's political capital and voracious consumer market, with about half its population made up of samurai and their employees. On this highly lucrative and competitive route the barrel barges had gained ascendency over their chief rivals, the *higaki kaisen,* distinguished by the diamond-shaped bamboo latticework along their bulwarks. So Sentarō had good reason to feel secure in his job.[6]

The *Eiriki-maru,* like other barrel junks, was a primitive version of today's efficient container vessels. To ensure profits in the highly competitive shipping business, the barrel junk was designed to carry a maximum cargo of sake barrels and to load and unload the barrels in minimum time. In the case of the *Eiriki-maru,* the cargo space was officially listed as fifteen hundred *koku* (a *koku* was about ten cubic feet), but the actual capacity was closer to two thousand *koku.* Its gross tonnage was about two hundred tons. Yet this behemoth—said to be thirty meters long (nearly one hundred feet)—required a crew of only sixteen, no more than the average junk.[7]

Aboard the *Eiriki-maru* Sentarō presided over his own little kitchen, a swaying, creaking galley where he boiled tubs of rice and prepared mounds of fish and vegetables for a hard-working crew. The position of cook was a lowly one, customarily filled by a teenager, but Sentarō must have felt proud to work the prized route to Edo on one of the largest ships he had ever seen.

In the fall of 1850 the *Eiriki-maru* left Osaka for Edo with a typical cargo. Listed in the manifest were

1,931 barrels of sake
150 barrels of soy sauce
240 barrels of sugar
20 rolls of paper
43 jars of tea
26 barrels of dried bonito[8]

Japanese junk at sea

The voyage generally took a month. Modern ships make that run overnight, but the cargo junks in the mid-nineteenth century skirted the coasts and made frequent stops. Commodore Perry observed that "they run from port to port, invariably seeking shelter on occasions of adverse winds or appearances of bad weather."[9] Though reasonably safe in calm inland waterways, the junks were clearly unfit for stormy seas. Taking a shortcut across a broad expanse of water was often the path to oblivion. Scores of disabled junks had been caught up in the Japan Current (called

Kuroshio, or "Black Current") and carried across the northern Pacific and even to American shores.

Japanese mariners had known better days. In the early 1600s Japan boasted a great fleet of ships plying the waters of Southeast Asia, even three-masted leviathans that carried as many as three hundred passengers. Two purely Western vessels built in Japan under foreign supervision crossed the Pacific Ocean to Mexico. But in the 1630s the Tokugawa shogunate, determined to extinguish Christian influence by a rigid policy of national seclusion, issued a series of edicts that forbade the dispatching of ships abroad. It even imposed the death penalty on Japanese who returned from abroad (the sentence was sometimes commuted). Western-style ships were destroyed, and Japanese-style junks were limited to the size of five hundred *koku.* Afterwards, for the sake of efficient coastal trade, the limit on junks was raised to fifteen hundred *koku* (roughly 150 tons), and as indicated above, fudging was allowed.[10]

Whatever its size, the Japanese junk was unfit for the high seas by virtue of its design. It was a cumbersome ship with little or no keel and with a high, open stern that allowed for the huge rectangular rudder, up to nine by twelve feet, to be lifted in shallow water. So though it was durable and economical to operate, the junk was hard to maneuver. The quarter-deck or poop-deck rose to an abrupt angle of fifty degrees from the main deck to the stern, forcing the helmsman to make a difficult balance. To Sir Rutherford Alcock, the helm resembled "the proboscis of a colossal elephant."[11]

The mariners who faced the perils of the sea on these clumsy vessels relied not only on their own skills but on luck and the help of the gods. Many sailors had the word *kichi* (good luck) as a part of their name. Every junk had its *funadama,* or ship's charm, placed in the cavity where the single mast was set at the time of construction. The charm consisted of diverse items such as coins, dice, grains of rice, and strands of hair (the hair might come from the shipowner's wife). In addition, the junk often had a miniature Shinto shrine.[12]

The guardian deity of seafarers was Kompira, a Buddhist-Shinto deity said to have its origins in an Indian crocodile god. The famous Kotohira Shrine near Marugame in Shikoku was dedicated to Kompira, but so were lesser shrines in virtually every seaside town and village. Every ship had a charm issued by the Kompira shrine where it was based. Many a seaman carried a small Kompira amulet on his body next to his skin. It was said that if a pious sailor caught in a storm at sea called upon this god in prayer, a mysterious light would guide him to safety.[13]

Sailors also looked up to their captain, a mortal whose command could make the difference between survival and death. The *Eiriki-maru*'s Captain Manzō, a native of Banshū (also called Harima and now Hyōgo Prefecture), was a patriarchal sixty years of age. His crewmen, by contrast, were in their thirties or below with the exception of the fifty-year-old steersman, Chōsuke (or Chōnosuke). Oriental culture put a premium on age as well as position, so Manzō commanded high respect. Yet he was more like a father than a commander. He and his hand-picked crew worked as a team.[14]

Manzō was also distinguished by the color of his skin. An anonymous writer who later saw him in America described him as "white," in contrast to his crewmen who, like the majority of Japanese, were "copper color." The writer speculated that this might be the result of Japanese intermarriage with Mongols captured during the thirteenth-century invasion or with Portuguese and Dutch a few centuries later. Whatever the explanation, it is estimated that up to 10 percent of many local populations in central Japan, where Manzō and his crew were based, have light skin color and other Caucasoid traits.[15]

Enter Hikozō (Joseph Heco)

En route to Edo the *Eiriki-maru* put in at Kumano on the Kii Peninsula. The junk *Sumiyoshi-maru* happened to be in port with a thirteen-year-old boy from Banshū, the home province of not only Captain Manzō but nine members of his crew. Called Hikozō or Hikotarō, the young teen had recently lost his mother and was making his first trip to Edo with his stepfather, the *Sumiyoshi-maru*'s captain. Manzō and his crew urged the lad to switch to their newer vessel for the voyage, promising him a sightseeing tour of the capital. So with his stepfather's reluctant permission, Hikozō transferred to the *Eiriki-maru*, unaware that the two junks would fail to rendezvous at Edo and he would never see his stepfather again. Whether happenstance or an act of the gods, the switch was his initial step toward a fabulous career as Joseph Heco, the first American of Japanese ancestry and one who shook hands with three American presidents, Pierce, Buchanan, and Lincoln.[16]

Before Hikozō came aboard, Sentarō was the youngest crewman on the *Eiriki-maru* and thus recipient of a cherished bit of indulgence from his seniors. The social dynamics changed when a thirteen-year-old was added to the roster. Bright, attractive, and endowed with a temple-school education, Hikozō became immensely popular with his new mates. To his credit, Sentarō seems to have stifled any feelings of jealousy and accepted the crew's new pet without complaint. He probably welcomed the boy heartily, for Hikozō served as apprentice cook, helping Sentarō with his chores.

Lumbering on up the coast, the *Eiriki-maru* made the required stop at Uraga, the customs station at the entrance to Edo Bay. Here inspectors verified that the crewmen and cargo were properly listed in the manifest. They also made certain that no women were hidden aboard, as required by a totalitarian regime that kept the wives and children of daimyo (feudal barons) hostage in Edo and exercised strict and intrusive control over the lives of all its subjects.

As the *Eiriki-maru* sailed up the bay and approached Shinagawa, where it would discharge its cargo, the crewmen could look beyond the island batteries and see the capital's low, wooded hills crowned with massive temples. Shinagawa was not only Edo's major port but its entry station on the Tōkaidō, the coastal highway running to the imperial city of Kyoto. More than 150 daimyo used this route when traveling with their miles-long retinues between Edo and their fiefdoms. So Shinagawa catered to swarms of sex-crazed seamen, foot-weary porters, and swaggering samurai. It had become a hellish paradise with an array of entertainment houses and rows of drinking and gambling dens.

Two of the crewmen steered young Hikozō past the seamy haunts of Shinagawa and into the heart of the world's largest city, its population in excess of one million.[17] Sentarō also must have gone sightseeing with some of his friends. There were so many trees and so much undergrowth that the city resembled a forest. But the autumn shedding of leaves had exposed the imposing mansions and gardens of the daimyo spaced at intervals along the way and enhanced the view of the gleaming, white-paneled wooden castle of the all-powerful shogun. Seemingly endless streets were thickly lined on both sides with two-storied houses roofed with ceramic tiles.

Eiriki-maru crewmen visited the Kannon temple at Asakusa, where they were jostled by the crowds and amused by tumblers and jugglers, mummers and mountebanks, storytellers and insect sellers. They enjoyed the stunning performances at a popular theater. Wherever they went they walked, since the alternative, riding in a *kago* (basket-like chair carried by porters), would put a strain on their wallets. Unlike America, Japan had no trains or trams or buggies. Wheeled conveyances for passengers—rickshas included—first appeared in the 1860s after the invasion by merchants and entrepreneurs from the West.

A mere four days after docking at Shinagawa, the *Eiriki-maru* began its return voyage to Osaka, stopping at Uraga to complete its cargo. As the cargo list indicates and as usual on a return voyage, the barrel junk now carried a different load that utilized only a third of its space.[18]

From Edo (Shinagawa):
    17 pieces of red flowers
    48 pieces of squid
    24 bundles of iron
    218 black whetstones
    9 pieces of hemp and ramie fabric

From Uraga:
    182 sacks of soy beans
    200 sacks of adzuki beans
    33 boxes of walnuts
    211 sacks of dried sardines (used for fertilizer)
    200 sacks of barley
    100 sacks of wheat

The Life-Changing Storm

Hampered by contrary winds despite clear weather, the *Eiriki-maru* beat about the coast down past the port of Shimoda on the Izu Peninsula and crossed Suruga Bay to Cape Omae. By then the winds had turned favorable. Since the fair skies gave every promise of holding out despite the whims of the weather, Captain Manzō chose to run a direct course to Ōshima on the Kii Peninsula, crossing the open sea called Enshū-nada. If there had been any inkling of trouble ahead, he would have prudently headed for the harbors on Ise Bay. But with scores of other vessels taking the shortcut, Manzō thought it a safe course. Like an army of lemmings marching mindlessly into a stretch of deep water, the hundreds of mariners were unaware of the perils that lay ahead.

On December 2, 1850, by the Western calendar, the evening sky turned eerily dark, rain began to fall in torrents, the wind became a roaring gale, and the rising waves threatened to swallow the ponderous junk. The crewmen lowered the huge flapping sail, but the boat "sped on like a flying bird."[19] It tossed and jerked without letup in the mountainous seas, and each plunge into a trough felt as though it would be the last.

So like the terror-stricken sailors in the Old Testament book of Jonah, Sentarō and his fellow crewmen cried out to their gods for mercy. They beseeched the miracle-working Kompira to calm the wind and waves that battered their ship. Some fingered their prayer beads and shouted *Namu Amida Butsu* ("Hail to Amida Buddha"). These perhaps included Chōsuke and at least three others who were registered at Jōdo Shin (True Pure Land) temples. Still others were affiliated with Tendai, Zen, and Shingon temples. Whatever their religious distinctives, all were said to make vows and seek divine intervention.[20]

The next day, following the centuries-old adage that the gods help those who help themselves, the crew jettisoned two hundred sacks of beans and grain and frantically discharged water from the flooding hold. The water reached an alarming depth of six feet, for bailing was inefficient and their hand pump was little more than useless. The junk still pitched and rolled dangerously in the heavy seas. The time had come for radical action.

As was often done when a junk was in peril of capsizing, the mariners proceeded to chop down the hundred-foot mast some two or three feet above the deck. After several hours of toil they leaped back as the giant timber snapped and toppled into the sea, leaving only a ragged stump three feet in diameter. The efficient keg junk now lacked effective means of propulsion. It was a floating, drifting hulk, a Noah's ark with seventeen humans but only one animal—a cat.

The crewmen sighted other dismasted junks moving in the same direction, but they were unable to extend or receive assistance. On the fifth day an island came into view, and some of the crewmen wanted to attempt a landing. Manzō disapproved. Perhaps the unknown island was the home of demons or cannibals who would devour them, he warned; it was safer to wait until they reached the mainland or an island they knew. Unconvinced and a bit defiant, some of the crew consulted divination sticks at the junk's shrine to ascertain the will of the gods. The oracle was ambiguous, merely prolonging the dispute until the island had passed beyond their reach.

Another island came into view that looked like Hachijōjima, located about one hundred miles southeast of the Izu Peninsula. Three of the crewmen—Yasutarō, Seitarō, and Iwakichi—had been on the *Sumikiyo-maru* ten months earlier when it was blown to that very island.[21] Unfortunately, the island lay off the *Eiriki-maru*'s path, and the crew was unable to steer their vessel to shore. It was the last landscape Sentarō and his comrades would see from their stricken junk. Hereafter their eyes would strain at monotonous seascapes day after day after day.

Resigned to their fate, the crew hauled in the heavy rudder, lowered two anchors at the bow, and let the ship drift stern first, pulling the anchors behind them. This stopped the creaking of the rudder, and the junk rode more at ease. The stressed-out men began to relax and to count themselves fortunate to be alive. Expressing their gratitude in the Shinto fashion, they washed their hands, rinsed their mouths, and offered prayers at the little shrine in the stern.

Sailors eating their rice

When free from essential duty, the crew caught and dried mackerel and other fish. They took walnuts from their cargo and squeezed them to obtain oil. Their efforts at distilling salt water were short-lived, since the process consumed too much fuel for the small yield of fresh water. Fortunately, as Sentarō reported later, they "managed to catch rainwater with pans and sheets." Even rainwater tasted salty, so saturated was the whole ship with brine.[22]

For weeks the junk drifted, through weather fair and foul, under skies a brilliant blue and as black as India ink. Since each Japanese month began with a new moon, on the twenty-third day the moon would be in the last quarter. In keeping with a Buddhist custom, Captain Manzō believed in staying up for the late moonrise that night and showing his respects. He took over Sentarō's galley and prepared rice cakes covered with soybean flour, which he offered to the moon ceremonially. Then all the crew ate the food with thankful hearts.

The next day two huge sharks approached the junk in formation. Some crewmen hailed them as messengers of the Shinto god Isobe, sent to protect them. But others quivered at the thought of being eaten by the sharks when the ship broke up, a peril they faced each time the weather took a turn for the worse. In one storm the seas ran so high that the crew dumped more of the cargo overboard. Some prayed and made vows, even cut off their hair. When the winds had moderated and the seas calmed down, the crew further secured the creaking hull with hemp rope, fearful that the nails would loosen too much.

The crewman Bunta, in later testimony to Japanese interrogators, praised the two cooks for their courage and composure. "We've cooked a lot of rice, so eat all you can," Sentarō and Hikozō told the others after an encounter with rough weather. "We don't know what the next storm will bring, but for now, there's food aplenty."[23] Probably Sentarō and his young partner experienced less tension than the others whose daily routine had been more disrupted. And they were more likely to think of the many sacks of beans on hand as well as the rice and whatever fish they could catch.

Saved by the Demons

On the fifty-second day of drifting, Yasutarō went up to the deck at daybreak for his morning ritual. After washing his body in salt water, he turned to the west, toward Japan, and prayed to his ancestral gods for deliverance, just as he had done while drifting on the *Sumikiyo-maru*. He was facing the junk's bow, which pointed to the west as the vessel drifted eastward stern first. Suddenly, far away in the morning mist, something white appeared. Yasutarō rubbed his eyes in disbelief, looked again, then alerted the whole crew.

"Wake up! I see a castle tower!" Yasutarō shouted as he burst into the cabin.[24] The whole crew scrambled to the deck and cast their weary eyes on a ship coming their way. It had three masts and many white sails, some square and some three-cornered, resembling a Dutch ship one of the crew had seen at Nagasaki. As the tall ship approached the *Eiriki-maru*, the sun rising above the opposite horizon made its white sails shimmer and glisten in sharp contrast to the black hull underneath. The Japanese attached a piece of cloth to a bamboo pole and waved it as their distress signal while shouting *Tasukete kure* (Help!) at the top of their lungs. Then they watched in amazement as the ninety-foot-long ship came to a fast and full stop on the high seas. No junk could maneuver like that!

The Japanese looked up at the strange creatures on deck, Hikozō recalled, "who might be, for all we knew, no human beings at all." Caucasians were like extraterrestrials to the Japanese sailors. Probably not one had seen a Westerner, unless at a distance in Nagasaki, and all were affected by the xenophobia that permeated Japan. Since the expulsion of Europeans in the seventeenth century (with the exception of a few Dutch traders confined to Dejima Island in Nagasaki Bay, as in a prison), Westerners were widely caricatured as demons and sub-humans. Popularly called *kōmōjin* (red-haired foreigner) or *ketōjin* (hairy barbarian), they were also variously regarded as wild beasts, monkeys, or criminals (who in Japan were not allowed to shave their faces or heads). One Japanese was to claim that 70 or 80 percent of the people in his country thought of Europeans as no different than dogs and horses.[25]

Despite their jubilation, Sentarō and his mates were reluctant to board the tall black ship. But after drifting more than seven weeks in a crippled junk whose structure might not hold through an eighth week of strain, they had no choice but to take the risk if they wished to survive. They hastily cut loose the small boat from the forward part of the junk and slid it down to the water. They threw in some of their precious rice, the captain's bedding, and a few other personal items. The younger ones tried to save yet more possessions while the older ones already in the boat threatened to cast off without them. After several flurried minutes, all were aboard. The only living creature abandoned with the junk was the feline mascot.

After sculling to the bark, a difficult feat in itself, the bedraggled sailors were hoisted up by rope one by one and welcomed at the gangway by the ship's captain, who stood nonchalantly puffing on a cigar through his mustache and beard. They knelt and bowed, their hands pressed together, symbolically pleading for humane treatment and expressing thanks for their rescue from an all-but-certain death. They would soon learn that the captain was William F. Jennings, and his ship was the American bark *Auckland*, en route from Hong Kong to San Francisco with a cargo of flour, sugar, and tea.

Captain Jennings later reported picking up the Japanese "nearly five hundred miles from their native land."[26] The precise location has been disputed, but what really matters is that two vessels happened to be in the same place at the same time in the vast expanse of the ocean, one crippled by storms, at the mercy of wind and waves, the other following its intended course, seaworthy and fit to save the helpless crew. This fortuitous encounter rescued both ships from the obscurity that otherwise would have been their fate.

Captain Jennings sent three of his own men back to the junk to retrieve additional items of value. But since the men took the Japanese boat that had come from the junk and were unable to control the unfamiliar craft on the rough seas, at length the mission was aborted. Sentarō and his friends, though glad for their rescue, grieved as their once-magnificent *Eiriki-maru*,

Eiriki-maru crewmen transfer to Auckland

bobbing like a cork in angry waters, faded from view. What was its fate? Sentarō was later understood—probably misunderstood—to say that a storm arose and sank the junk about thirty minutes after the rescue. Joseph Heco wrote more reliably of seeing the junk recede and disappear in the distance.[27] Did it sink to the ocean bottom, break apart on distant shoals, wash intact onto a sandy beach? Did anyone retrieve its precious coins and bundled flowers? How fared the cat? In popular superstition the cat was a creature endowed with magical charms. Did it survive? Its seventeen masters could only wonder.

Various features of the *Auckland*, built in 1846 at Medford, Massachusetts, amazed the Japanese. As Heco wrote, the ship "had a crew of only eleven officers and men, all told, and one man at the helm seemed sufficient to steer her."[28] Incredibly, the steersman, using sign language, informed the Japanese that the ship would reach port in forty-two days. How could he possibly know? Yet it turned out that he was correct to the very day. It would have been no less astounding to the Japanese to learn that the 204-ton *Auckland* was no match for the larger, sleeker clippers of that era. The *Challenge*, for example, once made the Hong Kong–San Francisco run in thirty-three days, less than half the *Auckland*'s current run of seventy days. But even this slower speed was awesome to the Japanese, and they were made aware that their ill-fated junk, though newer than the *Auckland*, was inferior in design and construction. Their marine technology lagged drastically behind that of the West.

For Sentarō and his crewmates, restricted to their own shores for generations, the expansive ocean was a new experience. They had been culturally conditioned to regard the confines of their own archipelago as the horizon of the world. But now they passed day after day without landmarks, looking at water that seemed to be endless. And in the strange new world of the *Auckland*, the language, hours of the day, food, clothing, personal habits—all were different. According to their calendar the Japanese had been rescued on the twenty-first day of the twelfth month of the third year of Emperor Kaei. By the Western calendar it was January 22, 1851.

Probably Sentarō had never folded himself into a chair, nor had he sat on a commode as opposed to squatting over a hole. He had never eaten with a knife, fork, and spoon, or drunk from a cup with a handle. Western clothing was a stunning sight if only because the Japanese adopted no new fashions in wearing apparel. The English spoken on the *Auckland* was a mere babbling that sounded like some kind of animal language. Sentarō and his cohorts could not help but feel alienated from the world of their upbringing. They had been removed from the "sacred space" of Japan to the "profane space" of the barbarian world.[29]

Each barbarian was peculiar in his own way. In contrast to the bearded, cigar-chomping captain, the first mate was a clean-shaven, tobacco-chewing man with black hair, red lips, and womanish looks. The second mate, garrulous but kind, was red-headed, fitting a demonic stereotype. A teenager who helped serve the castaways looked girlish but could scamper up the masts like a monkey. Whatever their individual traits, all these foreigners were no less exotic to the Japanese than the Japanese to them—and probably more so.

Sentarō's eyes were especially drawn to his counterpart, the *Auckland*'s cook. He was a Chinese who wore broad pantaloons, a wide-sleeved upper garment, and a queue that wound around his otherwise shaved head. This singular crewman proved invaluable to the Japanese, for he and the literate ones among them could exchange messages written in mutually understood Chinese ideographs, the different syntax notwithstanding. This helpful interpreter fell from their graces, however, when they saw him slaughter a pig for the mess. How barbarous it seemed to these Buddhists with reverence for four-footed beasts! His shocking deed made them wonder whether the Americans were cannibals—a popular notion about meat-eating foreigners—who would cook their human harvest from the sea if the food supply should run out. Not until they saw the well-stocked pantry did their fears subside.

The Japanese diet required boiled rice, bean paste, soy sauce, and fish. It included a rich variety of vegetables, among them beans, beets, carrots, cucumbers, eggplant, leeks, lettuce, mushrooms, peas, potatoes, radishes, spinach, tomatoes, turnips, and yams.[30] It had no place for meat, bread, and dairy products, all staples of the Western diet. So like Manjirō and other castaways, Sentarō and his comrades were appalled at what was set before them. The bread smelled like oil. The butter was revolting; it stank and had a vile, rancid taste. The meat was offensive religiously; eating it violated a Buddhist taboo. When Hikozō was told that the brown chunks in his soup were probably meat, he prayed the gods to forgive his unintended sin. Even familiar foods can be unpalatable if prepared differently. The Japanese grimaced at finding their rice salted, their eggs soft-boiled. Sentarō never salted the rice and always boiled the eggs hard.

Western meals were such an ordeal that the first Japanese embassy to America (1860) brought along their own cooks and utensils and a vast supply of native food. The USS *Powhatan,* which carried the ambassadors' group, provided a special place for the Japanese to prepare the great quantities of rice they consumed. On the *Kanrin-maru,* a Dutch-built clipper that carried the escort group, the original galley was removed and replaced with one adapted to Japanese cooking. In Washington, D.C., the embassy had access to a kitchen specially remodeled for preparing their own dishes. When their own food was inaccessible, they were often famished, even amid sumptuous feasts.[31]

Captain Jennings, reportedly kind and thoughtful, tried to accommodate the special needs of his unexpected guests. The Chinese cook boiled some of the rice they had brought aboard and served them vegetables and raw fish. Still, Sentarō must have longed for his own galley and provisions. He must have chafed at having to adapt to so different a way of life. Probably the adjustment was easiest for the young and intelligent Hikozō, but Sentarō too, about nineteen, had a clear advantage over the older crewmen.

This orphan of the sea would gradually absorb the new culture and make it his own.

Chapter 2

Pampered Ward of Uncle Sam

We met with nothing but the utmost kindness from all on board [the revenue cutter Polk*]. In fact, according to our notions we were treated over-well . . . And one would say to another that the strangers were fattening us for their future meat.*
                                                          —Joseph Heco[1]

THE *Auckland* arrived off the steep hills of San Francisco on March 4, 1851, six weeks after rescuing the Japanese from their stricken junk. "On approaching land," the *Alta California* said of the castaways, "they exhibited striking evidences of joy and devotion."[2] This emotional display was genuine, for Sentarō and his companions had been at sea for nearly a hundred days, including fifty-two days helplessly adrift. But their "joy and devotion" must have been tempered with a sense of foreboding at their prospects in a strange and foreign land.

As the curious Japanese watched from the *Auckland*'s deck, a little schooner hove to and sent aboard a harbor pilot, a bushy-bearded man dressed in a black suit and beaver hat. Captain Jennings greeted the fellow, took the pack of newspapers he thrust out, and disappeared below deck. Then the pilot took charge. Shouting orders through a trumpet, he guided the *Auckland* into a forest of masts—hundreds of tall masts rising from the water—and to an anchorage at North Beach below Telegraph Hill.[3]

When Captain Jennings reappeared from below, freshly shaved and clad in gentleman's attire, his appearance was so different that the Japanese momentarily wondered who he was. Jennings conferred briefly with two customs officers who had come aboard, then bade a warm farewell to his crew and Japanese wards. Sentarō and his fellows did not see him again for a week.

That afternoon two men in flannel shirts came aboard the *Auckland* and tried in vain to talk with the Japanese. After a conference with Mate Salters, the two managed to communicate by sign language that they wanted the Japanese to accompany them ashore. Sentarō was wary, for these men looked unimportant and their intentions were unclear. But three of his companions volunteered to go with the strangers. Some two hours later, to the envy of those who had stayed behind, the adventurous trio returned with glowing reports of the kind treatment they had received and the novel sights they had seen. The strangers had bought them fresh bread, pies, and cakes.[4]

All the Japanese began to eat better after fresh food supplies were brought to the ship. Sentarō was probably allowed to prepare meals more suitable to their palates than the alien fare they had endured thus far. But if their diet improved, another source of frustration remained: the language barrier. No interpreter was available to bridge the chasm between Japanese and English.

After a couple of days in port the *Auckland* moved up to the inner wharf alongside a battered old ship, no longer seaworthy, that served as a floating warehouse. Into this hulk the crew discharged the *Auckland*'s 700 barrels of flour, 4,000 mats (sacks) of sugar, and 7,352 boxes of tea. The Japanese pitched in and helped, anxious to repay the kind treatment they had received.[5]

The first Sunday after completing the cargo transfer, the full contingent of Japanese went ashore. Hikozō had been taken on a tour of the city after that first day when three of their number had dared go ashore with the flannel-shirted men. But this was probably the first visit for Sentarō and the others. As reported in the *Alta California,* the Japanese "appeared to be delighted with all they saw."[6]

Indeed, San Francisco was radically different from Edo and Osaka and any other city over which their curious eyes had roamed. Buildings were made of brick and stone as well as wood, and some of the streets were paved with fir-wood planks. Vehicles were pulled by horses, not men or oxen, and most were handsome turn-outs—carriages, buggies, chaises—bearing humans rather than assorted freight. The humans themselves were the most fascinating sight of all, at times shocking. Hikozō recoiled at the "fearful and dreadful" appearance of a black man. "I thought it was not human," he wrote, "and fancied it must be more akin to *Oni* (the Devil)."[7]

San Francisco offered a dazzling variety of skin color, facial features, body odor, dress, bearing, gestures, speech. The "negro dance houses" along Kearny Street bustled with not only Africans but Mexicans and Polynesians. The city had ethnic neighborhoods such as Little Chile, with immigrants from the Latin-American countries, and the notorious Sydney

Town, made up of lower-class immigrants and former convicts from Australia, among them the celebrated Sydney Slasher. On the wharves one would meet Spaniards, French, and Germans.[8]

The most clannish people were the Chinese. Despite their aloofness, these "Celestials" were admired for their industry, frugality, strict attention to business, and support of one another. They ran most of the restaurants and laundries in the city. When one of them died, some five hundred mourners would form a colorful funeral procession, a spectacle Sentarō may have witnessed. Besides those in residence, hordes of Chinese passed through the city going to work in the mines or returning to China with the money they had saved.[9]

Drawn mainly by the lure of California gold, San Francisco's thirty thousand people had come from all over the world. They were far more representative of humankind than Edo's one million.[10] So cosmopolitan a city could only have astounded Sentarō and his companions, members of a homogeneous race long cut off from the outside world.

One of the more confusing aspects of life in San Francisco was the absence of rigid hierarchical distinctions. The mayor of the city, or the governor of the state when he visited, was dressed no differently than other gentlemen. These officials traveled about without a retinue or other trappings of rank and power. Ordinary citizens could berate them without being struck down on the spot. There were class distinctions to be sure, but nothing like those in Japan where it was illegal, for example, for a commoner like Sentarō to wear silk.

On the same day Sentarō and company made their first group visit to the city, a representative of the *Alta California* visited them aboard the *Auckland*. The journalist described the Japanese as "a fine looking set of people." He learned from Captain Jennings and Mate Salters that "they rise at daylight every morning and bathe in cold water. They worship the sun, moon and wind, and pray to the sun regularly each day."[11] The Japanese faithfully observed their communal habits without regard to what others might think.

The journalist also reported on the articles saved from the *Eiriki-maru*. These included official documents, medicines, a chart of the coast of Japan, a compass "differing entirely from those in use among us," and a batch of Japanese coins—copper, silver, and gold. The report must have caught the eye of a clever thief, for the chart of the coast of Japan soon disappeared with some of the coins. Three weeks later the *Alta California* was still calling for the return of these missing items, especially the singular chart. Captain

Jennings took a fancy to the compass and gave it to a schoolmate as a token of esteem. The recipient, Captain Lee of the schooner *Elizabeth*, carried the instrument to New York, where the *Scientific American* deemed it "a curiosity of the most rare and interesting character."[12] The rescue of the Japanese and a few of their possessions had opened yet another peephole into mysterious Japan.

Foreign Freaks on Display

Two days after the journalists' visit, the captain of the storage ship to which the *Auckland* had transferred its cargo asked the Japanese to wash and shave in preparation for an evening out. He instructed those who were wearing Western clothes—mostly gifts from charitable strangers—to change to their kimonos. Then after supper the captain took them ashore. Probably he was Charles B. Macy. Years later Macy would write that Sentarō and his fellow castaways, upon arriving in San Francisco, "were placed under my special charge, and remained with me about a month."[13]

The captain led the clutch of Japanese to the California Exchange, a handsome brick edifice with stained-glass windows. It stood in a row of palace-like structures on the east side of Portsmouth Square, the city's spacious Plaza. He guided them upstairs to a lavishly furnished room where they walked on expensive carpeting with their outside footwear—conduct unthinkable in Japan. Suddenly Sentarō and his companions were confronted with another group of Japanese like themselves. All were dumbfounded, and some of their number were about to open a conversation with the strangers when they realized they were seeing their own images reflected in a mirror. The huge glass mirror, some eight feet wide and six feet high, offered a lifelike clarity unknown to their own little mirrors of polished bronze.

The Japanese now heard the music of a Western band, whose raucous, unfamiliar sound assaulted their ears no less than black skin astonished their eyes. Following the signals of their captain-host, they walked onto a stage behind a blue curtain and seated themselves on high benches designed for the huge American frame. Almost immediately the curtain opened, and to their horror the Japanese found themselves face to face with a hall full of spectators who laughed and gesticulated, making a shameless display of their fascination with a people long isolated from the rest of the world. Despite their obvious discomfort, the Japanese were then dispersed among the crowd, adding to the merriment of the evening.

This was the Grand Fancy Dress and Masquerade Ball. There were queer costumes aplenty, and some participants had cross dressed, men as women and vice versa. People danced, gambled at round tables set up for games, or amused themselves by placing little gifts—penknives, jewelry, money—in the hands of the Japanese. Since the gold rush of 1848, the flaunting of wealth in San Francisco was no less common than the raising of sails.

The masquerade ball had been promoted as a singular opportunity to see the shipwrecked Japanese appear in native costume and perform some of their favorite dances. "It will certainly be very amusing," the *Alta California* had announced, "independent of their own dancing, to see them engaged in dancing with the ladies of a civilized country." The paper had assumed that the pleasure would not be one-sided: "They will be treated with the greatest degree of respect by Mr. Cole and his associates, and will doubtless be highly pleased with the entertainment."[14] E. Cole was the California Exchange's proprietor.

In fact, Sentarō and his comrades were anything but pleased. They were not only dazed and flustered but deeply humiliated. It is virtually certain they had never seen a Western man before boarding the *Auckland*, and it is more certain they had never seen any "ladies of a civilized country" before landing in San Francisco. At the masquerade ball the women were dressed in low-cut gowns that left their shoulders bare, a shocking display to the Japanese. A kimono daintily revealed only the nape of the neck, the nearest thing to cleavage in their culture. True, men and women in Japan were accustomed to public nudity and even bathed together unashamedly. But Etsu Sugimoto, author of *A Daughter of the Samurai,* was shocked upon attending her first American dance to see women "publicly displaying bare skin just for the purpose of having it seen."[15]

Nitobe Inazō, who studied at Johns Hopkins University in the 1880s and took an American wife, described Western dancing as "the acrobatic hoppings of dizzy men and women in the crowded salon of a ball!" He condemned masquerades as "a violence to human dignity and nothing short of an abomination." This Western "muck" would eventually seep into Japan and gain a measure of acceptance, but Sentarō and his companions probably shared Nitobe's view. They might have described San Francisco as an American school book of that time described Osaka: "famous in Japan for the voluptuousness of its inhabitants."[16]

The Japanese were also offended by the privileged treatment women were accorded. Yanagawa Kenzaburō, who visited the United States with the embassy of 1860, was amazed that a man would remove his hat to a lady, let her go first, speak to her before speaking to a man. "In this country," he noted, "a lady is honored as parents are in Japan."[17] Indeed, it was shocking that a man would put his wife's interests before those of his parents, in violation of the code of filial piety. Often a husband seemed to be subservient to his wife, utterly reversing the roles observed in Japan.

Naturally some of the Japanese at the ball fumed at being taken advantage of so blatantly. They had been put on public display without warning. They had been exploited as the entertainment for the night, served up as a variation on the French Vaudeville offered other nights at the California Exchange. But Captain Manzō gently persuaded his men to disregard their personal feelings, at least outwardly, and cooperate with the foreigners who had saved their lives. "They appeared to be very much pleased with the music and dancing of the 'outside barbarians,'" the *Alta California* concluded, "and remained till a very late hour, being feasted and talked to by almost everybody."[18]

"OUTSIDE BARBARIANS." In his second biography of Sentarō's shipmate Hikozō, Chikamori Haruyoshi reproduced these English words in screaming capital letters—not once but thrice. He was impressed that Americans at the time understood the Japanese term used of foreigners—*iteki*—and could manipulate it humorously to their own advantage.[19] Despite Japan's self-imposed isolation from the outside world, a good bit of information passed in both directions.

Proprietor Cole, having pulled off a coup with the Japanese as top billing, now gallantly proposed returning them to their homeland. Cole offered to provide a suitable vessel and ship's master if the public would contribute the funds needed for a crew and provisions. He even staged a Japanese benefit ball at the Exchange. But the *Alta California* frowned on the scheme. While commending Cole's good intentions and liberal offer, the paper urged that the expedition be a national one, backed by the formidable power that only the republic could provide. It suggested that a local effort should be attempted only "if no more imposing method can be commanded."[20]

Meanwhile Sentarō and his comrades were learning to accept their celebrity status. A few days after the embarrassing masquerade ball, the *Alta California* noted that

> a number of the Japanese were on Long wharf having a jovial sort of a time. It seems that they have learned the value of our money and had

brought on shore a quantity of their coin . . . and were trading it off at an enormous rate of exchange for Spanish quarters, Yankee dimes and half dollars, of which in the course of the day they acquired a considerable quantity. This they expended for coffee and cakes, molasses candy, pea-nuts, and some elegant specimens of brass jewelry, with which they will probably initiate themselves into the good graces of the lovely damsels of Japan.[21]

The day was overcast and squally, but the weather did not dampen the spirits of the Japanese. Long Wharf, which extended two thousand feet into the bay at the end of Commercial Street, was "the noisiest spot in the city," a bustling place where bankers and brokers, auctioneers and hawkers, made their pitches and deals. Here Sentarō and company could interact with people from around the world and put their commercial skills to the test.[22]

On another occasion the Japanese donned kimonos and posed for daguerreotypes taken by H. R. Marks of Baltimore. These photographs are preserved only through numbered sketches based on them and published in the *Illustrated News* of New York. Figure number 7 is labeled "Simpatch (cook)." Apparently Sentarō identified himself as Sempachi, to use current romanization. As noted earlier, this name may well be the chief source of his sobriquet Sam Patch. His appearance suggests that Sentarō was the subject of the earliest extant daguerreotype of a Japanese, who is unnamed. The resemblance is striking (see pages 31 and 33).[23]

The daguerreotype method produced a picture like a mirror image. As Manjirō explained after posing in San Francisco several years later, in order to look properly dressed one had to arrange his kimono with the right side lapped over the left in front (which is done only when dressing a body for burial) so that in the picture the left side would be lapped over the right.[24] In the sketches of the *Eiriki-maru* crew, about half have their kimono properly arranged and half do not. Incongruously, Yasutarō seems to be wearing a necktie, and Tamizō sports a bow tie. There must have been some confusion about proper dress for the occasion.

American Hospitality at Its Best

Because the *Auckland* was preparing to leave port on its next voyage, the Japanese required new accommodations. The Collector of the Port, T. Butler King, placed them aboard the USR *Polk*, a four-hundred-ton vessel

Crew of the Eiriki-maru. *See Appendix for names*

of the Revenue-Cutter Service (now the Coast Guard). The *Polk* was a side-wheeler that had been converted to a bark, its machinery transferred to another cutter. It was to be home to Sentarō and his companions for the next eleven months.[25]

Watching their beloved *Auckland* sail for Honolulu gave the Japanese wards a deep sense of loss. They would never forget Captain Jennings and his crew for stopping to save them and for treating them well ever since. They had come to distrust Mate Salters for cheating Hikozō out of some money, but his dishonesty was an exception. The first foreigners they had ever met turned out to be a decent and humane bunch, worthy of gratitude and respect.[26]

Life on the *Polk* was frightening at first. The ship was made of iron, yet miraculously stayed afloat. The big guns (five 32-pounders) and military uniforms were ominous. The brass-buttoned officers wore swords, reminiscent of the haughty *yakunin* (government officials) in Japan. Several times a day all hands from the captain on down exercised with dumbbells to strengthen their muscles as though preparing for battle. But the Japanese soon had their fears allayed, for Henry D. Hunter, the *Polk*'s commander, was as thoughtful as he was disciplined. As though trying to outdo Jennings, Hunter authorized whatever supplies they needed and procured the vegetables they craved.[27]

Although Captain Hunter filled the role of surrogate father to his wards, the man who won first place in their hearts was Seaman Thomas Troy, a bewhiskered Irish-American, a member of the proud community that had recently celebrated St. Patrick's Day with a Shamrock Ball at the Eagle Saloon.[28] Though a fierce-looking fellow, Troy turned out to be as kind as the folklore hero who cared for the tongue-cut sparrow. He showed the Japanese to their quarters on the berth deck and helped them with their newly issued uniforms, underwear, caps, shoes, socks. Troy faithfully saw to their comfort as well as their needs, and even tutored them in English and arithmetic.

Joseph Heco's *Narrative of a Japanese* (1892) describes Troy as the ship's master-at-arms. The *Polk*'s "Muster and Pay Roll" lists him as only a seaman. But Heco is correct that Troy earned fifty dollars a month. All the seamen on the *Polk* were paid this amount, even though the designated compensation on revenue cutters was eighteen dollars for petty officers and fifteen dollars for seamen (the navy paid its seamen twelve dollars). Why such generous treatment of the *Polk*'s crewmen? "When, however, it shall so happen that seamen cannot be procured at the compensation herein established," said the Treasury Department regulations for revenue cutters, "the Collector is authorized to ship them for the time being, at the wages then current at the port." In booming San Francisco, Troy and his fellow crewmen enjoyed a windfall.[29]

Suffering from boredom and still burdened with *on* (sense of obligation), the Japanese volunteered their labor aboard ship and were granted work assignments. Hikozō waited on the captain, while others assisted the wardroom officers or did such chores as cleaning the decks. Sentarō may have helped in the galley. None wanted to be thought a freeloader. Still, they had much leisure and whiled away the time fishing. Seitarō recalled that they caught sardines, flatfish, gobies, and sea bream, which were served up in abundance at their dinner table. Since they caught more than they could eat, Troy sold the surplus fish, bringing them piles of coins and staunchly refusing any commission for his services.[30]

Troy took the whole group ashore twice, further orienting them to the city, then let them go and come on their own. Usually they did the town on Sundays and their fishing on other days. "The Japanese paid a visit to the shore yesterday," the *Alta California* reported in April, "and amused themselves by circulating around the Plaza. Some of them have adopted the Yankee style of dress, and look quite interesting."[31] Besides their *Polk*-issued outfits, the Japanese had civvies given them by friends.

Sam Patch (?)

The Plaza, nearly the size of two football fields, was an ornament to the city and the center of its life. Surrounding it were the California Exchange where the Japanese had been duped at the masquerade ball, specialty shops and little cafes, plush saloons and smoke-filled gambling dens, the post office and Justices' Court, and luxury hotels such as the Parker House, which housed the popular Jenny Lind theater. Above the Plaza, atop a 111-foot flagpole, Old Glory fluttered in the constant ocean breeze.[32]

For the Japanese the Plaza was like Edo's entertainment district Asakusa, a place where they could amuse themselves for long hours. The Plaza had organ grinders, candy peddlers, and assorted show-offs. A circus performed some evenings, and something no less exciting could happen anytime. During one of the frequent political gatherings, at which an elevated speaker would shout and gesticulate as though auctioning off fish in Nihonbashi, a spectator fell into the unsightly hole where an artesian well had been dug in vain. One Sunday evening a hundred sheep being driven across the Plaza toward the Presidio, there to be made into mutton, went on a rampage, invading the Italian Saloon and the El Dorado, scattering chairs and customers, spilling confectionary and whiskey. It was an event to be remembered.[33]

During the eleven months Sentarō and his comrades lived on the *Polk*, they might have visited a bathing establishment where for a dollar they could soak in hot water much as they had done in Japan. The salt-sea winds that howled daily out of the northwest and down from the sandhills encrusted everything and everyone with grit, making the baths a popular draw. They might have visited houses of ill fame, a respectable practice in Japan. Two of Sentarō's companions, Seitarō and Tokubee, mentioned San Francisco's prostitutes in the depositions they gave to government interrogators after returning to Japan.[34]

Even without going ashore, from their perch in the harbor the Japanese could observe a city on the move. Especially entertaining was the arrival of a steamer, which would discharge hundred of passengers into the waiting arms of family and friends. The steamers also brought mail and news from New York and Washington, from Europe and the larger world. Steamer days were like holidays, though filled with extra work, and like holy days, bringing personal messages of joy and sorrow to the lonely and anxious.[35]

Exciting in a different way than the semimonthly steamer days, and no less common, were the tremors that rattled the city. The Japanese, no strangers to earthquakes, dreaded them all. At least two of the quakes in May were strong enough to break windows and be felt by the ships in the harbor.

The Flowers of San Francisco

Neither steamer days nor earthquakes could match the drama of the awful fires that broke out several times a year. Some of these conflagrations devoured huge portions of the city. Sentarō and his companions had a grandstand view of the city's Fifth Great Fire that began a little after eleven o'clock on Sunday night, May 3, 1851. Incited by gale winds, the fire raged through the city for ten hours—until nine o'clock Monday morning—consuming about fifteen hundred buildings in a swath one mile long and half a mile wide. More than three-fourths of the city was blotted out, including nearly every remnant of the oldest part. The five-story Union Hotel burned like a furnace until its huge walls "pitched headlong into the street and over the wrecks of neighboring dwellings."[36] Observing the scene from the *Polk*, the Japanese must have thought of Edo, which had burned down so often that the colorful flames were nicknamed the "flowers of Edo."

Miraculously, the California Exchange was spared, but Long Wharf, where the Japanese had traded money and made purchases, was burned all the way to Battery Street. Three stationary storeships, *Niantic, Apollo,* and *General Harrison,* were destroyed. Even the shipping in the harbor was endangered for several hours. The *Audubon* had its sails set afire but extinguished the blaze.[37]

After the fire the *Polk's* Captain Hunter made available thirty men to join the California Guard and other groups in patrolling the streets. They were stationed in the vicinity of the burned Custom House.[38] How soon the Japanese were able to go ashore and survey the damage is unknown, but they must have been curious and eager for details. In addition to the vast property loss, the fire had left eight people dead, twenty injured, and thousands homeless and bereft of earthly goods.

During their visits ashore on Sundays, Sentarō and his friends must have wondered at the subdued mood of the city in contrast to the frenetic pace of other days. San Francisco, though far removed from its Roman Catholic roots and never a Puritan stronghold, was now observing the Christian Sabbath. "A year ago," observed the *Alta California,* "from the saloons upon the Plaza, sounds of music issued, and the jingling of dollars from the various banks chimed in with it. Many . . . were singing praises to the god of wine. Now the scene is changed. The gaming houses are closed; the city is quiet; the holy music of the church bell breaks upon the ear."[39] Those who did not choose to attend church were relaxing from their labor, taking a horse-drawn omnibus to the Mission Dolores or going on excursions around the bay.

Why the turnabout? The city's eighteen churches had a combined membership of only eight thousand, a mere quarter of the population. But the frequent hellish fires had sobered Christians and others alike into keeping the Sabbath as a safeguard against further judgment. Even when the city was furiously rebuilding after the fifth great fire, on Sundays "scarce a hammer or saw was to be heard."[40]

Sentarō and his buddies may have visited a church out of curiosity or at the invitation of others. In their later depositions some of the crew members described what happened on Sundays in San Francisco: "The people go to a place like a temple, where a person like a chief priest teaches in front of a metal Buddha, and the people give an offering of money." Their "metal Buddha" probably meant an image of Christ or Mary.[41]

But Sunday was not a day of worship or rest for the arsonists who menaced the city week after week. Instead, it was an opportune time for their hideous crimes. A little after ten o'clock on the morning of June 22, as worshipers were going to the city's churches, the dreadful cry of "Fire" rang out yet again. Fanned by the winds, the flames spread rapidly through the city, destroying fourteen blocks and about five hundred buildings and houses within four hours. Again the California Exchange was saved, though some of the other buildings on the Plaza were consumed. Once again the *Polk* did its part, furnishing twenty-five men to help combat the flames on Washington, Stockton, and Jackson streets.[42]

The *Polk* was also available to other ships in distress. When fire broke out on the *Leonora* at Clark's Point, Lieutenant McGowan led a boat's crew that helped extinguish the blaze. McGowan later responded to an emergency call from the steamer *Republic*.[43] No doubt Sentarō and his comrades were proud of their American friends who acted so nobly in times of need.

After the great fire of June 22, Sentarō and his friends saw burnt-out unfortunates leave for the mines to build up a nest-egg again. They saw tents and makeshift shelters spring up like mushrooms, a common sight in the fire-prone cities of Japan. This was San Francisco's sixth major fire in two years, its sixth time to embark on the painful process of rebuilding. Most if not all the fires had been the work of incendiaries, whose cruel and persistent efforts, fortunately, had failed more often than they had succeeded.

Arson was not the only crime plaguing San Francisco. Since 1849 there had been over five hundred robberies and twenty murders. The city was infamous for drunkenness, wife-beating, cowhiding, fistfights, duels, pocket picking, looting, furious driving in the streets, smashing of street lamps, and rowdyism of every sort. Dog fights were popular, usually two terriers snapping and biting one another. More bizarre were the ox and grizzly bear fights. And most worrisome of all, during the past year the city had been overrun by escaped felons from English penal colonies down below.[44]

One of the novel sights Hikozō reported was "over 50 men with chains on their legs all working hard at digging and carting the earth from the hill close by." This scene was new to the city as a whole. There had been complaints that prisoners were enjoying comforts denied to many law-abiding citizens, that they "sleep warm and well, they have their food supplied without an effort of mind or body, no cares, no labor, no sweat of the brow and blistering of hands."[45] In response, the Court of Sessions had established the chain gang.

The most gruesome of the novel spectacles were the public lynchings. The Vigilance Committee of more than five hundred citizens, taking the law into their own hands, arrested and tried an Australian named James Stuart for robbery and murder. Then in broad daylight they defiantly marched him to a gallows constructed on Market Street Wharf. His face uncovered, his hands clasped together, Stuart was lifted up and allowed to hang twenty minutes. "The decks and rigging of the vessels lying around the wharf were covered," said the *Alta California*, "and the wharf itself was one perfect sea of heads."[46] Sentarō and his shipmates were witnesses to the ugly side of American law and justice.

Crime became all the more real to Sentarō and his crewmates when the *Polk*'s Captain Hunter reported that his watch had been stolen. It was a valuable gold lever watch with a snake chain, a gift from his father. Hunter assumed that someone had boarded the ship at night, walked through the wardroom where the officers were sleeping, entered the captain's state-room, and taken the watch from his berth. The story seemed implausible, but eventually it was learned that a man named McCormick, brought on board by the port warden, had done just that.[47]

Destructive fires and relentless crimes notwithstanding, San Francisco carried on the hallowed traditions of a great and growing city. As usual, the Fourth of July was ushered in with the firing of cannon and the beating of drums. The several hundred ships in the harbor greeted the rising sun with a grand display of bunting: "the colors of nations, signals, pennants and flags of all kinds." Later in the morning bells rang out, and citizens assembled at the Plaza for something nobler than a hanging. In marched firemen, draymen, school children, Sons of Temperance, and other groups. The twenty-one-gun salute, reading of the Declaration of Independence, special oration, and other events filled the day. After dark the Plaza was alive with the popping, hissing, and whizzing of fireworks. Sentarō and his friends must have learned something of the meaning of "the rockets' red glare." They had seen patriotism on display in a foreign land.[48]

When an agricultural and mineralogical exhibition was held at the Verandah in October, the *Alta California* noted that the Japanese from the *Polk* were among the stream of visitors. Sentarō and his comrades saw a white-headed eagle with wingspread of nearly nine feet. They saw hundred-pound pumpkins, a forty-seven-pound beet, two-pound onions, three-pound potatoes, yard-long cucumbers. They saw specimens of oats and barley, marbles and granites—all impressive evidence that California, America's newest state, was up and coming fast.[49]

The observance of Christmas in San Francisco was a new experience to the Japanese, but New Year's had much in common with its observance in Japan. The custom of making New Year's calls was thoroughly established in the city. Every family was prepared for visitors, and citizens were moving about the city on horseback, in carriages, and on foot to visit acquaintances.[50]

February brought patriotism to the fore again with the celebration of Washington's birthday. The day began with the ringing of fire bells, the firing of a thirteen-gun salute, and the hoisting of national ensigns in the harbor. Later in the morning a parade commenced on California Street, with the city's associations, clubs, societies, and other organizations well represented by decorated wagons and carriages and marching groups. The citizens of the Celestial Empire marched behind a carriage bearing several Chinese musicians who wowed the crowds.[51]

For Sentarō and his comrades, their year in this dynamic city was one of incredible learning experiences. One writer has called the San Francisco of 1851 a "paradox town" of violent contrasts: "murderers and vigilance-committee members, gambling dens and churches, rum mills and fashionable restaurants, 'serious affrays' and benevolent societies, bullets and bloomers, horse thieves and *Harper's Magazine*."[52] It was a radically different world, a wonderland of novelties that surely no one back home would believe. The Japanese gladly would have swapped this surreal life for the familiar haunts of the homeland, but they must have felt fortunate to be fed and housed and even doted on. The pampering had to come to an end someday, and that day was drawing nigh.

Chapter 3

Voyage from Paradise to Hell

After we had boarded this ship [Susquehanna] the treatment was bad in all respects. They gave us not one grain of rice . . . sometimes they became angry and kicked us. Resentment was born in us and we harbored grievances; we worried, wondering what the future would bring.

—Joseph Heco[1]

A MERICA'S custody of the seventeen mariners coincided with a surge of interest in reclusive Japan, whose rugged archipelago—four main islands and some three thousand smaller ones—stretched like an obstinate barrier across the western Pacific. New England whalers wanted supply stations on its coast. Advocates of steam navigation sought access to its coal. Merchants yearned to exploit its markets. Missionaries were poised to extend to its thirty million people "civilization and Christianity." But the xenophobic samurai continued to repel foreign vessels that approached their misty shores. Sentarō and his comrades had barely arrived in San Francisco when the *Alta California* touted the presence of these unfortunates as "a good opportunity for attempting to open an intercourse with Japan."[2] As news of the rescue spread across America, so did the notion that these orphans of the sea could serve as useful pawns.

Commodore Matthew Calbraith Perry, the U.S. Navy's "Old Bruin" who roared out commands like a mountain grizzly, already had a Japan expedition on his drawing board. A leading proponent of steam navigation. Perry believed that well-armed steamships could force the Japanese out of its cocoon-like isolation. In January 1851, about the time the seventeen castaways were plucked from the sea, he shared his plan in writing with Secretary of the Navy William A. Graham. Soon afterwards he won the support of Secretary of State Daniel Webster.

Another enthusiast for a Japan expedition was Commodore John H. Aulick, who in February received orders to take command of the navy's East India Squadron. This command included East Asia. In early May, when he learned about the seventeen castaways in American hands, Aulick suggested to Secretary of State Webster "that this incident may afford a favorable opportunity for opening commercial relations with the empire of Japan; or, at least, of placing our intercourse with that Island upon a more easy footing." Webster concurred. Subsequently Aulick was appointed special envoy to Japan, and Navy Secretary Graham ordered that the seventeen Japanese be sent to Macao in a ship of the Pacific Squadron.[3]

The *Polk*'s commander had kept Washington informed about his Japanese wards, but whether the wards were informed about Washington's intentions is unclear. There must have been considerable speculation on their part. The *Alta California* had devoted long columns to articles on Japanese history, customs, and beliefs. It had discussed America's past dismal failures to open communications with Japan's "jealous and despotic" government and the proposal for a naval expedition.[4] Some of this Western perspective on their native land doubtless filtered down to Sentarō and his friends. By year's end they must have realized that their fate was directly linked with American efforts to establish formal ties with Japan. They could not help but be troubled and anxious for their future.

Japan's strict seclusion policy had been in effect since the seventeenth century. Only recently had its enforcement been relaxed to permit the repatriation of shipwrecked sailors who had been abroad. While the *Eiriki-maru* crew was in San Francisco, for example, Manjirō and two companions made their way back to Japan and lived to tell about it. Their punishment was nine months of confinement marked by frequent and intense interrogations. Twice they demonstrated their religious purity by trampling barefoot on *fumie,* brass plates bearing Christian images. But this information was not available to Sentarō's group at the time. They had no way of knowing how they might be treated.

One thing they did understand: the gravity of being tainted by the Christian faith. Whether the *Eiriki-maru* crewmen had been targets of proselytism is unknown. None of them admitted to a missionary encounter in San Francisco. The seventeen men doubtless observed Christians at worship, as noted already, but probably felt no pressure to convert if they ever entertained so radical a thought. To them the cross was a warning sign; the crucifix, a deadly snare.

In February 1852, after a cruise among the South Sea Islands, the sloop-of-war *St. Mary's* returned to the naval anchorage at Sausalito, just north of San Francisco. This was the vessel designated by naval authorities to convey the Japanese back across the Pacific. Sentarō and his cohorts heard about the *St. Mary's* from officers and crew of the *Polk*. Jubilant beyond restraint, they began packing their personal belongings and their souvenirs for family and friends back home. The empty glass bottles they had collected—glass was rare in Japan—and other oddities would not only satisfy the traditional obligation of travelers but would help convey to an insular people the wonders of a world beyond their own.

A day later Captain John A. Webster, who had succeeded Hunter as the *Polk's* commander, made the news official. The *St. Mary's*, he told them through Thomas Troy, would take the castaways to China by way of the Sandwich Islands. Then they would board another ship for the final leg of their journey to Japan. Webster was sorry to part with them, he said, but happy they could return to their homes.[5]

Two boats from the *St. Mary's* came alongside to fetch the Japanese and their luggage. The *Polk's* officers and men helped them transfer to the boats and gave them an affectionate send-off. But as the Japanese approached the *St. Mary's*, accompanied by Troy, a fresh wave of trepidation washed over them. The 958-ton, 149-foot vessel was much larger than the *Polk,* and far more ominous. Guarded by armed, pacing sentinels, this black sloop-of-war carried twenty-two guns and ten times that number of men.[6]

The Japanese were welcomed aboard politely, then shown to their quarters and assisted in stowing their luggage. Then they returned to the deck to bid a sad farewell to Thomas Troy, who left with an emotional "Goodbye and God bless you."[7] Troy wanted to accompany them to Japan but felt he could not afford to quit his job and pay the expenses of the trip.

Providentially for the Japanese, the departure of the *St. Mary's* was delayed two days. Sentarō and his companions seized the opportunity to revisit the *Polk*. They told Captain Webster that no one on the new ship understood their language, that it was imperative for Troy to accompany them. Webster asked Troy his wishes. The Irishman said that he would go if he could be paid a seaman's wage of twelve dollars a month. Webster promptly wrote to George A. Magruder, captain of the *St. Mary's*, who agreed to Troy's request. Sentarō and his comrades were ecstatic.

After the two-day delay so propitious for the Japanese, the *St. Mary's* sailed at six A.M. March 1, aroused by a breeze from the southwest. Captain Magruder and Lieutenant James S. Biddle walked to and fro on the quarter-deck shouting orders, the lieutenant with a trumpet in his hand. The anchors were weighed to the music of drum and fife, and all the sails, in "man-of-war style," were hoisted simultaneously at one command. Half an hour later the ship passed by the *Polk*, whose officers and crew were gathered on the deck to wave handkerchiefs and shout farewells. The Japanese returned their salutations and watched their cherished friends fade away as the *St. Mary's* glided through the Golden Gate and into the open sea.[8]

Crossroads of the Pacific

Three weeks later Sentarō caught his first glimpse of Hawaii, the largest of the Sandwich Islands. The *St. Mary's* sailed into the deep-channeled bay of Hilo, called Byron's Bay after the British sea captain who had surveyed the harbor a generation before. Strung along the crescent beach were lofty cocoa palms and thatched houses set against a charming background of living green. Towering over the scene were the snow-mantled peaks of Mauna Kea and Mauna Loa, each taller than Mount Fuji though no match for its conical splendor.

For Sentarō and his comrades, the stunning beauty of this island paradise and the excitement of their first visit were clouded by a tragic loss. Their beloved Captain Manzō died at 9:15 Sunday night, March 21, the day they sighted land.[9] Manzō had been psychologically devastated by the loss of his new junk, having lost another one the previous spring. Forced to adjust to eating and living habits radically different from what he had known for six decades, he had borne the onus of responsibility for sixteen crewmen in a strange new world. The strain had taken its toll on his aging frame. In a picture taken in San Francisco his face looks sallow and deeply lined.

In poor health for the past six months, Manzō had perked up for three or four days after leaving San Francisco but had declined ever since. The sixty-three-year-old captain spoke his last words to Jisaku (also called Tora): "No more." Then he "died as easy as an infant," an eyewitness wrote. According to a later report, Manzō "died of a broken heart," the result of "despairing of ever getting home, and feeling great solicitude for the lives of those under his care." A deposition given by some of his crewmen after their repatriation more than two years later hinted at tuberculosis as the immediate cause of death.[10]

Following Manzō's death the Japanese placed a pot of water and a pan of rice at his head, which were to nourish him on his way to the land of bliss. The next day they bathed his body, shaved his head and face, and dressed him in new white clothes. The casket was a square box the ship's carpenter had made to their specifications. The Japanese placed their captain's body in the box in a sitting position, then packed his clothes and part of his bedding around him.

Two boat crews carried the sixteen mourners ashore with their precious burden. Scantily clad "Kanakas" cleared a wide path through thorny bushes to a freshly dug grave. An audience of two hundred watched as the odd-shaped casket was lowered into place and the Japanese began their curious rites. Each one sprinkled three drops of fresh water on the box, then together they placed a hat on it. After filling up the grave they laid a pan of rice and a spoon on the dirt. Their solicitous but sad work done, the Japanese roamed over the area, relieving their pain with a sightseeing binge. Heaven shone upon them with fair skies in a town notorious for its many wet days.[11]

The next day the Japanese returned to the grave and affixed a headboard inscribed with the words *Namu Amida Butsu Nihon Manzō* ("Hail Amida Buddha; Manzō of Japan") and the date of death. Kiyozō had done the writing. Bunta recalled that an American wrote something in English—about twenty letters—on the other side of the board. This inscription is unknown, for the wooden board has long since vanished. Joseph Heco recalled that Manzō was laid to rest in the "public graveyard." Whether that should be identified with Homelani Memorial Park or the cemetery of St. Joseph's Catholic Church is a matter of dispute. There is no trace of Manzō's grave in either place.[12]

Sentarō and his party were not the first Japanese seen in Hilo. Seven survivors of the drifting junk *Chōja-maru* were aboard the American whale ship *James Loper* when it stood in port for three days in September 1839. But Manzō seems to have been the first of many Japanese buried there. A later influx of Japanese pioneers helped develop the town.

Troubles in Asian Waters

After ten days at the crossroads of the Pacific, the *St. Mary's* sailed on to Hong Kong, arriving May 1, 1852. Great Britain had seized the island ten years before as a booty of the First Opium War. The vast harbor now hosted warships, trading junks, and merchant craft from around the world, as well as little market boats with richly colored sails. The city stretched for a mile along the shore at the foot of Victoria Peak, which rose like a Gibraltar to a height of eighteen hundred feet. The Japanese newcomers could not help but note the contrast between the "beautiful" houses of the foreigners and the "shabby" houses of the Chinese.[13] Indeed, many foreigners lived in opulent splendor, their mansions equipped with every conceivable luxury and tended by swarms of highly trained and specialized servants.

Two days later the *St. Mary's* sailed over to Macao, some four hours and forty miles to the west. A Portuguese colony for more than two centuries, Macao was graced with convents and cathedrals whose bells rang out over the poverty and decay of this once thriving port. In the bay's shallow waters the *St. Mary's* rendezvoused with the *Susquehanna*, flagship of America's East India Squadron. The side-wheel steamer had arrived at Macao in February, bringing Commodore Aulick from the United States by way of the Cape of Good Hope.[14]

One day after Aulick paid a visit to the *St. Mary's,* the *Susquehanna* "rcd on board 16 Japanese & an Interpreter" from that ship, which the commodore afterwards sent on a mission to Batavia (now Indonesia).[15] Once again Sentarō and his comrades were separated from friends they had come to admire. Captain Magruder and his crew had treated them so well that from their perspective the *St. Mary's* actually had a saintly aura about it. Commodore Aulick showed promise of similar benevolence when he permitted them to go sightseeing in Macao. But trying times lay just ahead.

The *Susquehanna* was huge, 250 feet in length and 44 feet in beam. Its paddle wheels were 30 feet across. Each time the Japanese had changed ships, from the *Eiriki-maru* to the *Auckland* to the *Polk* to the *St. Mary's* to the *Susquehanna,* they had moved up to a larger one. The last one, the coal-burning behemoth, proved to be the most unbearable. Their quarters were cramped and hellishly hot, especially now that they lay below the Tropic of Cancer and summer was coming on. Adding to the misery, for the first time in their lives they were deprived of rice to eat. Still worse, Heco wrote, "the *Susquehanna* people were rough and unkind to us." If there were exceptions among the three hundred officers and men other than Troy, Heco did not mention them. Once when the Japanese were resting in the shade on deck with some other sailors, seeking relief from their steamy, stuffy cabins, "the officer of the watch kicked us with his shoes and [drove us down to our quarters] like a herd of swine."[16]

Thomas Troy fumed at the abuse heaped on his wards but had no authority to stop it. He told them that the officers and crewmen of the *Susquehanna* had been in China several months and were accustomed to pummeling the Chinese, who would submit to being "kicked and beaten like beasts" in exchange for the money they earned working on foreign ships. The Americans were merely treating the Japanese in the same manner they treated the Chinese, Troy explained.[17] So great was the contempt Westerners had for the yellow race that young British crewmen were sometimes issued long bamboo poles with which to crack the skulls of sluggish "coolies."

It may be, as a Japanese scholar claims, that the Japanese were mistreated mainly because Commodore Aulick had been unjustly relieved of his command. The victim of malicious gossip, Aulick had been informed that Perry would replace him as commander of the East India Squadron and that he must return to Washington to account for two alleged breaches of decorum. Dismayed and disgruntled, he came to regard the Japanese as a nuisance, an unwanted burden to the squadron. Without the protective cover of Aulick's favor, Sentarō and his companions were at the mercy of the worst elements on the ship.[18]

Whatever the extent of Aulick's complicity in the abuse, the Japanese felt that in their status as wards of the government they had no recourse, and that any complaint to the commodore or the ship's commander, Franklin Buchanan, might incite recriminations. Anger gnawed at their insides like a rodent. They would have agreed with Herman Melville that "the Navy is the asylum of the perverse."[19] Increasingly they yearned to escape from the ship as from a prison.

The Japanese had been on the *Susquehanna* two weeks when the ship steamed over to Hong Kong. Among the visitors allowed on board was a dark-skinned man in Western clothes who looked like a Malay but was in fact a Japanese. He startled his fellow countrymen by addressing them in their own language and identifying himself as Rikimatsu. Like them, the thirty-one-year-old Riki was a shipwreck survivor with a harrowing tale to share. In 1835, when he was a teenager, his junk was carrying a load of sweet potatoes from the Amakusa Islands in Kyushu to the port of Nagasaki when it was battered and disabled by a storm. The ship drifted thirty-five days, considerably fewer days than the *Eiriki-maru,* but food and water were so short that only four of the crewmen survived.

The nightmare cruise ended on the inhospitable shores of northern Luzon in the Philippines. Dark-skinned "devils" stole the crewmen's tools and even snatched away the tattered clothing they wore. Yet these natives also provided food that saved their lives. Turned over to Spanish authorities a month later, the four survivors—Captain Harada Shōzō, Kumatarō, Shisaburō, and Rikimatsu—were taken to Manila and, in 1837, to Macao. They were so despondent that they considered suicide.[20]

American merchant Charles W. King of the Olyphant Company learned of these "Amakusa drifters" and placed them in the custody of Karl F. A. Gützlaff, a Prussian-born missionary. Gützlaff worked for the British superintendent of trade as Chinese secretary and interpreter but continued to preach the gospel indefatigably even while in government service.[21] He and his English wife were caring for three shipwrecked sailors from Owari province who had arrived the year before. So the four Japanese brought from Manila and placed in their care were united with fellow countrymen who had survived a similar ordeal.

The British government was providing support for the three earlier castaways. The Olyphant Company, together with the American Overseas Mission, undertook support of the Amakusa four. In 1837 Charles King took all seven aboard his brig *Morrison* in an ill-conceived attempt to return them to their homeland. Gützlaff went along, as did missionaries Peter Parker and S. Wells Williams. At Uraga, near the entrance of Edo Bay, and again at Kagoshima in southern Kyushu, the ship was repulsed by cannon fire.

After these two failures, King offered to deliver the seven Japanese to Nagasaki, the one port where foreign ships were allowed. They refused. Having seen their ship bombarded twice in sneak attacks, with one direct hit and several near misses, they were too filled with dread to entrust their lives to a government that ordered such attacks. They preferred to return to Macao as permanent exiles from their homeland. The superintendent of British trade granted to each of the seven a purse of thirty Mexican dollars with which to make a fresh start in life.[22]

"They are uneasy people," Williams wrote of the seven castaways, "for they love their fatherland as much as any nation, and do not at all relish their unwitting exile. However, they are fain to make the best of it at present." And since they were resigned to living abroad, without hope of repatriation, they were no longer immune to the Christian faith. Their natural resistance to missionary outreach began to wear down. Five of the seven participated in prayers at Wells Williams's home for nearly two years. Rikimatsu, the youngest of the Amakusa four, convincingly embraced the Christian faith. So did Otokichi, the youngest of the Owari group of three. These two young men, Williams claimed, were "the first fruits of the Church of Christ in Japan."[23]

Having made the quantum leap to Christian baptism, incompatible with his nationality, Riki swore loyalty to the British crown and took an American wife. She bore him three children. Currently the family lived in a spacious home near the harbor, next door to Captain Shōzō, who had recently left for San Francisco. The other two Amakusa survivors, Shisaburō and Kumatarō, had died. Karl Gützlaff had also died, and Riki was working for his widow at her late husband's publishing office. Two years later he would be employed as interpreter to a British squadron, though it was said of his interpreting that he "rendered the substance of all conversations in such patches and shreds that it was an exercise of ingenuity to sew them together."[24] Riki's services were in demand despite his shortcomings, so scarce were persons with any knowledge of both English and Japanese.

The *Susquehanna's* log book reveals that on May 25 Captain Buchanan "gave shore liberty to 12 of the Japanese & their interpreter."[25] Probably this marks the first opportunity for his countrymen to visit Riki's home. Whether Sentarō was among them is unknown. The lucky dozen met Riki's white-skinned, good-natured wife and enjoyed food seasoned with soy sauce, an ingredient they had sorely missed. But the cheerful atmosphere turned solemn when Riki recounted the terror-filled hours on the *Morrison* when it was under attack and warned his new friends that they could experience a reception no less hostile. He urged them to stay and settle in Hong Kong.

The expatriate Japanese who passionately offered this advice was blessed with secure employment, an attractive family, and a home with amenities far beyond the reach of most seamen. Sentarō and his companions, though they had been in the custody of foreigners for a year and a half, realized for the first time that permanent exile was a viable option. But the more nationalistic ones among them saw in Riki something of a traitor. All along they had been reticent to learn English. They had tried to block the incursion of foreign influences into their lives. Now they were confronted with a Japanese who had not only compromised his national traits but had sold out completely to the barbarians. Was he not a devil?

Indeed, Riki the Christian was playing the role of the serpent, tempting his countrymen with forbidden fruit, opening their eyes to new possibilities, putting their innocence at risk. And though he convinced no one to stay in Hong Kong, he in effect drove a wedge into their granite-like unity as a crew. They generally had acted as with one heart and mind in their dealings with foreigners, though perhaps with less dedication and firmness after losing their captain in Hawaii and being disillusioned by their rough handling on the *Susquehanna*. But having encountered the charming Riki, they could no longer play as one team.

The split burst into the open one Sunday after they learned from a Chinese priest that it was possible to return to Japan on a Chinese junk. By writing characters that some of the Japanese could read, the priest explained that they could take a sampan to Kowloon, travel by land through Canton and Nanking to the port of Chapu (near Shanghai), and there board one of the junks that regularly sailed to Nagasaki. Some were excited at the prospects, so the group huddled all night at Shōzō's house, next door to Riki's, and thrashed out the matter. More than half set out for Canton in the early morning rain while the others returned to the *Susquehanna* and made excuses for their missing companions. Whichever group reached Japan first was to contact the families of the others.

In Heco's account, "the eight strongest and most robust of our party" struck out on the arduous overland journey, while the other eight, himself included, returned to the ship. But Bunta testified that nine went, himself included, and seven stayed behind. He even supplied the names of those in each group. A staunch nationalist, Bunta lauded his own group as true patriots and rapped the stay-behinds, Sentarō among them, as "America-lovers."[26]

Even if thought cowardly or disloyal, Sentarō had nothing to regret. Before the day was over, the brave patriots returned by sampan to the *Susquehanna* and sheepishly reclaimed their stifling quarters on board. En route to Canton they had been surrounded by fifty or sixty armed ruffians and stripped of all their belongings—money, pocket watches, clothing, souvenir photos from America, letters of introduction. Probably some of them lost those "elegant specimens of brass jewelry" purchased in San Francisco amid speculation that with this finery they would "initiate themselves into the good graces of the lovely damsels of Japan."[27] They were a pitiful looking lot, each wearing only a shirt and a pair of drawers, each downcast and empty-handed. Their alibi to the ship's officers was that they had been victims of a shady deal with prostitutes.

A Permanent Split in the Ranks

Thomas Troy meanwhile grew weary of waiting for his Japanese wards to be taken to their homeland. He pined for his former life in San Francisco where better money was to be had. His term of enlistment was flexible; as the *Susquehanna*'s muster roll noted, he "was to be discharged at the discretion of the commanding officer."[28] So in August, while the ship was moored at Cum Sing Moon north of Macao, Troy requested and was granted permission to leave. He asked Hikozō to accompany him at Troy's expense, arguing that if the teenager learned English and American ways he could be of valuable service to a newly opened Japan in the years ahead. Hikozō consented to go on the condition that one of his mates went also. Thomas selected Kamezō. Then Jisaku asked to join them, and Thomas gave his consent.

The other thirteen *Eiriki-maru* members did not take lightly to the loss of three teeth from their comb of camaraderie. Only after hot debate did they consent to the separation, and then with mixed feelings. With frustration running high, most of them would have welcomed the chance to return to America rather than endure mistreatment on the *Susquehanna* and face a possibly worse fate in Japan. But they lacked the money for passage and understood that Troy could not afford to take more of them even if the commodore were to give his consent.[29]

As recorded in the *Susquehanna*'s deck log, the captain "allowed 'Kaw-me-tho,' 'G. Saw-Kov,' & 'He-Ko-Tho' (Japanese) to leave this ship at their request." The crude spellings adequately identify Kamezō, Jisaku, and Hikozō. Troy, formally discharged from service the previous day, left the ship with the three. When they were boarding a hired sampan that would take them to Macao, some of the other Japanese, Hikozō would recall, "waxed jealous and made objections to our leaving them." The contention within their ranks was still alive. There could have been a prolonged altercation had not the deck officer ordered Troy's group to cast off at once.[30]

Troy and his charges checked into a Macao hotel run by a Portuguese, then made their way to Hong Kong and took steerage on the British bark *Sarah Hooper* bound for San Francisco. In California, Jisaku obtained a seventy-dollar-a month position on the revenue cutter *Argus,* and Kame worked on the surveying cutter *Ewing* at sixty dollars. Hikozō, after a few unpleasant months on the revenue cutter *Frolic,* worked in a respectable boarding house for thirty dollars and then won the patronage of the wealthy Collector of Customs, B. C. Sanders, who placed him in a Catholic school in Baltimore and set the talented youth on his meteoric rise to fame. As for big-hearted Troy, he was employed on the *Argus* at his former salary of fifty dollars a month.[31]

While three of the *Eiriki-maru* crewmen were headed for these rewarding jobs in the United States, the thirteen still aboard the *Susquehanna* suffered mounting boredom. They were listless and melancholy. The ship left Cum Sing Moon and moved back and forth between Macao and Hong

Kong. Shore leaves were granted at both ports, but whether any Japanese were included is not indicated in the deck log. Then in the latter part of December Aulick took the *Susquehanna* to Manila, where he "allowed 51 men to visit the shore on liberty, and two of the Japanese."[32] A few days later a large number of Spanish officers and ladies boarded the ship and stayed till evening, helping to brighten the atmosphere and relieve the boredom.

The Philippine archipelago under Spain was increasingly important to the United States because of its growing exports of hemp, sugar, and indigo to California, and Americans involved in the trade welcomed the war steamer's visit as a demonstration of their nation's power. But to Sentarō and his companions impatient to return home, this voyage to the far south was another irritating delay beyond their comprehension. Making matters worse, the *Susquehanna* was beset with breakdowns. When it limped back to Hong Kong at the end of January 1853, Commodore Aulick himself was down with an illness. He finally left Hong Kong in March, taking the overland route to Europe and thence to the United States.[33]

In February "five of the Japanese left the ship for the purpose of visiting the shore."[34] Then after another trip up the Pearl River, Sentarō and his companions likely had further opportunities to explore Hong Kong and see colonialism at work. When possible they visited a temple to pray for a quick and safe return home, but they had little choice but to be patient and submit to their captors on the ship. Chinese caulkers were often aboard, as many as 154 at one time, so the Japanese also observed the treatment accorded their fellow Orientals. Meanwhile, Commodore Perry, Aulick's replacement, was en route on the USS *Mississippi*, coming from Norfolk around the Cape of Good Hope.

On to Shanghai—and Japan

Commodore Perry still had not arrived when on Sunday, March 20, the *Susquehanna* made the four-hour run over to Macao to pick up Humphrey Marshall, the new U.S. Commissioner to China. A hardheaded Kentucky colonel short on diplomatic skills, Marshall had commandeered the vessel to convey him to Shanghai, where he expected to gather firsthand information about the Taiping Rebellion then sweeping the southern half of China. He boarded the *Susquehanna* the next morning to the welcome of stirring airs from the band and a thunderous salute, after which the ship immediately stood out to sea. Marshall shared his handsome cabin in the

stern with a three-man suite. Commodore Perry's son Oliver H. Perry II
was his private secretary. Dr. Peter Parker, the medical missionary who had
sailed on the *Morrison* with the seven Japanese castaways, was serving as
Secretary of Legation and Chinese interpreter. Bayard Taylor was a
renowned traveler and writer who still mourned the loss of his wife two
years before.

As the steamer plied the Formosa Channel, the thirteen Japanese were
summoned in a body to the quarter-deck to pay their respects to Marshall,
the "big mandarin." As Bayard Taylor noted, the Japanese "made a very
profound inclination of the head, removing their caps at the same time."
Peter Parker tried speaking Chinese to them but drew a blank. Then he
managed to communicate by writing in Chinese characters that a few of
Sentarō's comrades could read. The Japanese "appeared cheerful and in
good condition," Taylor added. "They were nearly all dressed in sailor
costume with clothes which the officers and men had given them . . . They
wore their hair shorter upon the crown and front of the head, but hanging
loose and long at the back and sides."[35] One could wish for a daguerreotype of this motley crew in ill-fitting naval garb incongruent with their
unkempt native hairdos.

The next day the Japanese sent a note to the commissioner addressed
to "the American king." It was apparent that the writer, possibly Kiyozō,
was limited by the small stock of Chinese characters in his possession. The
terse note read: "We, thirteen Japanese men, have fathers, mothers, young
brothers, old brothers, wives, children. You go to Shanghai: go to Japan!"[36]
The mariners had endured ten unhappy months on the *Susquehanna* and
their patience was wearing thin. Homesickness was taking its toll.

Three days later, having further mulled their dilemma, the Japanese
requested a second interview with Commissioner Marshall. They desired
to leave the ship at Shanghai so they could make their way to Chapu and
take one of the regular Chinese junks to Nagasaki. Probably they had
learned that Chapu was located on the north side of Hangchow Bay less
than ninety miles from Shanghai. The mariners were feeling desperate and
anxious to seize the opportunity Rikimatsu had laid out before them.[37]

Approaching Shanghai, the *Susquehanna* ran aground but worked itself
free, then maneuvered up the Whangpoo River through a forest of Chinese
junks and anchored in front of the three-story American consulate in the
foreign settlement. Controlled by the French, British, and Americans, the
settlement spanned three-quarters of a mile of riverfront property and was
adorned with stately mansions and lush gardens. A broad quay along the

water called the Bund served as a favorite gathering place, especially in the evenings, to talk business or share gossip. Apart from the missionaries, Taylor reported, about 170 foreigners lived in the settlement. Only fourteen were women, an unbalance reminiscent of San Francisco.[38]

To the south of the settlement lay the native city, nearly three hundred thousand people squeezed into a walled circumference of five miles. The contrast with the plush settlement was stark. Although some parts were fairly decent, much of the city consisted of foul streets and dirty hovels. The Japanese would have noticed in their ramblings, as did journalist J. W. Spalding, "the horrible ghastly emaciation, and foamy mouths, of dead and dying beggars, in filthy tattered rags, to whose presence the passers-by seemed utterly indifferent."[39] They would have realized that their own adverse circumstances could be far worse.

The Clever Otokichi

While the *Susquehanna* lay at anchor, hundreds of Chinese were allowed to visit the ship, and as happened at Hong Kong, a Japanese also came aboard. He was Otokichi, one of the three "Owari drifters" who had been united with the four "Amakusa drifters" in Macao. Oto worked as a gatekeeper for Dent and Company, a large British trading firm that handled opium. He also served as a linguist at times, even though his reading of Japanese was limited to kana (syllabary writing) and his translations were piecemeal and flawed.[40]

Like Rikimatsu in Hong Kong, Otokichi went all out in entertaining his fellow countrymen. They were impressed with his spacious home, well staffed with Chinese servants. They marveled at the exotic birds in cages, the decorative flowers and fruit made of precious stones, and the windows made of glass, a rarity in Japan. Here was a former seaman like themselves living like a daimyo (feudal baron). And no less astonishing, Oto was well informed on America's planned expedition to Japan (he read the English press). His guests found themselves warming to him far more than to Rikimatsu. They were wiser now, able to accept Otokichi not as a traitor but as a victim of circumstances who had made the most of his fate.[41]

Oto's guests listened spellbound as he told a tale more incredible than even Rikimatsu's. In 1832, perhaps the year of Sentarō's birth, Oto and thirteen crewmates on the *Hōjun-maru* were caught in a storm while crossing the Enshū-nada, the open sea where the *Eiriki-maru* met disaster eighteen years later. Their junk drifted, not two months and five hundred miles, but fourteen months and five thousand miles—all the way across the Pacific. The drinking water supply ran out, and rainfall was scant. Scurvy struck, and "their limbs swelled like barrels."[42] When at last the junk washed ashore at Cape Flattery in what is now the state of Washington, only the three youngest of the fourteen crew members were still alive: Iwakichi, Kyūkichi, and fourteen-year-old Otokichi. Makah Indians seized what cargo and possessions remained, smashed the ship, and enslaved the three survivors. The harsh welcome was akin to that of the Amakusa group in Luzon, a far cry indeed from the warm reception accorded Sentarō's group on the *Auckland*.

In time news of the enslaved castaways reached John McLaughlin, chief factor (agent) of the Hudson's Bay Company, who sent a rescue party to fetch them. During several months stay at Fort Vancouver, the emaciated sailors recovered their health and attended a school run by Cyrus Shepard of the Methodist Mission of Oregon. As Shepard reported, "they were remarkably studious, and made very rapid improvement."[43] The castaways also were befriended by nine-year-old Ranald McDonald, who later won fame as a captive English teacher in Japan.

In 1835 McLaughlin sent the shipwrecked sailors to London by way of the Sandwich Islands and Cape Horn. While kept aboard ship in the Thames River, they were allowed one day of sightseeing, becoming the first Japanese known to set foot on English soil. Their signatures are preserved in a Foreign Office document.[44]

From London the three men were sent to Macao, where Karl Gützlaff took them under his wing. This master of a dozen tongues quickly learned enough of their coarse sailors' language to translate the Gospel of John. Printed in Singapore in 1837, this work is the first extant book of the Bible published in the Japanese language (Jonathan Goble's Gospel of Matthew [1871] is the first published inside Japan). Gützlaff followed it up with the Epistles of John. In recognition of the contribution "the three -kichis" made to these pioneering scripture translations, in 1958 the Japan Bible Society erected a monument to their honor in Onoura, a village at the tip of the Chita Peninsula south of Nagoya. Here is located also, in Ryōsanji Temple, the tombstone inscribed with the names of all fourteen members of the *Hōjun-maru* crew.[45]

After the harrowing, futile voyage of the *Morrison*, the three -kichis were used in British service, with Iwakichi and Kyūkichi working in Gützlaff's office in Hong Kong. Afterwards Iwakichi went to Ningpo as servant to the British consul at that place, where he disappeared and was presumed dead.[46] Otokichi, the least intelligent of the three, settled in Shanghai as we have noted.

Like Riki before him, Oto warned his new friends not to return to Japan on an American warship. His words carried more weight that Riki's. He had encountered Japanese ferocity not only when on the *Morrison* but more recently when serving as interpreter on the HMS *Mariner,* which in Edo Bay had been surrounded by more than fifty boats during the night and threatened by shore batteries set up by the light of ominous fires. Oto's advice was also more practical because Chapú, the port from which Chinese trading junks sailed to Nagasaki each year, was now accessible, and he had sent his fellow countrymen back to Japan on six previous occasions. Oto was experienced, dependable, and more than willing to help his new friends. Persuaded one and all, the *Eiriki-maru* crewmen asked Oto to arrange their escape from the *Susquehanna.*

American consulate, Shanghai

As a first step, Oto obtained permission from Captain Buchanan for four of the Japanese to remain in Shanghai. On April 1, just before the *Susquehanna* weighed anchor to convey Commissioner Marshall up to Nanking, these four, in the words of the log book, "left the ship at their own request." Such leniency on Buchanan's part seems to have been out of character. He was nicknamed "Old Million" for insisting that the only way to deal with the Chinese was "to give them a million shot a minute." Later he became furious at Commodore Perry for commuting to life imprisonment the death sentence of a *Susquehanna* crewman guilty of mutinous behavior. But perhaps his release of these wards was not a matter of kindness toward the Japanese. "Neither Capt. Buchanan nor the Commissioner," Taylor reported, "had the authority to keep them on board." Whatever the precise reason for their release, the four men were elated. Speaking through Otokichi, they thanked the officers and men of the ship from their hearts, and said they would never forget their kindness toward them. Taylor added that "two of them wept like children when they left." In light of their gross mistreatment, it was a stellar performance.[47]

The other nine Japanese, including Sentarō, remained on the *Susquehanna,* which ran aground upstream and had to abort its plan to reach Nanking. After the ship's return to Shanghai, "all the Japanese but one were permitted to leave the ship at their own request."[48] That one was Sentarō.

Chapter 4

Conscript and Volunteer

Poor Sentarō! He must feel like a bird in a cage with its feed all gone.

—Bunta[1]

ON April 9, 1853, two days after seeing the last of his *Eiriki-maru* crewmates leave the *Susquehanna*, Sentarō joined the U.S. Navy—probably the first from his country to do so. "Shipped Sam Patch one of the Japanese as (Landsman) at his own request," says the ship's logbook.[2] The log uses the phrase "at his own request" routinely as if to protect the ship's commander from charges of wrongful coercion. In Sam's case, should it be taken literally? Was he a volunteer?

"The Japanese all preferred to remain in China," Perry's *Narrative of the Expedition* asserts, "lest if they returned home they should lose their lives, with the exception of Sam Patch, who remained on board."[3] This is a half-truth at best. Sam's twelve crewmates preferred to remain in Shanghai when the *Susquehanna* left for Japan because they wanted to return home *without* losing their lives. In fact, all but one sailed to Nagasaki on the first available junk.

Was Sam Patch all that different from the others? Is it conceivable that the docile cook chose to go alone with the expedition while his companions chose to return home by the only means permitted under Japanese law? This would have been contrary to Japanese group psychology and his own dependent nature. Willfully going alone would have been no less audacious—or foolhardy—than the American Sam Patch's final leap at Genesee Falls. Japan's Sam Patch was of a different stripe. Indeed, his companions testified that the so-called exception was shanghaied at Shanghai.

"Sam Patch was the only one of the group," writes Arthur Walworth, "who had been able to endure the rough handling that the petty officers of the *Susquehanna* habitually gave to Orientals."[4] Perry's *Narrative* may imply as much. But was Sam tougher than his crewmates, more tolerant of abuse?

If their testimony is credible, it was a matter not of endurance but of duress, an explanation more rational than American claims to the contrary. Still, the question remains, why would Sam be shipped against his will?

Some Japanese writers have assumed that Commander Buchanan kept Sam as hostage to ensure the return of his companions from shore leave. But the ship's log implies that he allowed the others to leave the ship permanently, and Bayard Taylor states unequivocally that Buchanan and Commissioner Marshall lacked the authority to keep them aboard. Buchanan doubtless remembered that Commodore Aulick had released three of the Japanese at Cum Sing Moon. Perhaps the commander regarded the remaining wards as of minor importance to the expedition and thought a token one would suffice. Perhaps he reasoned that having one in custody would make it easier to coax some of the others back should Perry want them. The truth may never be known.

There is another question yet to be answered. Why was Sam kept aboard and not one of the others? Why not one of the officers, Chōsuke or Jimpachi? With their experience and expertise, either would have been far more useful to the expedition than Sam. Surely Buchanan would not have selected the cook from among the thirteen sailors. Did Sam volunteer for the onerous duty? Did his mates choose him by lot? Did they presume on his docile nature, knowing he would submit and not rebel? Was he singled out because he was the youngest? Whatever the reason or reasons, Sam kept a lonely vigil aboard ship while his mates earned money at jobs Otokichi had arranged. Six of them worked the night shift at Dent and Company, secretly loading opium. The other six, armed with hatchets, patrolled the streets of the International Concession against possible disturbances arising from the Taiping Rebellion. None would have forgotten their comrade's plight.

On the very day Sam was orphaned on the *Susquehanna*, Commodore Perry arrived at Macao and Hong Kong on the *Mississippi* and learned that his intended flagship had been preempted by Commissioner Marshall. "Old Bruin," who could split the air with invectives, was furious that his orders to await his arrival had been overridden. His anger had hardly subsided in early May when the *Mississippi* caught up with the *Susquehanna* at Shanghai. There the commodore exploded yet again when he learned that of the seventeen Japanese shipped from San Francisco to be placed at his disposal, only one was still under naval jurisdiction. Commander Buchanan frantically tried to retrieve the dozen men ashore, but the sanguine Otokichi, smugly entrenched under British protection, refused to surrender his wards. Buchanan offered to settle for two or three, but Oto brazenly sought even Sam's release. On May 17, 1853, the *Susquehanna* and the *Mississippi* chugged out of port with none of the twelve Japanese whom Oto had dispersed in taverns and brothels where they would be hard to ensnare.[5]

Thus the *Eiriki-maru's* illiterate cook became the only Japanese to accompany the Perry expedition to Japan. "Sam went with fear and trembling," the *Narrative* relates. True indeed. Rikimatsu in Hong Kong and Otokichi in Shanghai had warned him repeatedly against returning to Japan on a foreign warship, and his fellow sailors on the *Susquehanna* kept teasing him about the fate that awaited him there. Yet he took his place "as one of the crew," the *Narrative* adds, and "won the good will of his shipmates generally by his good nature."[6] Unable to control his own destiny, Sam acquiesced in his fate. In that sense only was he a volunteer.

The solitary Japanese was but one of many foreigners under Perry's command. Shipping a non-American was routine in the navy. The squadron included a German artist, a French chef, and an Italian bandmaster, each ranked as an acting master's mate at twenty-five dollars a month. Among the many Chinese on the *Susquehanna* muster rolls were Ahtuck, a landsman from Hong Kong; Awai, a "first class boy" from Shanghai; and various servants and deckhands. One cabin boy, of unidentified nationality but doubtless black, was entered as "Jim crow," place and time of enlistment "unknown." These aliens, especially the Chinese, were usually "paid off," not "discharged," when no longer needed.[7]

En route to Japan the *Susquehanna* stopped at Naha, Okinawa. Here Sam came under the influence of S. Wells Williams, who had come directly from Macao on the *Saratoga* and then transferred to the flagship. Earlier Perry had persuaded Williams, against his wife Sarah's will and his own, to join the expedition as an interpreter. The commodore had accepted the missionary's stipulation that he "should not be called on to work on the Sabbath, and should have comfortable accommodations on board ship." Williams brought along his fifty-five-year-old Chinese teacher, Sieh, but in vain. The emaciated opium addict, who had given only two days' service since leaving Macao, grew delirious en route to the Bonin Islands and was buried at sea with his pipe.[8]

Although Williams missed old Sieh, a Japanese teacher would have served him better. Sixteen years had passed since his accompanying Rikimatsu, Otokichi, and five other castaways to Japan on the *Morrison*. Nine years had passed since he tried to use their language. "I have been looking over the Japanese phrases I once wrote out with Giusaboro [Jusaburō]," Williams wrote, "but they do not easily recur to mind. I have forgotten almost all the phrases I once had at my tongue's end."[9] Indeed, after so long a time of disuse, his Japanese, never substantial, was almost obliterated from memory. Strangely, there is no indication in his journal that Williams ever sought instruction from Sam Patch during the many months they were on the same ship. Though not as able as Jusaburō and others who assisted Williams earlier, Sam had something to offer as the only member of the squadron whose native tongue was Japanese.

Return to Edo Bay

More than a month after reaching Okinawa, the *Susquehanna*, accompanied by the *Mississippi* and the sailing vessels *Saratoga* and *Plymouth,* departed for Edo Bay. On a beautiful Friday morning, July 8, 1853, the sacred landscape of Japan came into view, graced with the towering cone of Mount Fuji. Sam's heart must have pounded at the splendid sight he had

S. Wells Williams as seen by a Japanese artist

missed for two long years. That afternoon the four vessels anchored off the coast of Uraga, the customs station from which Sam's junk had embarked on its final voyage. Now he saw the town from a smoke-belching warship that looked like a floating volcano to the frightened Japanese staring at it from little boats and points along the shore. No steamship had ever been seen in those waters. Sam himself had every reason to be terrified. He must have recalled how the *Morrison* with his countrymen aboard had been bombarded in these very waters. The forts and batteries on the shore were starkly frightening. How vastly different from his previous visits to Uraga on a commercial junk!

The four black ships stood in battle formation, their crews on high alert. Native guard boats and other small craft quickly formed cordons around the intruders, and nimble men tried to scamper aboard, only to face pikes, cutlasses, and pistols. In time the boats were forced away by threats of attack with the exception of those that brought local officials to the flagship. Sam cowered below deck like a frightened rabbit in its burrow.

When several officials came to the ship on the squadron's first Sunday in Japan, they were sternly turned away. This day, they were told, was reserved for Americans to worship God. Actually the day was little different from others except for the 10:30 divine service conducted by Chaplain George Jones. The service was historic. When the two or three hundred present sang a hymn accompanied by the ship's band, the music swept through the fleet and echoed across the shore. "The Japanese listened with wonder," wrote John S. Sewall, captain's clerk on the *Saratoga*. The audience included brown-skinned boatmen clad only in loincloths as they passed by in cargo junks or hovered in little fishing boats a safe distance away.[10] Sam had heard Sunday services aboard American vessels numerous times, but this was the first Christian worship openly conducted within earshot of his homeland in more than two hundred years.

During the following days Kayama Eizaemon, whose richly embroidered robe bespoke his rank as the governor's aide, came aboard often with his suite to inspect the ship, hold discussions, and tipple the proffered drinks. One of Kayama's interpreters noticed some of the Chinese deckhands who had been hired at Shanghai. "Is it possible that you have Chinese among your men?" he asked. Antón Portman, Perry's Dutch interpreter, replied, "These men are the servants of our sailors."[11] If any of the visitors had spotted a Japanese attached to the American vessel, they would have been shocked and alarmed. But Sam Patch remained out of sight, as did Commodore Perry to ensure respect of mythic proportions from the baffled Japanese.

Commodore Perry

When negotiations were completed, Perry emerged to present a letter from President Millard Fillmore to representatives of the shogun. In a colorful ceremony at Kurihama Beach, Toda, prince of Izu, and Ido, prince of Iwami, accepted the letter and responded with a written acknowledgment. Perry and the princes were guarded by well-armed troops—about 250 Americans and several thousand Japanese—whose movements Sam probably watched discreetly from the *Susquehanna's* deck. Wells Williams, in his account of the events of the day, expressed confidence that he had made progress in the language. "I have now learned more fluency by my practice," he told his journal, "and did considerable side talking." It was later reported that he used the conjunction *tadashi* so frequently that the Japanese called him *Tadashi Sama* (Mr. But).[12] Whatever his limitations, Williams doubtless improved rapidly from contacts with samurai whose language was more refined than Sam's.

The next afternoon Perry transferred his pennant to the *Mississippi* and took Williams and Sam Patch on an exploratory cruise up the bay toward Edo. Presumably Sam could identify places along the way, having sailed this route on his junk. But his observations proved of little value, for as a cook on the *Eiriki-maru* he had paid more attention to pots and pans than to navigational aids. When asked to identify a peculiar structure in the bay that "looked like a steamer coming end on, with an enormous smoke pipe," Sam said it was "a tree on an islet," and estimated it was three or four *ri* from Edo (one *ri* is 2.44 miles). But he knew so little that Perry probably fumed anew that he had been deprived of the navigator and others whom Buchanan had released at Shanghai.[13]

Perry turned the *Mississippi* around at a point near the present Haneda Airport lest he cause undue alarm by too close an approach to the capital. That evening he returned nonchalantly to the *Susquehanna,* followed by Williams and Sam. The commodore was unaware that Edo had been in panic, with soldiers rushing to defend the city, residents fleeing the coast, the price of rice soaring. Sam was unaware that one of the marines on the *Mississippi,* who might have stood before him that day, would afterwards change the course of his life. That marine was Jonathan Goble.

A Companion for Sam

The first stage of its mission accomplished, the squadron returned to Okinawa and thence to Hong Kong. In January 1854 it embarked on the second cruise to Japan, again by way of Okinawa. When the fleet lay off Naha a native sailor named Kamata Nōju offered to work for the Americans. Kamata first swam out to the sloop *Vandalia* but was turned away. Undeterred, he paddled by night to the *Susquehanna,* which took him aboard and hoisted in his canoe. Commodore Perry asked B. J. Bettelheim, a resident missionary doctor, to interrogate the Okinawan. Bettelheim, a gifted linguist who was persona non grata to the local government but secured under the British crown, grilled Kamata three days in a row, the latter two days in the commodore's presence.[14]

"I am not asking asylum," Kamata insisted, "for I have committed no crime." The thirty-year-old renegade only wished to attain a better life by working as a servant at the American coal shed in Naha. His wife and child and other family members had forsaken him, he claimed, after he had swum out to the *Vandalia* and returned with a silk handkerchief. Kamata divulged some gossip about "fifty concubines in the palace at Thuy," Bettelheim noted, and spoke of the bad women of his country "in a way I can impossibly commit to writing." Kamata even volunteered information on Okinawa-Japan relations and the spy signals used on the junks from Kagoshima in southern Kyushu. He was privy to this intelligence because he belonged to the sailor's guild and had traveled to Japan.[15]

Kamata's request for employment struck Bettelheim as ill-conceived and highly suspect. Perry thought it unsafe to hire him locally but was willing to have the runaway in his employ aboard ship. He offered Kamata a chance to return ashore, which was declined, then authorized a two-year term in the U.S. Navy. The Okinawan was added to the *Susquehanna*'s muster roll as Jack Canoe, a sobriquet used by the crewmen who had hauled his small craft aboard.[16]

The muster rolls of the *Susquehanna* and later those of the *Mississippi* list Canoe with the rank of cabin boy or second-class cabin boy. The deck logs of both ships refer to him as landsman. His name varies between Jack Canoe and John Canoe. To a lonely Sam Patch, unable to communicate in depth with anyone else on the ship, Jack was a godsend. His Ryūkyū dialect differed sharply from Sam's Geishū dialect, but his linguistic skills had been enhanced by contacts with Japanese sailors from the Satsuma (Kagoshima) clan. The two men had enough in common to forge a friendship of mutual benefit.

In February the squadron proceeded to Edo Bay, this time with ten ships instead of four. Upon arriving, Commodore Perry moved to the *Powhatan* because the *Susquehanna* was under orders to return to China at an early date. Transferred with him were "13 men & 2 Chinamen (boys)." Sam was sent aboard one week later, "by order of Commodore Perry." The logs overlook Jack Canoe, who also made the change. Wells Williams had moved to the *Powhatan* during the stopover at Okinawa, accompanied by his new Chinese teacher Lo, said to be free of the opium scourge that had debilitated Sieh.[17]

Edward Yorke McCauley, acting master's mate on the *Powhatan*, discovered that both Sam Patch and Jack Canoe were "stanch supporters of the dignity of the American flag." The pair constantly reiterated that they considered themselves Americans and not Japanese, "evincing their ill feeling to the latter by getting their heads out of the ports and shaking their fists at their countrymen in the boats alongside."[18] Apparently Sam had been infected with Jack's disloyalty toward his own people.

But not toward all of them. Sam wrote a letter to "his friends," the *Narrative* reveals, which Flag Captain Henry A. Adams turned over to Kayama Eizaemon. Kayama promised to deliver the letter as directed. Since Sam was illiterate, probably unable to write even the syllabary script (kana), doubtless someone took his dictation. This might have been his buddy Jack, who likely was sufficiently literate to serve as the scribe. Another possibility was Wells Williams, who could write both kana and kanji. Perry's remark the previous June that Williams "cannot himself write the Mandarin language" was probably a deduction from the missionary's habit of dictating to Sieh. Williams would later serve as professor of Chinese language and literature at Yale University.[19]

Whoever the letter's amanuensis, the friends to whom it was addressed were probably the twelve crewmen Sam had left in China ten months before. He would have asked whether they had reached their homes and how they were faring. What happened to the letter is unknown. Sam's shipmates were still in Chapu, where the sailing schedules had been disrupted by the Taiping Rebellion. They were stranded in a place where the facilities were crude and the food was terrible. Even though Otokichi and his wife visited them and showed them every kindness, earning their lasting gratitude, the homesick sailors could not help but bemoan their fate. But at last, in August, they would embark for Japan.[20]

Trembling before the High and Mighty

Kayama desired to meet Sam and asked Adams to arrange an interview. At the appointed time Sam was brought to the aft deck and presented to three lavishly robed officials. With Kayama were Nakajima Saburōsuke, of lesser rank, and Moriyama Einosuke, a newly added interpreter who had learned English from the American castaway Ranald McDonald during the latter's imprisonment in Nagasaki. Moriyama was known to share titillating tidbits about his five marriages, current attractive wife, and his "bye-wife."[21]

In the presence of these stern-looking dignitaries, Sam's American bravado crumbled. The terrified sailor "turned a ghastly green i' the face," dropped to his knees, and pushed his face to the deck. His prostrate form trembled all over. Captain Adams ordered Sam to rise, assuring him that he was perfectly safe aboard an American man-of-war. Sam got up but could barely stand on his shaking limbs.[22]

Kayama noted in his diary that Sam "wore American clothing and had the appearance of an American, with his hair only half cut." The description tallies with E. Y. McCauley's, who wrote that Sam "wears Govt. slops and lets his hair grow all over his head like a christian."[23] The shabby looking youth with the unkempt hair contrasted sharply with the well-attired officials, their heads properly shaven on top, and the hair at the back and sides neatly oiled, gathered, and tied.

In the interview Sam identified himself as Kurazō, a native of Aki, and twenty-three years old. He was not lying. The name Kurazō is consistent with Kurajirō, the name by which he was registered at his home temple. Aki is another name for Geishū, which roughly corresponds to the present Hiroshima Prefecture and encompasses Ikuchijima, the island where Sam was born. The age of twenty-three is fully consistent with the twenty-four Sam would claim the next year in New York State. The only uncertainty is whether he stated his age by Western or Japanese reckoning on these occasions. By the latter, a child is one year old at birth and two years old on the first New Year's following birth.[24]

Nitobe Inazō wrote that Sam "was asked by the Japanese officials to stay in the country and engage in building 'black ships.'" Probably Nitobe's only source for this intelligence was Perry's *Narrative*. One cumbersome sentence in the *Narrative* tells us that Kayama was "instructed to build a vessel after the model of the storeship Supply" and that the Japanese commissioners invited Sam "to land and rejoin his family." If the two statements are connected in the sense that Nitobe apparently understood them, which is unlikely, Kayama and the other commissioners assumed too much about Sam's potential. Two of Sam's shipmates later built Western ships, but only a miracle could have transformed Sam into a marine architect.[25]

The interview had hardly begun when the Americans abruptly packed Sam off "to spare him further discomfort." Kayama was disappointed. It was beyond one's comprehension, he told his diary, that a Japanese castaway would not seize the opportunity to return to his home. Surely the claims of one's native land, he wrote, should override any obligation to a foreign country that had given one succor and protection. In the conversation with Adams that followed Sam's dismissal, Kayama ridiculed the idea that the seaman's family might be punished for his self-alienation.[26]

As for Sam, he was so shaken by the encounter, McCauley said, that "no coaxing has been sufficient to make him get into a boat, or go any where near his compatriots since."[27] Sam's confrontation with his nation's authorities left him unnerved if not psychologically devastated. He was unable to comprehend, let alone accept, Kayama's guarantee of immunity from the punishment meted out to returnees from abroad. He cringed within his foreign sanctuary as though he might be seized and whisked off to prison.

Samuel Eliot Morison's account of the Kayama interview in *"Old Bruin"* adds that Sam later visited his family ashore. Morison was a scholar who dispensed with footnotes in his torrent of books, and in this instance the source is not apparent from his bibliography. In view of Sam's display of terror, his anti-Japanese stance reported earlier by McCauley, and his status as an only-child orphan, there is reason to suspect that Morison was misinformed about the visit with family ashore. In the same paragraph he writes that Sam Patch and Jonathan Goble both died in Japan, although Goble actually died in St. Louis more than a dozen years after permanently leaving Japan.[28]

The report of Sam's dramatic encounter with Japanese officials must have spread like wildfire among the people of the region, for there would have been tremendous interest in the revelation that a Japanese subject was among the crewmen on a black ship. The laborers who provided supplies to the *Powhatan* would have passed on the news. Indeed, a boatman named Nanzō, of Kakizaki Village, reported meeting a Japanese on the steamer when he delivered fuel and water. The Japanese had been "a sailor on the *Eiriki-maru*, a ship belonging to Matsuya of Nada," Nanzō reported; he worked in the open during the day but stayed below deck at night. This could only have been Sam Patch.[29]

At month's end, March 31, 1854, Perry and his Japanese counterparts signed the Treaty of Kanagawa, an accord of peace and friendship between the United States and Japan. The expedition had achieved its goal. Though spurred by the recovery of seventeen castaways from the *Eiriki-maru*, potential bargaining chips in the negotiations, the expedition in no way depended on Sam for its outcome. If any castaway exerted influence, it was Manjirō. He later told Samuel Damon in Honolulu that he had been hidden away in an adjoining room during the negotiations and kept busy translating the documents passed back and forth between the two sides. Though Manjirō was not allowed to have any contact with the Americans or even to make his presence known, his command of both languages apparently kept negotiations moving swiftly to a successful conclusion.[30]

The treaty wrapped up, Perry made yet another provocative trip up the bay to within sight of Edo. Then he ran about eighty miles down the coast to Shimoda, the last port which the *Eiriki-maru* had passed before it was rendered helpless. The Treaty of Kanagawa immediately opened Shimoda for the purchase of supplies. After nearly a month of frustrating negotiations there to work out numerous details not covered in the treaty, Perry took his fleet to Hakodate, which was to be formally opened the following year. Upon returning to Shimoda he moved from the *Powhatan* to the *Mississippi*, accompanied by Sam, Jack Canoe, and two Chinese servants.[31] Once again Sam was on the same vessel as Jonathan Goble, this time to stay.

The Final Refusal

With more important matters settled, Japanese officials again turned their attention to Sam Patch. Interpreter Moriyama Einosuke, in company with Nakadai Shintarō and others, formally asked the commodore to permit Sam to remain in Japan. Perry consented on two conditions: that Sam make the choice without coercion, and that the officials give a written pledge that he would not be punished in any way. They in turn offered to give whatever guarantee was required, and they pledged that "he should be treated kindly and provided for, under the immediate protection of one of them."[32]

When Sam was called before the officials, he fell abjectly to his knees, repeating his obsequious behavior at Kanagawa. He would have remained on the deck had not Lieutenant Silas Bent ordered him to rise to his feet. Sam appeared ill at ease, but less frightened than before. Under prodding from Moriyama, he made excuse for declining repatriation while at Kanagawa in March. "It is not that I was unwilling to return to my country," Sam explained. "I did not feel accepted at the time." Nor had his fears subsided, for he had since traveled about the country as far north as Hakodate on an American warship. "Besides," he added, "I have a moral obligation to the Americans who have taken care of me, and before returning home, I want to confer with my companions who are still in America and China."[33]

Moriyama turned on his charm. The gist of his argument, according to his own record, went like this: "You could have been repatriated last spring if the Americans had been willing to release you. True, you have visited various parts of Japan on a black ship, but that is no ground for punishment. As for your obligation to those who took care of you, I understand why it weighs on your mind, but the protection of castaways is a mutual obligation among nations, by no means a rare thing. The truly human thing to do after being rescued is to return to one's own country, to one's parents and friends."[34]

Sam agreed. He conceded that life among foreigners was trying, that the language barrier was formidable and the ship's food unpalatable. Still, he liked his work—at nine dollars a month—and felt that the time had not come to go home. As Perry's *Narrative* puts it, "all the eloquence and persuasiveness of the Japanese were insufficient to induce him to leave the ship." "He would not accede to my words," Moriyama lamented, "and I had to give up." His diary further indicates that Antón Portman told him Sam had grown up without an education and did not understand reason.[35]

However simplistic his thinking, Sam was convinced that life was more secure with the Americans than it would be in his homeland after long exposure to foreign ways. And his intransigence made a mockery of Japan's rigid feudal system. It is ironic that a high-ranking samurai found himself powerless before a low-ranking sailor who, after initial servility, spoke his own mind decisively. Sam's firm stand could have been based on growth in self-awareness no less than on a passive and fearful nature. Would he have acted differently had Jack Canoe not paddled into his life? Whatever the reasons, the conscripted landsman was now a bona fide volunteer.

In Edo Bay, Sam had cautiously kept to his ship. Did he venture ashore at Shimoda, after tensions had been relaxed? The official *Narrative* seems to imply that Sam did not. The many journals kept by expedition members are silent on the matter. A Japanese document notes that Sam questioned the water carriers who came out to the ship, hoping someone might remember the *Eiriki-maru,* but the document throws no light on whether he went ashore.[36]

The famous Black Ship Scroll, painted by curious on-lookers, offers a fascinating view of the squadron's visit to Shimoda. A form of folk art rich in humor, the scroll pictures Commodore Perry, Captain Adams, and some other men of rank who are identified by name. But the scenes mostly show the ordinary sailors and marines as they dance, do their laundry, dally with harlots, hull rice, or butcher turtles. The only enlisted man identified by name in the scroll is Jonathan Goble, who is shown in his marine uniform peering through a telescope. Next to him is pictured a bull-necked black man. In other scenes Chinese servants appear.[37]

One intriguing character is "Japanese interpreter Matō." Since no such person was attached to the expedition, it is widely assumed that this interpreter was Sam Patch by yet another name. But Matō's picture hardly resembles the known sketch of Sam. Interestingly, Matō's facial features vary slightly in the different copies of the Black Ship Scroll, as do other aspects of his picture. One conspicuous variation is the number of buttons on his jacket. In the scroll owned by the Honolulu Academy of Arts, Matō's jacket has six buttons. In the scroll owned by the Japan Society of Northern California, the jacket has twelve buttons. In two pictures of Matō in Japan, there are sixteen buttons and no buttons. Yet the pictures seem to be variations of one original.[38]

Japanese interpreter Matō. Detail from the Black Ship Scroll owned by the Honolulu Academy of Arts

If Matō was not Sam Patch, who was he? Haruna Akira has identified him as Otokichi, who visited Uraga and Shimoda in 1849—five years before—as interpreter on the HMS *Mariner*. If Matō indeed represents a Japanese interpreter who visited Shimoda with Commodore Perry in 1854, he might have been Jack Canoe (Kamata Nōju). Kamata could have picked up considerable English during the four months he had been with the squadron. It is also worth remembering that Sam's former crewmate Iwakichi visited Shimoda four months later on the *Susquehanna*. If Sam Patch himself was the mysterious interpreter, which seems unlikely, the picture is evidence that he had garnered the courage to go ashore.[39]

After leaving Shimoda, Sam had occasion to put his language ability to good use. The *Mississippi* lay off Amami Ōshima for three hours while two boats in charge of Lieutenants William L. Maury and William A. Webb went ashore to inspect the island. Sam seems to have been in Maury's boat. As the Americans approached the beach, they were met by a band of natives intent on blocking their approach. One was armed with a matchlock, another brandished a sword, and still others carried stones, sticks, or spears. "Sam Patch soon undeceived them," said Wells Williams, "and stated the pacific intentions of the boat." The natives, whose dress was common to Loochooans, turned friendly and exchanged five fowls and a quantity of potatoes and other vegetables for thirty pounds of pork and one hundred pounds of bread brought by the foreigners. They offered no resistance as the strangers reconnoitered their land—thanks to the assurances Sam was able to give.[40]

The *Mississippi* steamed to Hong Kong by way of Naha, then pushed up the river toward Canton as far as Whampoa. After the ship's return to Hong Kong, Sam and his shipmates bade farewell to Commodore Perry, who traveled to his home in New York via Europe. The *Mississippi* was destined for New York but by the longer route across the Pacific and around South America.

To America Once Again

The *Mississippi's* first stop on the return voyage was Shimoda. Whether Sam went ashore during the previous visits is murky, but surely he would have availed himself of this last opportunity to tread the sacred soil of his native land. Relations between the Japanese and the Americans this time were all sugar and spice. There was a flurry of shopping and socializing, with smiles and bows galore.[41]

Sam must have been aware that this could be his final opportunity to reclaim his heritage as a Japanese and return to his family and childhood friends. Surely he thought of the twelve shipmates who had remained in China when he was forced to sail without them to Japan. By refusing repatriation, he had in effect broken his part of the mutual agreement to reunite in Japan. But after sixteen months of separation, he could not even know for sure whether they were alive.

As noted above, all twelve had planned to return to Nagasaki by Chinese junk, but the Taiping Rebellion had disrupted the sailing schedule. Iwakichi ran out of patience and sneaked back to Shanghai. The other eleven endured life in a Chapu dormitory until they sailed at last in August 1854. One day before their arrival at Nagasaki, Yasutarō died of illness. He was buried in Nagasaki. While Sam was at Shimoda, the ten returnees were undergoing the intense, lengthy interrogation inflicted on Japanese who had been abroad. They were grilled twenty-one different times. Before the ordeal had ended, Kyōsuke died, further reducing the ranks to nine.

The survivors were allowed to go to their homes but not simultaneously. Bunta went first, arriving in Tottori in early December. Five others, Asagorō, Seitarō, Jimpachi, Kiyozō, and Tamizō, were home by the end of the year. The remaining three, Tokubee, Chōsuke, and Ikumatsu, returned by the end of February 1855. Seitarō and Asagorō, like Manjirō earlier, were elevated to samurai status, becoming Honjō Zenjirō and Yamaguchi Asagorō. They served their clan, Himeji, by building the Western-style ships *Hayatori-maru* and *Shingo-maru.* Along with Tokubee and Bunta, they also contributed to our knowledge of their adventures through depositions preserved at Nagasaki.[42]

The independent-minded Iwakichi, having deserted his fellows at Chapu, chose to visit the United States again. In July 1854, when the *Susquehanna* called at Shanghai after the mission to Japan, Commander Buchanan signed him on as a landsman for the return cruise to America. The muster rolls list him as Dan Ketch. Although the *Susquehanna* lay in the harbor at Shimoda when the *Mississippi* arrived from Hong Kong, there would hardly have been a chance for Dan and Sam to meet even if they had known of their proximity to one another. The *Susquehanna* was already coaled and ready for sea.[43]

The *Mississippi* remained at Shimoda ten days, until October 1. Then at two P.M. it left with a fanfare that bode well for Sam's future. The locals exploded firecrackers, beat gongs, and waved handkerchiefs. The Americans responded with three rousing cheers for their hosts.[44] But the passage across the Pacific was anything but pleasant, for one week out of port the ship was caught in a typhoon. Mammoth waves crashed over its deck for three hours and brought the whole crew face to face with death. Sam must have relived the disaster that struck the *Eiriki-maru* four years earlier. The *Mississippi* limped into Honolulu with a fractured crank pin and other needed repairs.

More than a hundred whalers were in port, but Sam's eyes were likely drawn to two familiar warships, *St. Mary's* and *Susquehanna,* evoking a blend of fond and painful memories. Although the *Susquehanna* remained in port another week, Sam still may have had no contact with Dan Ketch. Dan traveled to America on the *Susquehanna,* not on the *Mississippi* as implied by Perry's *Narrative* and asserted in a number of books. Preceding the *Mississippi,* the *Susquehanna* sailed via San Francisco, Valparaiso, and Rio de Janeiro. After the ship's arrival at the Philadelphia Navy Yard in mid-March, Dan was honorably discharged from the navy and brought under the protection of Commodore Perry in New York.[45]

While at Honolulu, Sam may or may not have met Samuel Chenery Damon, the seamen's chaplain who earlier had shown kindness to Manjirō and other Japanese castaways. The mild-mannered Damon was editor of the *Friend* and pastor of Bethel Union Church in the Seamen's Chapel at the corner of King and Bethel. He reported meeting Jonathan Goble, who contributed a dollar to the Seamen's Chapel Fund and talked about his plans for missionary work in Japan. Damon made no mention of Sam Patch.[46]

King Kamehameha III visited the *St. Mary's* and the *Susquehanna* but not the *Mississippi,* which was coaling and repairing damages at the time. Having missed out on a royal visit, the *Mississippi*'s Commander Sidney S. Lee gave a general invitation to the residents of Honolulu to visit his ship the day before he left port. Men and women crowded aboard, among them the U.S. commissioner, foreign consuls, high government officials, and the captain of the *St. Mary's* (the *Susquehanna* was no longer in port). Lowly sailors like Sam enjoyed the festive atmosphere and the sweet music dispensed by the ship's lively band.[47]

The *Mississippi* chugged on through rough seas to San Francisco, a city in decline, its land values falling. The yield from the gold mines had reached its peak; the mining era had waned. The brighter side was that San Francisco's population was more fixed and its economy more stable. Numerous improvements had been made since Sam's departure nearly three years before. The fir plank roads and sidewalks had been greatly expanded and the oil lamps replaced with gas lights.[48]

Sam's shipmates Jisaku and Kamezō were living in the city, and it is likely that he visited with them. This contact was probably the motivation for Sam's expressed desire some two years later to leave New York State and join his crewmates in California. Heco arrived in San Francisco one week after Sam, coming from Baltimore with his patron B. C. Sanders. Heco probably did not know that Sam was on the *Mississippi,* and the ship was not easily accessible while its dead engine was being repaired at the Benein Iron Works. He knew that Jisaku and Kame were there but made no mention of them in his record of the visit. The eighteen-year-old Heco had been baptized a Catholic two days before leaving Baltimore, so he may have been reticent to face his crewmates. Two weeks after his arrival in the port, and a few days before the *Mississippi* stood out to sea, Heco entered a local Catholic school.[49]

On its long swing around South America, the *Mississippi* put in at Valparaiso, Chile, then passed through the straits of Magellan, dropping anchor in a cove called Plaza Parda. Sam later recalled that it was "an awful cold place," surrounded by mountain snow and glaciers. After an extended stop at Rio de Janeiro for coaling, caulking, and taking on fresh provisions, the ship arrived at New York harbor Sunday, April 22, 1855, and stood up the East River for the Navy Yard. The next afternoon Commodore Perry came aboard for thirty-five minutes and received three cheers from Sam and the other crewmen. On April 26 the colors were hauled down and the old war steamer decommissioned.[50]

Sam Patch later reported collecting two hundred dollars when he left the ship. Probably he had drawn little money from the paymaster during his two years of service, and since August 1854 his monthly pay as landsman had increased to twelve dollars. Sam was better off financially than at any previous time in his life. He checked into the Sailors' Home established by the American Seamen's Friend Society, to which Chaplain Damon belonged. Doubtless he was admitted to the main facility on Cherry Street rather than the Colored Sailors' Home on Dover Street. After sleeping aboard ships for more than four and a half years, Sam was entering a new life on terra firma. Another four and a half years would pass before he would set foot on a ship again.[51]

During the historic expedition Sam had grown better acquainted with the religion of the Americans. Matthew Perry, for all his faults, was an Episcopalian who "made it a point to read through the Bible on every cruise."[52] Sam heard hymns sung, prayers prayed, sermons preached. He had frequent contacts with missionary Wells Williams, who may well have discussed religion with him. Any missionary-minded Christian such as Jonathan Goble might have tried to convert him. But the linguistic and cultural barriers were high, and Sam was far from prepared to embrace a religion he had been taught to abhor.

At the Sailors' Home, he later told E. W. Clark, Sam was "picked up and befriended" by Goble.[53] Was this his first encounter with the zealous marine? The two had been on the same ship for ten months, ever since Sam transferred to the *Mississippi* with Commodore Perry. But Goble's personal journal, which he kept until the ship was ready to leave Hong Kong for New York, makes no mention of Sam. Nor does Damon's report on his encounter with Goble in Honolulu. The first meaningful contact between them seems to have occurred after they left Honolulu, although Goble may have had an eye on Sam earlier. By the time they reached New York Goble clearly had designs on the Japanese seaman as a potential convert and missionary to his own people. Sam welcomed the attention, unaware that under Goble's protective wing he would encounter fresh storms that would change his life yet again.

Chapter 5

Immersion in an Icy Creek

I trust my heart all to God—cloud gone—all bright—great load gone—head light—feel just like fly away.

—Sam Patch[1]

HIS pockets bulging with U.S. dollars, Sam Patch accompanied Jonathan Goble to the ex-marine's hometown, Wayne Village, in the interior of New York State. Traveling with them was John Davies, a pious sailor who had become Goble's closest friend on the *Mississippi*. Their train passed through Albany and Syracuse, which Sam later described as "very queer places." Albany he remembered as "that kind of flat place down on a river with some big law houses on the hill behind it."[2] The first Japanese seen in those parts, Sam doubtless drew many stares.

Wayne Village, in Steuben County, overlooks Keuka Lake, one of the Finger Lakes that were created—mythically—when God placed his hand on this beautiful portion of the state. The trio from the *Mississippi* called on the Reverend Philetus Olney, who had baptized Goble seven years before and had corresponded with him during the expedition to Japan. Exuberantly supportive of Goble's missionary commitment, Elder Olney urged him to obtain the needed preparation at Madison University, a Baptist school in Madison County. The last of three terms in the school year was about to commence. So Goble, with Sam and John in tow, traveled a hundred miles back in the direction from whence they had come.[3]

Madison University, situated in quaint Hamilton Village, is known today as Colgate University. It was so named in 1890 to honor the soap-making Baptist family that had lavished funds on the institution. In the 1850s, when the Goble trio enrolled, the school was more church-oriented than at present, offering thorough training for Christian ministry at home and abroad through its two-year academy, four-year college, and two-year graduate course in theology.

Goble, Davies, and Sam all entered the academy, or preparatory school. Sam was listed in the student register as "Samuel Sintaro, 24." Thus his Japanese name was raised to surname and the first part of his nickname was expanded to its dignified form. Sam's home was given as "Scoku, Japan." Probably he claimed Shikoku because it was adjacent to his birthplace and known abroad as one of Japan's three principal islands along with "Kiusiu" (Kyushu) and "Nippon" (Honshu). The fourth principal island, now Hokkaido, at the time was merely the isolated and sparsely populated Yesso or Jesso. The spelling "Scoku," based no doubt on Sam's pronunciation, is phonetically accurate to a remarkable degree when compared with "Sitkokf" in Commodore Perry's *Narrative of the Expedition* and "Sikokf" in *The New American Cyclopaedia* of 1860. In those days of confounded, nonstandardized spellings of Japanese names, Sam was smart not to claim Ikuchijima as his home.[4]

Madison University's third term, which ran from May to August, was an awkward time to enter the academy. The main courses, notably Latin and Greek, assumed mastery of the material covered in the previous two terms. As a solution to this difficulty, the faculty assigned Goble and Davies to "private lessons" and Sam to a "private class."[5] These makeshift arrangements proved unfeasible, however, and within days the trio returned to Wayne Village to await the start of the school year in the fall. They had made the long trip in vain.

In a census taken at Wayne Village June 4, Goble, Davies, and Sam were counted as boarders in the home of forty-nine-year-old farmer Gilbert Ganong and his wife Maria. Sam's entry reads, "Samuel Sintarro, 24, born in Japan, 1/12 year in Wayne, sailor, alien."[6] Jonathan afterwards moved to the parsonage at the invitation of Elder Olney but continued to look after Sam and see that his protégé attended the local Barrington Baptist Church, later known as the Wayne Village Baptist Church.

Academically Challenged

When the surrounding hills were ablaze with autumn leaves, Jonathan and Sam returned to Madison University without Davies and formally entered the academy as first-year students. Sam's name and residence were recorded with new spellings: "Samuel Sentharo" from "Sekokf, Japan." The registrar must have read up on Japan and learned a more recognizable spelling for the alien's home place, a spelling more flawed than the phonetic "Scoku" recorded in the spring. The school's curriculum, besides

Latin and Greek, included English grammar, arithmetic, geography, and American history. Likely Sam had the status of special student with a tailor-made program. It is unlikely that he attempted Latin or Greek.[7]

Madison's campus was dominated by two four-story buildings made of limestone. The Western Edifice, one hundred feet long and forty wide, housed the chapel, library, classrooms, and dormitory rooms for fifty students. The Eastern Edifice, slightly smaller, provided space for classrooms, the two literary societies, and accommodations for a hundred students. All the students, whether in the academy, college, or seminary, were mingled in the two dormitories and had one common life.[8] Sam roomed with Jonathan in 36 Eastern Edifice, a room that later became 306 East Hall.

When Sam entered the academy, Madison was all male and had a total enrollment of 224, about the same as Princeton and half that of Virginia, the nation's largest university.[9] Colgate now claims 2,800 students. The Department of East Asian Languages and Literatures lists four teachers of Japanese who regularly offer courses from elementary to advanced levels. In Sam's time, by contrast, Japan was virtually unknown, and there was nary a soul on campus with whom he could communicate in his native tongue.

But Sam had learned enough English to survive in an alien culture, especially in a pietistic school where faculty and students alike were generous with their help. But handling English for academic purposes was another matter, too demanding for one of sparse intellect and language aptitude. One list of the fifty students who entered Madison in 1855 is arranged in descending order according to how long the students remained in school. Sam is number 48, third from the bottom.[10] His advisors, realizing that he needed McGuffey, not Caesar and Xenophon, transferred him to the public school at a level more in keeping with his sparse verbal skills.

Probably Sam continued to live in the dorm with Jonathan Goble until the following spring when his roommate took a bride. She was Eliza Weeks, whom Jonathan had met in Wayne Village the previous summer. After the newlyweds obtained a private dwelling in Hamilton, they took Sam in and used him as general flunky. They also kept several boarders to help pay the bills.[11]

Goble's plunge into matrimony had serious repercussions for his education. Since one of Madison's regulations forbade students to marry while enrolled in the school, he had automatically forfeited his academic standing. Apparently he had blithely assumed that the faculty would pardon and reinstate him because of his age (twenty-eight) and his valued experience with the Japan expedition that made him a prime candidate for missionary work. But Jonathan was mistaken. He was merely allowed to attend classes as an auditor with no hope of graduation. This was the only concession he could wring from a faculty sympathetic to his plight but unwilling to bend the rules.[12]

Before joining the Marine Corps, Goble had spent two years in Auburn Prison for sending a threatening letter to a Syracuse grocer. His incarceration had followed years of misbehavior as a rebellious youth. Influenced by chapel services, religious books, and the rigors of prison discipline, Jonathan had experienced a conversion that seemed to tame his wild nature as well as set him on a course toward missionary service overseas.

But the old nature remained, imbedded in Goble's psyche. He had a short fuse, and his dynamite temper could still explode. All it needed was a blasting cap such as Goble's expulsion from school. The leathery marine, with a solid build of five feet nine and a half inches, began to abuse his diminutive protégé. "He pounded me, he beated me, most every day," Sam complained to George W. Eaton, Madison's president. Though a man of massive intellect and unbounded love, Eaton was at times inept in handling delicate personnel matters. His reluctance to deal firmly with offenders—Goble in this case—left Sam with little recourse. The violence harked back to Sam's early weeks on the *Susquehanna* when crewmen accustomed to kicking Chinese coolies applied their bruising boots to the Japanese as well. Even the frail Eliza Goble, a great-grandson claimed, had a hot temper and grew irritated at having the Japanese menial "forever under foot, especially when least desired."[13]

Once when his ill-treatment grew intolerable, Sam slipped away to a wood at West Eaton, about eight miles away, and attempted suicide by drowning. S. J. Douglas, a Madison student who heard Sam's own account of the experience, recalled that when Sam entered the water, "he thought it was too cold to drown in with any comfort." His clothes dripping wet, Sam made his way to a nearby house, whose occupants proved to be good Samaritans. They took him in, provided dry clothes, and kept him for a week. Sam abandoned his suicide wish and returned to the Goble home with an air of resignation.[14]

Irresistible Grace

President Eaton had announced in 1856 that Sam "entered college with
a view to return, some day, as a missionary to his native land." Goble had
made similar statements in soliciting donations for his own support. Perry's

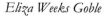

Eliza Weeks Goble

Jonathan Goble

Narrative of the Expedition, published in 1856, had spread this expectation far
beyond Baptist circles. "One of the marines named Goble, a religious
man," the *Narrative* said, "had taken a special interest in [Sam Patch];
finding in his docility and intelligence promise of good fruit from a
properly directed religious training, Goble had begun with him a system of
instruction which he hoped would not only make the Japanese a fair
English scholar, but a faithful Christian."[15]

Yet after two years under Goble's wing in the isolated Baptist sanctuary
at Hamilton Village, Sam was yet to become a Christian, much less a
candidate for missionary service. Although he attended Hamilton Baptist
Church and its Sabbath school, he resisted all efforts to convert him, and
this frustrated Goble's long-standing plan to exploit him for the promotion
of missions. Timid, artless Sam was less intelligent than widely assumed,
but his soul was no easy catch. Though submissive and compliant, he had
a mind of his own.

When the Japanese embassy of 1860 was visiting Washington, D.C., the
New York Times reported that several ministers of various denominations
"thrust themselves at divers times upon these people, with the benevolent
object of converting them immediately to the doctrines of Christianity."[16]
These clergymen were especially active with their proselytizing in a back

parlor at Willard's Hotel where the Japanese were housed. They seemed unaware that the embassy was tribal in nature and, like some Communist delegations a century later, its members were expected to spy on one another, being especially careful that no one was infected or even tainted with the "pernicious" Christian faith. The arduous, well-meant efforts to evangelize these Japanese were futile.

Even in the Baptist enclave where Sam Patch was entrapped, there was skepticism as to whether the lone Japanese would embrace the Christian faith. As reported by Matthew Kempsey, a student correspondent for the *American Baptist*, "Some felt that it was presumption on the part of those who encouraged him to come here that he might be converted, and feared that if for no other reason than this, he never would be born into Christ's kingdom."[17] This pessimism was probably reenforced by Goble's maltreatment of his ward.

Goble failed to comprehend that Sam was a vigorous personality who suffered frustration at the deepest level. The waif groveled before Jonathan, as he had groveled before two-sworded Japanese officials, but he longed to rise above his minion status. He remembered his fellow crewmen of the *Eiriki-maru*, especially the two in San Francisco, Kamezō and Jisaku. He somehow knew that Kamezō had saved up fifteen hundred dollars. He may have known that Jisaku, a playboy who lived day by day and saved nothing for the future, was said to spend two dollars on pleasure for every one dollar he spent on food and clothing. It was Sam's dream to join his countrymen and accumulate some wealth of his own—or at least enjoy a better life. Several times he tried to run away, "hoping to reach California by some means or other," only to fail. Ultimately, though, his aim was to rejoin his mates in Japan. And he knew the peril of returning as a Christian. "Not only would he lose his own life," Kempsey sympathized, "but also endanger those of his own friends."[18]

Even so, Sam had little in common with the members of the 1860 Japanese embassy. A castaway isolated from his country against his will and unavoidably marred by outside influences was more vulnerable to evangelistic zeal. Rikimatsu in Hong Kong, Otokichi in Shanghai—both were Christians. So was Sam's own crewmate Joseph Heco. Conversion to the foreign faith was not unthinkable. The crucible of his shipwreck experience and ensuing events had already transmuted the castaway into a runaway.

Sam had been isolated from his own people for nine years and virtually imprisoned in a Baptist bastion for over two years. Should the conflicted alien renounce his Japanese identity and cast his lot with the Americans? His head was spinning, his heart in turmoil. He was trapped in a sinkhole of agony. "Being a member of our Sabbath-school," Kempsey wrote, "he drew a book from the library to read, which seemed to impress him with the fact that salvation was by Christ alone." Cornered and coerced, bombarded with "irresistible grace," Sam at last succumbed to the mounting pressure. To escape feelings of wretchedness and despair, he agreed to be baptized.[19]

Candidates for baptism at the five-hundred-member Hamilton Baptist Church customarily made a public profession of faith at the monthly "covenant meeting." This was also the occasion for pledging obedience to the church covenant, which defined the conduct and lifestyle expected of members. Sam made his profession Saturday, March 6, 1858, by coincidence the day of Commodore Perry's funeral in New York City. Standing before the congregation, no doubt trembling, he said, "I trust my heart all to God—cloud gone—all bright—great load gone—head light—feel just like fly away." Two other students and a girl of eight or nine also gave their statements of faith. The next morning the Reverend Hezekiah Harvey immersed the four new believers in Chenango Creek near the railroad station, probably close to where the creek now runs under Lebanon Street. To be baptized by this English-born cleric was an honor. Harvey, age thirty-six, served as the church's pastor only one year before his election as Professor of Church History and Pastoral Theology in the Hamilton Theological Seminary. It was a year crowned with sixty-four baptisms. Once thwarted by disease from going to China as a missionary, Harvey blended high scholarship with a passion for winning souls.[20]

Sunday, March 7, was a bitterly cold day for an outdoor baptism. When Pastor Harvey lowered him into the icy waters, Sam may have recalled the time he entered similar waters at West Eaton in a failed suicide attempt. This time he followed through on his commitment. Through the pictorial rite of immersion, Sam died to sin, was buried with Christ, and rose to newness of life. He was duly entered in the church roll as "Samuel Sintaro."[21]

As is usual in a conversion experience, Sam's life was now deepened with new meaning, enlarged with new purpose. His burden was gone, the painful struggle over. A deep peace filled his heart. He would say in prayer meeting, "Love Jesus, so happy." His broken English would evoke laughter from some of the students until Alexander M. Beebee, professor of logic and English literature, intervened. Though physically weak and one who by temperament and disposition was an effective comforter of the sick, Beebee spoke with intensity, and students knew better than to ignore him. He convinced them that Sam's confession was no laughing matter. "What a wealth of soul that expresses," Beebee said, "for that once dark heathen mind in which the light now shines!"[22]

Nitobe Inazō wrote of Sam that "the poor heathen was dubbed a Christian by being dipped in water."[23] The cynical tone is understandable, given the pressures on Sam to convert. But Sam was no "rice Christian." To strike out for Japan as lackey to an aggressive missionary—and this is exactly what he would do—required a serious commitment if not a willingness to die for his new faith. This commitment would be renewed in San Francisco and again in Honolulu, where Sam would bypass opportunities to bail out and enjoy the security of a free society. His remaining life would confirm that both his conversion experience and his commitment to missionary service were genuine, however limited his capacity for fulfillment. Sam "lacked Yankee pluck," as Nitobe wrote, but his Christian convictions seemed to have a core of steel.

Captain Macy, who had helped look after Sam and his shipmates in San Francisco following their rescue at sea, read that Professor Harvey had baptized a Japanese youth. When he learned that the convert was one of the Japanese he had befriended seven years before, he invited Sam to spend his school vacation at the Macy home in New York. Sam stayed about two months. "I was delighted to hear him speaking in our own language," Macy wrote, "and telling in broken accents of the wondrous love of God."[24]

Setting His Face toward Home

Back in Hamilton, Sam made preparations for the long anticipated return to Japan. He accompanied the Gobles to New York where a council of Baptist pastors examined Jonathan as a candidate for missionary service. The council recommended Goble's ordination to the gospel ministry and his appointment to Japan under the American Baptist Free Mission Society. The double recommendation was carried out in a special service November 3, 1859, at New York's Laight Street Baptist Church. Sam's presence added spice and color to the occasion.

A reporter for the *New York Evening Express* wrote:

The missionaries arrived at the appointed time. One of them, the Japanese convert—being almost a solitary Christian among millions of his race—was naturally enough, the "observed of all observers." Independent of his nativity, he would have attracted attention. His dress consisted of a light blue calico coat, joined together by a single lapel in front, a gray vest, buttoned almost up to the neck, and pants of a printed material so light as to be serviceable only under a tropical sun. The sight of his apparel would have chilled a sensitive Northerner at this season. Considered apart from his Japanese extraction, it might be deemed fantastical; but an observation of the quiet, unassuming appearance of Sentharo would have instantly dismissed such an opinion. It was simply the apparel of his sunny land, and he loved it for her sake.[25]

The reporter seemed unaware that Japan is no sunnier or more tropical than the United States. The climate of Japan's Pacific coast, the arena of Sam's life before his shipwreck, roughly corresponds to that of America's Atlantic coast. The reason for the out-of-season dress is as unclear as its appearance was misleading to the reporter. Perhaps it was a donated suit, something from the "missionary barrel," that Sam had taken a liking to. Perhaps the Gobles or other advisors planned his outfit to draw attention to Japan as exotic. Clearly, it was unauthentic. Sam's appearance would have drawn more stares in Edo than it did in New York.

One of the prayers offered during the service included a petition for "the Japanese guide," asking "that God would make him the humble instrument to lead his countrymen to Christ." Jonathan himself, in remarks following his ordination, expressed thanks that his Japanese friend "would also go with him, for he would be very useful—and perhaps advance his work."[26]

Then the focus shifted to the Japanese youth who all through the program had been eloquent in his silence. Sam was now invited to stand in the limelight and make some remarks. The trembling waif started out in Japanese, then at Pastor William S. Hall's request switched to English. His utterance "was accompanied by some declamation." Sam was heard to say: "I trust in Jesus—he save me—the world all wicked, tossing, tumbling, lying in wickedness—Jesus call me—send his Holy Spirit—old things pass away—behold all things become new—in the resurrection shall see him—Jesus see me then—he save me."[27]

Assuming that the published transcript fairly represents what Sam actually said, it appears that he had barely learned to piece together the most common Sunday school phrases in his four years at Hamilton. But to his credit, Sam's words were intelligible enough to be recorded. The more gifted castaways Manjirō and Heco, the best Japanese-English interpreters of their time, had their own limitations. Samples of their writing reveal that their English was hardly grammatical or idiomatic. Though less than fluent, however, they handled more complex ideas than Sam and managed to put their English skills to good use.[28]

The people who heard Sam's childlike testimony probably took it for granted that he could articulate the gospel effectively in his native tongue. This was assuming too much. Sam did sing a hymn in Japanese for the congregation, which must have been his own crude rendering of an English hymn. The performance was a fitting close to the service, a lasting thrill for those present. Goble's protégé was a celebrity in his own right.

Sam had already endeared himself to Baptists in his brief travels. Several churches and Sabbath schools in New York and New Jersey had sent him offerings ranging from twenty-five cents to twelve dollars, and the Seamen's Bethel had added its gift of $10.50. Two gentlemen named Raymond and Hoadley paid his passage to San Francisco, and other friends had furnished him with a liberal outfit. As a new Christian and potential missionary to his own people, Sam was pampered in New York much as he had been in San Francisco when regarded as a potential pawn in diplomatic efforts to open his country to the West.[29]

While in New York Sam stayed in the Sailors' Home as he had done upon leaving the *Mississippi*. One day Captain Macy visited the Sailors' Home and inquired how the bill was to be paid. "Write [Sam's story] for the readers of the *Life Boat*," he was told, and "the children will pay it." *Life Boat* was a four- and eight-page monthly published by the Seamen's Friend Society for the use of Sabbath schools. Macy's account, of interest to adults as well as children, was copied in the *Sailors' Magazine* and the *Friend* of Hawaii.[30]

Sailing day was Saturday, November 5, 1859. Sam rode in a carriage to the North River at the foot of Canal Street and boarded the steamer *Baltic* with Jonathan, Eliza, two-year-old Dorinda, and nearly a thousand other passengers. As the huge ship pulled away from the dock at two P.M., he waved goodbye to beaming, familiar faces, especially those from the Laight Street Church. He must have felt both joy and apprehension as the ship chugged out into the Atlantic on the first leg of his journey back to the homeland he had renounced. The sea was so rough that even globe-circling Jonathan was among the many who fell sick. Sam weathered the squalls with aplomb.[31]

After a weeklong voyage the *Baltic* reached Aspinwall, Panama. The passengers went ashore by launch and boarded a six-coach steam train for the three-hour, fifty-seven-mile ride from ocean to ocean. They passed through a lush land of palms where Sam's tropical outfit worn at the Laight Street Church would have been appropriate. Upon reaching the Pacific, the passengers took launches to the steamer *Sonora*, which carried them on to San Francisco in thirteen days.

Goble rented a room for his family in a widow's residence. Sam apparently found lodging with his former shipmate Kamezō, one of the three who had left the *Susquehanna* at Cum Sing Moon and returned to San Francisco with Thomas Troy. Kamezō had been alone in San Francisco for about eight months. Jisaku, formerly employed as a clerk in Wells, Fargo & Company's San Francisco office, had sailed to Hakodate, Japan, on the bark *Melita*. Heco had returned to Japan as interpreter for the U.S. consulate in Kanagawa.[32]

"Samuel has found one of his countrymen here," Jonathan reported, "and I do not know but we shall have two, instead of one, to go home with us."[33] It was his impression that Kamezō might join his party for the return to Japan. He was mistaken. Kamezō, though initially delighted to meet Sam again, probably feared to return in the company of a Christian "priest" and a fellow countryman who had defected to a faith not tolerated in Japan.

After Sam's departure, however, Kamezō grew increasingly lonely and anxious to return home. About a year later he obtained work on a cargo ship bound for Hong Kong, where he had the good fortune of meeting up with the Japanese embassy en route to Japan on the USS *Niagara*. Using the name Kamegorō, he requested and was granted permission to accompany the embassy home. One of its members, Nonomura Tadazane, thought the Westernized Kame looked like a Portuguese. The castaway arrived at Shinagawa in November, the last of the surviving *Eiriki-maru* crewmen to return to the homeland.[34]

While Jonathan tried to book passage to Japan, Sam had ample time to look over the bustling city, now in its second era of prosperity. The population had jumped to seventy thousand, though with men still outnumbering women three to one, and the city was claiming to be more cosmopolitan and advanced than many of the larger cities of Europe and America. The huts and shanties had been replaced with stone and brick structures, and many streets paved with stone blocks. But there were still muddy roads from the "late spell of wet weather," some near the wharves being barely passable. Several hotels were under construction to meet the growing demand for lodging. Crooked lotteries were on the rise. Eight hundred grog shops were in business. Among the persons arrested in November were 205 drunks.[35]

The churches were thriving. Sam probably attended the First Baptist Church on Washington Street with the Gobles, who chafed at hearing the Reverends J. L. Shuck and T. P. Crawford as visiting preachers. Both were slavery-tainted Southern Baptist missionaries. Doubtless Sam and the Gobles participated to some extent in the traditional week of prayer, January 9 to 15, which featured daily prayer, praise, and preaching services, both union and separate, in the various churches of the city. The peace of their last Sunday in San Francisco was shattered by immense quantities of firecrackers exploded by the local Chinese in celebration of their New Year.[36]

The Broad Pacific Again

Several trading ships arrived from Japan, bringing pears, sweet potatoes, and pea beans, but Jonathan was unable to book passage on any of them for the return voyage. The charterers of the schooner *Page* and the bark *What Cheer* turned him down, the *Alta California* reported, "probably on the ground that the attempt of Mr. Goble to convert the natives to Christianity might possibly prove a hindrance, in some way, to the trade and commercial operations which the charterers had in view." The *Polynesian* was to report that the *Onward* also turned him down.[37]

As Goble was an avid reader of newspapers, he probably noticed that *What Cheer* conveyed a young man named Frank P. Knight to Yokohama. Knight had recently visited Japan and formed a copartnership with Joseph Heco for a shipping and commission business. He was now going to Yokohama with ten thousand dollars in cash to launch the firm of Knight & Heco. Because of his association with a missionary, Sam was denied travel on the ship that bore his former shipmate's business partner.[38]

With better options closed, Goble booked space on the bark *Frances Palmer* sailing for Honolulu, hoping to find there a whaler or trading vessel that would convey them on to Japan. "We pay $130 for our passage to the islands," he wrote, "and Sentharo goes as cabin boy." Sam was overjoyed to find Thomas Troy aboard the *Frances Palmer*. Troy was his hero, one who would jump to Sam's defense if Goble should strike him.[39]

Also on board was C. A. Williams, owner of a first-class Honolulu mercantile house. He told Goble he was interested in going to Japan to establish a branch house and that if he went, he would take the Goble party in his ship. After arriving in Honolulu, Williams indeed arranged to travel in his bark *Zoe* to obtain "beautiful specimens of Japanese workmanship." And true to his word, he offered Sam and the Gobles the "opportunity of getting to the field of their missionary labors."[40]

In Honolulu the Bethel chaplain and *Friend* editor who had met Jonathan in 1854 showed the Gobles and Sam every courtesy. Samuel Damon arranged for "Samuel Sentharo" to lodge in the Sailor's Home, a three-story wooden structure with verandas on each level. The weekly charge for lodging and meals was six dollars at the officers' table and five dollars at the seamen's table. Thanks to Damon, Sam Patch paid nothing. This outstanding missionary would be honored by his alma mater Amherst

with a doctor of divinity degree. Though intensely interested in Japan, he would not realize his desire to visit that country until 1884—ten years after Sam's death, two years after Goble's final return to the United States, and one year before his own demise in Honolulu.[41]

Sam did not forget the generous aid. "It was our privilege," Damon later reported, "to receive a letter written by this Japanese, in the English language, and dated Kanagawa, April 24, 1860."[42] The letter was brought by the *Zoe* on its return trip, along with a letter from Goble. Damon published Goble's letter in the *Friend* but not Sam's, which was likely a childlike expression of

Samuel C. Damon with wife and son

thanks for Damon's kindness. The original letter, if extant, would be valuable as a sample of Sam's handwriting. Apparently it is lost.

Four decades of missionary activity apparently had transformed the Sandwich Islands into a semi-Western, semi-Christian realm. Twenty-two thousand of the seventy-five to eighty thousand inhabitants were members of evangelical Protestant churches. "Forty years ago," one writer noted, "nothing was more common than for a ship, as soon as it had cast its anchor, to be surrounded by twenty, or thirty, or fifty women, nearly if not entirely naked, swimming around the vessel, and climbing up its sides. This has long since ceased, to the great indignation of wicked men, who naturally hate the religion which caused the change . . ." Still, there was evidence aplenty that missionary influence had its limits. One member of the Japanese embassy that visited Honolulu within the month reported visiting a brothel, and another wrote that "the native women are very lewd and don't mind sexual intercourse even during the day."[43]

On February 19, a Sabbath day when all rum dens and businesses of every kind were closed and quiet was observed, Sam accompanied the Gobles to the Kaumakapili Church. This native Hawaiian church was under the pastoral care of the veteran missionary Lowell Smith. The visitors were unable to understand the language used in the service but attempted to sing the strange words printed in the hymnal. Perhaps Sam, as well as Goble who had learned a little of his language, noticed the similarities between Hawaiian and Japanese. The vowels and consonants were pronounced generally the same, and in both languages the words and even the syllables all ended in a vowel sound (with the exception of the *n* sound in Japanese).[44]

The following Saturday the commissioner of the United States, James W. Borden, had an audience scheduled with King Kamehameha III. Because the king was "indisposed," Queen Emma held court in his place. Commissioner Borden presented ten visitors to the queen, nine of them Americans including "the Rev. Mr. Goble and his lady." The tenth person so honored was "Mr. Samuel Santhare (*sic*), a native of Japan."[45]

Likely Sam was more favorably impressed with Hawaiian royalty than was Fukuzawa Yukichi, who visited Honolulu in May aboard the *Kanrin-maru* en route home from San Francisco. To Fukuzawa, who saw King Kamehameha as well as Queen Emma, the natives were "miserable" and brought to mind the word "barbarian." That the royal couple would display as their treasure a rug made of bird feathers disappointed this proud Japanese. "The king of Hawaii," he wrote, "seemed to me more or less the headman of a village of fishermen."[46]

The Goble party also attended a Monday evening gathering at the Fort Street Church at which several visiting missionaries gave addresses. Goble, the first speaker, lectured on "the civilization, refinement, superstitions and government of the Japanese," then introduced "Samuel Sentharo, a native of Japan." "This man," Jonathan said, "went with me to the United States, has lived in my family while I was pursuing my studies at Hamilton, and I hope has also become a true follower of the Lord Jesus Christ. He is, so far as I know, the only Japanese who has ever truly embraced the religion of the Bible."[47] Goble's "religion of the Bible" clearly excluded the Roman Catholic faith introduced to Japan in the sixteenth century, but did it exclude the Protestantism embraced by Rikimatsu and Otokichi? He was sufficiently well read to have known about the earlier Protestant converts. If so, he was speaking in a sectarian manner, as Baptist Goble often did.

After being introduced, the Japanese convert sang a hymn in his native tongue. Then he uttered a few broken sentences in English that were barely understood. Damon's ears caught the following: "I hope in Jesus. He save my soul. The Holy Spirit make my heart new. I go back to Japan to tell my people about Jesus."[48]

Two days later the *Zoe* under Captain Bush sailed with seven passengers: owner C. A. Williams, his bookkeeper F. S. Pratt, Thomas Troy, the Goble family of three, and Sam Patch.[49] If they had waited five more days, Sam would have seen the USS *Powhatan* arrive in Honolulu. The volcano-like black ship that terrified the inhabitants along Edo Bay when Sam was aboard was now carrying the first Japanese embassy to the United States.

The *Zoe* reached the coast of Japan March 30, 1860, thirty days from Honolulu, but it was tossed about for two days in storm and fog before entering Edo Bay. The ship sailed past familiar landmarks Americanized as Perry Island, Plymouth Rock, Saratoga Spit, Susquehanna Bay, Mississippi Bay, and Treaty Point. It was past midnight when the *Zoe* dropped anchor off the faint, eerie shoreline of Kanagawa. For Sam Patch, the place would have been scary. Unlike on his previous return visits to Japan, he lacked the protection of an American naval uniform and the big guns of a war steamer. He needed whatever courage and comfort he could muster from his Christian faith—here a forbidden faith. His pounding heart resonated with the midnight gloom.

Chapter 6

Protection under the Flag

Samuel, our Japanese boy, is permitted to land safely under the protection of the American flag.

—Jonathan Goble[1]

Daybreak unveiled a long sweep of drab wooden houses and budding trees against a backdrop of picturesque hills. Strung along the higher elevations were massive Buddhist temples, their grey cemeteries offset by lovely gardens with cryptomeria and camellias in bloom. It was a familiar scene to Sam Patch, who had sailed along this coast on the *Eiriki-maru, Mississippi,* and *Powhatan*. But one striking feature he had never seen before. Above four of the temples hung foreign national flags—the stars and stripes among them—such as he had seen on ship masts in San Francisco and other major ports. The quaint but growing town of Kanagawa, population thirty thousand, now had diplomatic and commercial ties with the barbarian West.[2]

The four flags identified the temples in which the American, British, French, and Dutch consuls had installed themselves after the port's opening in July 1859. Most foreigners other than these consuls lived in nearby Yokohama, where the Japanese government had built a well-protected settlement complete with two stone wharves. The practical minded merchants and entrepreneurs preferred this location to Kanagawa proper, where the waters were shallow and the surroundings so congested that xenophobic swordsmen could hardly be contained. But the legalistic diplomats, insisting on a strict interpretation of the Harris Treaty, had denounced the Yokohama settlement as illegal and demanded housing within the old town of Kanagawa itself. Since temples were the only available buildings secure and large enough to meet their needs, the Japanese government had yielded these sacred structures, expelling the priests and their venerated gods.

The pioneer missionaries, all Americans, chose to cooperate with their consul in Kanagawa, E. M. Dorr. Unlike the defiant expatriates in Yokohama, their objectives lay outside the realm of business and profits. With Dorr's assistance they had obtained two of the seven Buddhist structures thus far leased to foreigners. Dr. and Mrs. James C. Hepburn of the Presbyterian Board and the Reverend and Mrs. Samuel Robbins Brown of the Dutch Reformed Board shared the facilities at Jōbutsuji, a Pure Land temple. They split the rent of twelve dollars a month. Dr. and Mrs. Duane B. Simmons, also Dutch Reformed, resided at Zen-related Sōkōji. Now it was Jonathan Goble's turn at temple hunting for his family and Sam Patch.[3]

On that first morning anchored off Kanagawa, Sam remained aboard the Zoe with Eliza and daughter Dora while Jonathan visited Consul Dorr at his lofty perch in Hongakuji. The stout, hard-drinking consul informed the newcomer that he faced an uphill battle for living space in the town, since the Japanese government was pressuring the few foreigners residing there to move to Yokohama. For the present time the Gobles would have to impose on another missionary family. Leaving Hongakuji, Jonathan made his way down a path through rice paddies, vegetable gardens, and fragrant rape blossom fields, passed Jōsōji, the temple that housed the British consul, and entered the grounds of Jōbutsuji, home of the Hepburns and the Browns. Though at a lower elevation without the magnificent view of the bay that Dorr enjoyed, this temple stood well above the Tōkaidō, the coastal highway that intersected the long straggling town.

Dr. Hepburn and his wife Clarissa—or Clara, as he called her—occupied the temple proper at the end of a stone walk leading from the compound gate. They had divided the forty-two-square-foot building into eight rooms and installed western furniture, including a wood-burning Franklin stove. One room was occupied by a long-term boarder named Francis Hall, a brilliant journalist, businessman, and Dutch Reformed layman. Another room was given over to Mrs. William Culbertson, a Presbyterian missionary visiting from China for a few weeks.[4]

Connected with the temple proper by a covered walkway was the sprawling, irregularly shaped priests' house. Here lived the Brown family: Robbins, his gentle wife Elizabeth, their grown-up daughter Julia, and two smaller children, Howard and Hattie, whom the Japanese regarded as "great curiosities."[5] Another child, Robert, was attending Rutgers College. The Browns were keeping Caroline Adrian, a single woman who had accompanied them from New York as a self-supporting missionary and would later transfer to the Dutch Reformed mission in Amoy, China.

Despite the strain it would put on their household, the Browns offered to make room for the Gobles until they could find a place of their own. That afternoon Jonathan, Eliza, and Dora moved from the *Zoe* to the compound. Dirty, bare-legged "coolies" transported their baggage, much of it slung from bamboo poles resting on their shoulders.

Sam stayed behind. "We have not yet got Sentharo on shore," Jonathan wrote at week's end, "as it is thought best to keep him on board, out of reach of danger, until the consul has arranged with the government . . . We expect all will be soon settled, so that we can have a home and take him with us." One writer has called Sam a "coward" for remaining aboard ship.

Jōbutsuji

Sam was timid and cautious by nature, but his acquiescence to consular advice in this instance was hardly cowardice. Given his lack of clout, he had little choice but to comply.[6]

After three weeks aboard ship, Sam was brought to Jōbutsuji "under the protection of the American flag," as arranged by Dorr. This special status was crucial. Unlike his shipmate Joseph Heco, now a Yokohama business-man and Dorr's part-time interpreter, Sam lacked the immunity from arrest guaranteed by American citizenship. Technically, he was still a Japanese subject. So even the consul's assurances could not relieve Sam's apprehension altogether. "When he first landed," Goble wrote, "he was both happy in the thought that after ten years' absence he was once more permitted to set his foot on his native soil and afraid that he might be seized and punished according to the ancient law and custom of the empire, with regard to those who by any means have seen foreign countries."[7]

Apparently Sam took the precaution of using a new alias in his dealings with the Japanese. Perhaps he thought it unsafe to use earlier names such as Sentarō or Sempachi, by which he was known to his junk mates, or Kurazō, by which he was known to Japanese officials while with the Perry expedition. A map of Kanagawa dated Man'en (1860 was the first year of Man'en) lists the residents of Jōbutsuji as "Hepburn-Brown" and "Goble-Unosuke." Unosuke almost certainly refers to Sam.[8]

Every precaution was justified. The castaway Manjirō, who had endured two years of interrogations before being allowed a brief visit with his mother, had just returned from San Francisco and Honolulu after serving as interpreter on the *Kanrin-maru*. While in Yokohama he accepted an invitation to go aboard an American vessel. Consequently he was accused of secretly disclosing information to the foreigners and, despite claims of innocence, was fired as an instructor at the naval school and for a time confined to his home.[9] Such was the climate of suspicion that Sam faced in Japan.

There was a greater peril still. A Japanese Christian in government hands would face the choice between recanting his religious beliefs or enduring prison and abuse. Sam's own shipmates, like Manjirō, had been required to trample on a Christian ikon to prove they were not contaminated by the dreaded faith. Sam could have met this requirement easily had he accepted repatriation while with the Perry expedition, but no longer. His life had changed, and being a Christian meant to the Japanese that he was subversive. Special protection was a must.

The Feel of Cold Steel

Worse still for Sam, not even the guarantees that Dorr arranged could shield him from the razor-sharp blades of the *rōnin*. These masterless, unbridled samurai thrived on wild rumors. The alien intruders had come, it was said, to destroy morality, practice sorcery, and drain the country of its goods and produce because their own lands were sterile. They used Japanese blood to dye their clothes red. The feet concealed in their boots were like horses' hooves, toeless and incompatible with thonged sandals. They were like hogs because they trampled on Japanese floors with their boots on (too often true). Such tales fueled the burgeoning movement known as *jōi*, "expel the barbarians."

So Sam had less to fear from Japanese law than from lawless swordsmen. In Yokohama, despite strategically placed guardhouses and gatekeepers, two Dutch shipmasters and three Russians had been slashed to death on the streets at night. More ominous for Sam was a murder committed in the middle of the day. The Chinese servant of José Loureiro, a Portuguese serving as vice consul for France, was chased through the streets by a man with drawn sword. Before the hapless servant could reach the safety of a foreign compound he was slashed and gashed beyond repair. He lingered but a few days.[10]

One month before Sam came ashore, the *tairo* (great elder) who had signed commercial treaties with the United States and four other Western powers paid for this brashness with his life. Ii Naosuke was riding in a stately palanquin that was surrounded by a small army of attendants and armed guards on a snowy Saturday morning. When the procession reached the Sakurada Gate of Edo Castle, eighteen bystanders suddenly threw aside the cloaks hiding their swords and slashed their way to the palanquin, making off with Ii's severed head.[11]

Another murder that took place earlier that year was the most frightening one of all for Sam. His shipmate Iwakichi, also called Dankichi and nicknamed Dan Ketch, had been slain just outside the gate of the British consulate general in Edo, where he was employed as linguist and confidential servant to Sir Rutherford Alcock. Attacking from behind, the assassin thrust his short sword with such force that it was buried to the hilt in Dan's body, the point emerging above the right breast. "These gentry strike home," Alcock commented, "and require no second blow to complete their work."[12] Dan staggered a few paces toward the compound gate, where the porter pulled out the sword before the victim collapsed in a bloody heap. Within ten minutes he was dead.

The gruesome deed was carried out on a Sunday afternoon in broad daylight, in full view of the men, women, and children who happened to be at the scene. Dan was said to have been playing with the children, helping them fly their kites. The murderer, his face reportedly covered by a basket-like straw hat, fled like a deer and got away with his crime. More frightening for Sam, the murder happened directly under the British flag that flew above the consulate general's gate. A British subject, Dan was protected under that flag more securely than Sam under the American flag. But he proved defenseless when attacked.

Why was Dan singled out for death? "The immediate cause," Alcock reported, "was probably some personal enmity, added to his unpopularity with the whole class of officials, who looked upon him as a sort of traitor to his own country; because, speaking both English and Japanese, he was . . . suspected of giving me information not otherwise obtainable nor always palatable to them." Alcock also acknowledged that more was involved than Dan's glaring status as a turncoat. The linguist was "ill-tempered, proud, and violent." His privileged status as longtime American resident and then British subject seems to have gone to his head and brought out the worst in him. "He was puffed up with the pride of place," wrote Francis Hall, "and became insolent and abrasive to the people." He wore European clothes ostentatiously and played up his Western identity with a vengeance. When insults were hurled at him—Dan comprehended the words as foreigners could not—he responded in kind with impunity. He lashed out at proud samurai in their own language, which was far more provocative than being cursed in English or French.[13]

Dan's flamboyance and overweening manner were symptomatic of gross indiscretion. Hall noted Dan's "unfortunate intrigue with a tea house damsel which resulted in her imprisonment, and that of her family, and his being shunned in every tea house he entered." Was he utterly indifferent to the growing resentment against him? At the public bathhouse, Alcock was told, some patrons in Dan's own hearing had talked about designs on his life. Joseph Heco had warned him repeatedly to be more careful. But Dan had been overconfident if not arrogant, far from prudent or discreet. He had relied too heavily on good luck, the British flag, and the Colt revolver at his side.[14]

His glaring faults notwithstanding, Dan as murder victim was honored with a splendid Buddhist funeral and buried at Kōrinji, on the left bank of the Furukawa River in Takanawa not far from the British legation. His grave is marked by a tablet that reads "Dankirche, Japanese linguist to the British Legation, murdered by Japanese assassins on January 21, 1860." Nearby is the grave of Henry Heusken, the Dutch-born interpreter to the American Legation in Edo, who was ambushed by a band of swordsmen a year later. His mistress and friends had urged the popular Heusken to be more circumspect, but he too had not taken heed.[15]

Like Dan Ketch, Sam Patch had adopted Western dress and ways, but he was more restrained by temperament and far less likely to arouse anger and resentment. Yet even Sam had taunted his fellow countrymen while aboard the *Mississippi*. Moreover, he was a Christian. Although Dan had retained a number of Bibles and prayer books given him in America and China, unlike Rikimatsu, Otokichi, Heco, and Sam, Dan had successfully resisted the most zealous efforts to convert him to the foreign faith. Religion was not a factor in his demise.

As for Sam, his subservience to foreigners as a baptized Christian could be seen more as karma than a crime, as more deserving of pity than scorn. But he could not depend on this sympathetic view. And no matter what cautions he might exercise to avoid ruffians, no matter how tightly he might cling to his foreign protectors, the possibility of a horrible fate hung steadily over his head. He must have cringed quite often at the thought of cold steel piercing his body or slashing his throat. No foreigner or lackey of foreigners was exempt from the ire of ruthless swordsmen.

Joseph Heco, who traveled extensively in the region and frequented the theater with Francis Hall, sensed this danger increasingly. Like Dan, he was told that *rōnin* were out to cut him down. So the next year, after the warnings "waxed far too frequent for my comfort," Heco prudently departed for the United States. In San Francisco he told Robert H. Pruyn that he was regarded by his countrymen "with great jealousy if not constant suspicion and so much so that he cannot do business there nor live there in safety."[16] Pruyn was to succeed Townsend Harris as U.S. minister to Japan.

Sam was safer than Heco because of the tight security imposed on Jōbutsuji. The authorities had surrounded the temple grounds with a stockade fence and erected a guardhouse at the gate. Two-sworded officials, called *yakunin*, kept a careful check on persons entering or leaving the enclosure. But the *yakunin* also marched into the compound frequently to make inquiry of the occupants, and Sam must have wondered at times whether he might be seized. His life was unsettled also because the Gobles still had no house of their own. They were guests of the Browns, occupying a small room finished off for them in a detached

S. R. Brown

area described as the "woodhouse/kitchen."[17] Where Sam lodged is unclear, but his makeshift quarters must have been no more ideal than those of the Gobles.

Many were the difficult adjustments Sam had to make, not having lived in his homeland for nearly a decade. For seven years, ever since being separated from his shipmates at Shanghai, the expatriate had seldom been with other Japanese people. "He had almost forgotten his native tongue," Goble noted, "and even yet he forgets and speaks English to his own countrymen."[18] His use of English in this way could have been a ploy to mount and maintain a safety barrier between himself and other Japanese. Sam had not abandoned his language altogether. In both New York and Honolulu he had sung a hymn in his native tongue. He had conversed with Kamezō during their weeks together in San Francisco. At times he had tutored his patron. Goble had "acquired a tolerable acquaintance with the Japanese language," Damon wrote during the Honolulu stopover, "so that he can both read and write the same, and also converse in it. He has acquired this knowledge from books, and intercourse with Samuel Sentharo."[19]

After reaching Japan, Goble looked to others for instruction in the language. He reported learning katakana from a young samurai he employed briefly (the authorities drove the tutor away). He also engaged a few other teachers, only to have the authorities intervene. It is apparent from Goble's efforts that Sam had little to offer with his crude, low-class Japanese. The British diplomat Ernest Satow, who studied the language with Robbins Brown, described one of his Japanese teachers as "stupid and of little assistance."[20] He might have described Sam as of no assistance whatever.

Sam clearly lacked the drive and confidence of the slain Dan Ketch, whose language ability, however modest, was helpful to Alcock at a time when Japanese-English interpreters were scarce. He lacked the intelligence and versatility of Joseph Heco, who engaged in trade, published the newspaper *Kaigai shimbun,* and worked for the Ministry of Finance. He lacked the practical skills of three other junk mates who built Western-style ships. To quote Nitobe again, Sam was destined to be "a poor house servant" the rest of his life. Even so, this was no dreadful fate, no cause for pity or tears.

Not All Servants Are Equal

At Jōbutsuji the Hepburns and Browns had a bevy of servants to sweep the grounds, clean the buildings, draw water from the compound well, cook meals, do laundry, run errands. All of them were Japanese, in contrast to the diplomats' cooks and washermen, who were mostly Chinese or English. Some of the Japanese helpers were exceptional in ability, coming from good families but willing to do menial tasks in order to learn the language and culture of the Americans. "The servants are quick to learn and are active and pleasant," wrote China missionary John L. Nevius, who with his wife Helen lodged with the Hepburns in July. "They walk rapidly and noiselessly through the home without shoes, sliding back the light partitions."[21] Some missionaries would keep the same servants for decades and come to love them as members of the family.

The compound employees were all males with the exception of "a roguish eyed little Japanese girl" Dr. Hepburn had engaged. The authorities frowned on this deviation from the norm and threatened to take the girl away. Whether they did so is unclear.[22] Sam Patch, though male, was a deviation in another sense, a queer misfit who occupied a sort of undefined space at the temple complex. He could not be taken away by the authorities, but neither could he be dismissed in short order. His identity was fuzzy and confused.

But Sam had a great deal to offer. Despite his meager intellect, as a servant in foreign homes he clearly had the edge on his competition. Sam had lived among Americans long enough to be familiar with their language and culture. The Hepburns and Browns, who spoke Japanese "only with a stammering tongue," were surely pleased to have someone on the compound who could understand English fairly well and interpret for them in a pinch. Yet this was one of the lesser advantages Sam had over the other servants.

Tokugawa Japan had a pervasive system of espionage that was an accepted part of life under the feudal regime. Everyone of any importance was subject to the constant gaze of the *metsuke*, the prying eyes of a despotic government determined to squelch dissent lest it become sedition. Every official was "duplicated," with one spying upon the other. "No one is safe from his neighbor," wrote a correspondent for the *New York Times*. ". . . The two crimes most abhorred in Ireland are here not only commonly practiced but honored—unchastity and 'informing.'"[23]

Thus it was general knowledge that Japanese servants doubled as spies. Whether they had applied for the job on their own accord or had been planted as trained eyes and ears, they had to report to the government officials charged with gathering intelligence on the foreign intruders. Sir Rutherford Alcock commented that "spies habitually invent more than they ever discover."[24] This must have been true of some of the servants' accounts of the exotic creatures inhabiting the Jōbutsuji compound. Sam Patch himself must have been a titillating subject for intelligence reports.

The missionaries, forced to tolerate this irksome situation, tried to look on the bright side. The servants not only reported out, they also reported in, sharing useful news and rumors from the surrounding community. And in reporting out, whether formally to stern officials or informally to curious neighbors, they sometimes cleared up misunderstandings about their employers. Perhaps they challenged the widespread assumption, for instance, that Caroline Adrian, who lived with the Brown family, was Mr. Brown's concubine. Perhaps they testified that the so-called barbarians were not so barbaric after all. One of Dr. Hepburn's servants confessed that he had taken the job for the purpose of murdering him, but after a few weeks of observing the doctor's character and conduct, the would-be assassin had scrapped his evil intent.[25]

No matter how dependable the other servants might be, only Sam was exempt from interrogation by the authorities about the personal activities of his masters. Because of his unique protection under the American flag, he could not be arrested or detained. True, the authorities refrained from making any arrests within the sacred temple enclosure, but they could and did seize servants without explanation when they were outside the compound. So if Sam did not cringe in fear at the presence of the *yakunin*, as the other servants did, he at least would have shown them cautious respect.

Sam was preferable to Japanese servants also because of his sobriety. Doubtless he had savored his cups of sake with his *Eiriki-maru* shipmates and his rations of grog with American sailors. But his four years with the Gobles, mostly in the strict Baptist enclave at Hamilton, had distanced him from alcohol, and his conversion in that Puritanical setting implied a lifelong commitment to abstinence. As a dry domestic, Sam was a rarity in Japan.

In this "nation of drunkards," to use Hepburn's term, foreigners on their rambles were often terrorized by intoxicated men. On one occasion Clara Hepburn, despite being accompanied by guards, was dealt a heavy blow on the shoulder by a pole-wielding drunk. Later another sot who followed the Hepburns blatantly insulted them and menaced them with a short sword. The compound servants were rarely a threat in this way, but they were no less given to drink than many a swaggering blade. A couple of months after Sam's arrival at Jōbutsuji, a tippling servant named Kami had become so worthless from his addiction that Mrs. Hepburn dismissed him and asked her husband's language teacher, Honda Sadajirō, to find a sober replacement. Honda brought her a candidate but declined to recommend him. "All that are active and intelligent drink and all that do not drink are fools," he said. Brown's language teacher, Yano Mototaka, agreed.[26]

To Francis Hall, this "national vice" was so pervasive that one simply had to accommodate it whenever possible. After seeing his horse groom so intoxicated that he could not mount, Hall opined that it was "useless to dismiss a servant for drunkenness unless his habit becomes troublesome. A new one might be just as bad."[27] The groom, Hikozō, kept his job.

When the Anglican bishop George Smith was a guest of the Browns that summer, he observed that one of the servants "became so maddened by sakee . . . that two other Japanese were compelled to hold him during the paroxysms of his drunken frenzy and boisterous clamour." In Goble's eyes, the Browns themselves were partly to blame. "Missionaries here," the teetotal Baptist charged, ". . . attend public dinners, drink wine and porter, give and receive toasts." Brown did drink wine in moderation, as William Griffis also pointed out, but he encouraged total abstinence among sailors for whom one drink led to the next and the next and the next. Brown saw no contradiction in this stance, but Goble viewed it as deleterious compromise. "The effect is already apparent among the natives," he claimed, "for while their servants are frequently getting drunk and making them trouble, we have no difficulty of the kind in our house." Since Goble was at times a brute who would whack a tipsy servant and boot him out the door, his underlings were more likely to remain sober. And while he had Sam Patch under his finger, Goble probably employed only one or two others at most.[28]

Yakunin (an official)

Indeed, it was customary for the best of servants to go out frolicking in the evening and come home reeking of spirits. This included Tomi, a former peddler who seemed to know everybody. At least he managed to put off his indulgence until evening, Hall reported, and to render good service during the day. Tomi left Jōbutsuji before the year-end and worked as a guide for the English botanist Robert Fortune, who resided for a time at the French consulate. Tomi looked red about the eyes in the mornings, Fortune noted, but "he kept sober, for the most part, during the day."[29]

Still, terrible things could happen at night. After the Hepburns moved from Jōbutsuji to Yokohama, the doctor prudently warned his four booze-loving servants that the alcohol he kept for medical purposes could be fatal if swallowed. But the servants conspired to steal into his dispensary one night and help themselves to the fiery liquid. Even though they took the precaution of diluting it with water, the four men drank themselves into a stupor and lost consciousness. One had a wife, fortunately, who came searching for her missing husband. She alerted the doctor, who in his usual compassionate manner rendered medical assistance to the servants and, upon their recovery, accepted their suffering and shame as full atonement for their crime of theft.

The prevalence of theft in Japan was another reason Sam was a prize of a servant. Young men in need of extra money for their recurrent visits to houses of prostitution, if not for alcohol, would steal out of desperation. Those employed by foreigners were easily tempted by their ready access to imported, exotic goods. On one occasion the trusted Tomi secretly cut off a slice of a quarter of beef he carried to Jōbutsuji from the boat landing. In a more serious case, the servant Kako, teenage son of Brown's teacher Yano, pilfered some trifles and then went so far as to take Japanese coins worth about forty dollars out of Brown's safe. His fellow servants exposed him lest they be implicated in his crime and land in jail themselves. Even though Kako returned most of the loot, the other servants still wanted him dismissed, but his father pled that he be given another chance. Faced with this dilemma, Brown took the boy to Edo and made new arrangements for him there.[31]

Another advantage Sam had over other servants was the dress code he had learned in America. "I wonder what a New York lady would do," Hepburn wrote, "to go into her kitchen and find the servants cooking or scrubbing in a state of almost entire nudity." As bug-eyed visitors to Japan liked to recount in their journals and letters, male laborers preferred to work clad only in a loincloth, lower-class women often went about nude above the waist, and children played stark naked. Both sexes of all ages stripped and washed themselves in their yards and streets or engaged in "indiscriminate tubbing" at the public baths. Dr. Hepburn spoke for many prudish Westerners when he called such habits "repulsive and shocking to our sense of what is proper and decent." He and Clara broke their own servants of the habit of showing up for work in scanty clothing, but such restraints were not always easy to enforce.

Further to Sam's advantage, he had been provided Western medical care for several years and apparently was free from various ailments that affected the Japanese. One common ailment was the itch, which Doctors Hepburn and Simmons treated frequently. "It is almost impossible to get a domestic servant free from this loathsome disease," Rutherford Alcock complained, "or keep him so."[33] Sam was an exception.

Again, Sam was adept at preparing Western as well as Japanese dishes. His years of experience with the Gobles added handsomely to his value as a cook. While boarding in the Hepburn home, Francis Hall complained that "the fish came on to the table dripping with oil in which it had been cooked unscaled and uneviscerated." The four servants at the time (Tomi, Kami, Kuni, Kimpachi) were "awkward louts as ever served." When Kuni tried to make some hot rolls, Hall said, they turned out heavy and flat. Not surprisingly, Hepburn wrote that his wife "had a heavy load of housekeeping in her having to teach new servants to wash and to cook."[34]

Sam's familiarity with Western appliances also added to his value in foreign homes. The servants in the English legation at Edo "lit a monstrous fire in the dining-room stove," Alcock wrote, which resulted in "sad destruction of tiles, roof, and ceilings." Had it not have been for a large pond close at hand and the fast arrival of the fire brigade in response to the clang of the temple bell, the whole building might have been destroyed by their carelessness.[35]

One habit of servants by no means harmful but nonetheless annoying was their obsequiousness. They bowed and prostrated themselves to their foreign masters in the same abject manner as to Japanese officials. There was little the foreigners could do to change this time-honored practice, though they could decline customary pampering such as being fanned constantly in the summer heat. Sam, who had prostrated himself before Japanese officials on the *Susquehanna,* no longer behaved in this manner. To the contrary, it is likely that the servants at Jōbutsuji prostrated themselves before him when he first appeared in Western dress.

Good-bye Gobles

Despite his superior worth as a servant, Sam was a burden to the Gobles, themselves a burden to the Browns. Each time Jonathan struck a deal for renting a house or temple, Japanese officials squelched the transaction, in one case arresting the would-be landlord. Consul Dorr kept protesting to the governor and making unveiled threats, but to no avail. The Gobles were increasingly frustrated and stressed out, and the many rainy days that May only added to the gloom.

"Samuel is still with us," wrote Jonathan after seven trying weeks at Jōbutsuji, "and desires to remain. When we have expressed our fears as to getting a house he has said, 'No fear, the Lord will give us a house.'"[36] Clearly, Sam's childlike faith was still intact. His expression of confidence in Providence fittingly marks his last appearance in all of Jonathan's voluminous correspondence.

Indeed, Sam's expectation was soon fulfilled. Jonathan and Consul Dorr conspired to move the Gobles' furniture into a house at the back of the compound whose owner was willing to rent. Then they managed to foil all government attempts to evict the Gobles. Dr. Hepburn described the "rear house" as "small and uncomfortable," but Jonathan hired some carpenters to renovate the place and make it liveable. Still, there was no room for Sam. The Gobles had to accommodate Jesse and Eliza Hartwell, Southern Baptist missionaries to China, who showed up with their infant son and a nurse and stayed four weeks to recruit their health. The Hepburns and Browns had guests of their own. The untimely, unwanted visit of the Hartwells, whose proslavery stance was anathema to the Gobles, trumped the misery of mosquitoes and the scorching July heat.[37]

The Gobles had room for Sam after the Hartwells had left, but they could not afford his keep. Even though the Hartwells paid for their board and Jonathan received honoraria for his Sunday preaching to the crews aboard ships anchored in the harbor, the Gobles were so strapped for cash that they borrowed money from Robbins Brown. They had arrived in Japan with only two hundred dollars, more than half of which had come as an unexpected gift from Christians in Hawaii. Not until November did they receive any funds from America, and then only $450 from the Free Mission Society—a half year's salary and fifty dollars for mission expenses. In the interim, house renovation, rent, and other expenses quickly ate up their two hundred dollars. Jonathan later wrote that he and Eliza "were in deep poverty, much in debt, mending shoes to get a little food."[38]

Not that food was expensive. After a meal with Dr. Simmons and another friend, Francis Hall noted that "a roast chicken cost 7¢ flanked by boiled rice, squash, egg plants, value of the vegetables 2¢." But a foreigner's overall living expenses were high. The face value of one's money was reduced by the complicated process of currency exchange, and its purchasing power was diminished by Japan's double-price system by which foreigners were charged more. As Ernest Satow put it, there was "a fixed price for the foreigner wherever he went, arbitrarily determined without reference to the native tariff." For example, Japanese traveling from Kanagawa to Yokohama boarded the public ferry boat. Foreigners had to take a sculling boat, paying sixteen times as much. The more brazen barbarians who forced their way onto the public ferry boat learned that the boatmen would refuse to stir until they had disembarked.[39]

Foreigners also paid more for servants. Dr. Hepburn gave each of his a monthly salary of eight *bu,* or about $2.62 (the *bu,* also called *ichibu,* was a rectangular silver coin worth about 32 cents). The servants provided their own food. "I paid my cook and his wife," wrote D. B. McCartee, "between four and five dollars a month, (they feeding themselves), and my *betto*, or horse-boy, for wages, and horse feed, six dollars a month." The McCartees, missionaries from China, were living temporarily in Yokohama after spending a few days with the Browns.[40]

Whether in Kanagawa or Yokohama, working for a foreigner was lucrative. In a Japanese home, average wages were only three or four *bu*. A woman servant, Hall was told, "would receive her living, clothing, and one or two ichibus per month." But the salary gap was partially offset by a special government tax on the servants' wages. The servants at Jōbutsuji were compelled to pay half a *bu* monthly, while those in Yokohama were charged one and a half *bu*. The government kept more detailed records on the servants of foreigners than on others, adding to government expense and allegedly justifying the tax.[41]

How much Sam Patch was paid is unknown. Doubtless he commanded more than other servants. His final employer, E. W. Clark, paid him four times as much as a Japanese servant. All that is clear at this point is that Goble could not afford him. Brown could. His annual salary was $800, the same as Goble's, but the Reformed mission board provided an additional $300 for his wife and $150 for their three children. If allowances for house rent and two teachers' wages are included, Brown's total financial package was $1,538, far more generous than Goble's.[42] Even so, Brown lived beyond his income and, like Dr. Hepburn, made up the difference with private funds. Goble had no savings, no reserves to draw on. He could barely scrounge enough to support his sickly wife Eliza and their little Dora, much less Sam Patch. Sam had to go.

In November 1860, when the USS *Niagara* brought the Japanese embassy home from America (this ship also brought Goble's long awaited remittance from the Free Mission Society), many of the sailors, as was their bent, went on a drunken spree. While they made a nuisance of themselves at Yokohama with blasphemous talk and bloody fights, some of their sober crewmates visited Jōbutsuji and enjoyed fellowship with the missionary families. These pious ones conducted a rousing worship service that delighted Robbins Brown and Sam Patch. "We don't know any but one Japanese Protestant Christian in the country," Brown wrote, "and that individual was present on that occasion. He is our cook, was converted in America & now lives safely here, dressing as a foreigner & he shows unmistakable evidence of piety. His feelings were much wrought upon by the scene last night, as he sat listening to the addresses, & prayers & songs of the seamen."[43]

Here it is clear that Sam had become the Browns' cook, that the transfer had occurred while Jonathan was financially strapped and awaiting his first remittance from abroad. Probably from the beginning Sam's presence on the compound proved beneficial to the Hepburns and Browns, especially the Browns, with whom the Gobles resided two months. Whether gradually or at a particular time after Sam's first few months in Japan, Robbins Brown assumed responsibility for his support. Whether or not the Gobles were glad to let him go, probably Sam was pleased to have a more reliable, more considerate employer. He may well have been troubled by Goble's aggressive evangelism, fearing it could endanger his own life as Goble's convert. There was a truculence about Goble that contrasted sharply with the civility of Brown, a highly educated and cultured gentleman who represented New England at its best. Brown's gracefulness made Goble look gauche.

Though his employer might change, Sam was committed to a life with foreigners. As a Christian in Western garments, he would not dare visit his home in Ikuchijima. He was assumed dead, and it was best to leave it at that. His best deal in life was to utilize the cooking skills he had honed on the *Eiriki-maru* and enhanced in the service of foreigners. Supported by the well-to-do Browns, he could cook with a flair.

From the outset of his residence at Jōbutsuji, Sam attended the Sunday morning services held in the Hepburns' house and heard preaching by Robbins Brown or a visiting clergyman. The services drew some twenty or thirty Westerners from Kanagawa, Yokohama, and vessels offshore. Sam also attended the Thursday evening prayer meetings. In July the Sunday services were moved to a rented room in Yokohama, where the congregation increased to about forty. Brown shared the preaching duties with John Nevius, who resided in the temple that Dr. and Mrs. Simmons had vacated. Sam probably went to Yokohama each Sunday in company with other residents of Jōbutsuji.[44]

While living on the temple compound Sam saw some outstanding visitors come and go. Numa Morikazu and Ōmura Masajirō, destined to hold high government positions, came regularly to Dr. Hepburn for English lessons. The famed castaway Manjirō called on the Browns in July to get some instructions on how to use the sewing machine he had brought from California. Thomas Troy likely dropped by to check up on Sam. One evening in August the kind Irish-American was seen outside the U.S. consulate playing the clarinet, and the next year he was working in Yokohama as a clerk at Heco's company.[45]

Heco had resigned his full-time position as the consul's interpreter earlier in the year and gone into business with Frank Knight. But until he left for America in the latter part of 1861, he continued to interpret whenever his services were needed. As often as he was in the area, he must have visited Jōbutsuji.[46] Heco was a close friend of Francis Hall, who lived with the Hepburns at Jōbutsuji several months before moving in with Dr. Simmons (Mrs. Simmons had returned to the States). Hall also filled in for the U.S. consul on occasion.

Heco's relationship with Sam is mystifying. Judging from his two autobiographies, which make no mention of this crewmate, Heco had no interest in Sam whatsoever. While at Canton in 1859, before coming to Yokohama, he met Iwakichi for the first time since their dramatic parting in 1852. He could have learned from Iwakichi that Sam served in the Perry expedition, and that Iwakichi afterwards joined the crew of the *Susquehanna*. Then Heco went on to Shanghai and saw Otokichi. This was the man who had secured the release of twelve *Eiriki-maru* crewmen from the *Susquehanna* but had been unable to free Sam. But according to Heco's *Narrative*, Otokichi told him that all thirteen had sailed to Japan with Perry and that the commodore had brought them back to Shanghai after they had declined to meet with Japanese officials at Uraga. Otokichi then applied to the Chinese authorities, Heco alleged, and "the thirteen castaways were taken to Nagasaki on one of their junks."[47]

It is highly unlikely that Otokichi would have given Heco this false information in 1859, only a few years after the events took place. Probably when Heco prepared his *Narrative* with James Murdock's assistance in the early 1890s, he had no written record of his conversations with Iwakichi and Otokichi, and his memories of those conversations were faded and dim. His failure to recognize that Sam and Sam alone accompanied the Perry expedition to Japan suggests that his fellow cook Sentarō had made little impression on his agile and absorbent mind.

Chapter 7

Nurse for the Children

In March of 1866, I set out on my first visit home, accompanied by our faithful, though inefficient, servant Sentarō, "Sam Patch."

—Margaret Ballagh[1]

I spent much more for the stay at San Francisco, freight on her baggage, and nurse to wait on the children home.

—James Ballagh[2]

A year and a half after Sam's return to Japan with the Gobles, an attractive young couple who would impact his life joined the missionary community at Jōbutsuji. James Hamilton Ballagh and his wife Margaret Tate Kinnear, like the Browns, were sponsored by the Dutch Reformed board. They moved in with Dr. Hepburn, who welcomed their companionship because his wife had recently left for the States to care for their troubled son Samuel.

James Ballagh was twenty-nine, close to Sam's age. A graduate of Rutgers College and New Brunswick Theological Seminary, he was better educated than Goble but less scholarly than Brown or Hepburn. Ballagh was both a muscular outdoorsman and a paragon of piety who spent hours on his knees interceding for individuals by name and for causes around the world. He could be firm, even obstinate, but unlike Goble he kept his fists under control. His mother had married with the intention of raising up missionaries, and four of her nine children pursued that calling. James, his brother John, and sisters Carrie and Anna all served in Japan, the first generation of a dynasty of missionaries in service to the present time.[3]

Margaret Ballagh, like Clara Hepburn, was a Southerner who cheered the Confederates in the War between the States. Orphaned as a child, she was raised by a childless, well-to-do aunt in Brownsburg, Virginia. Her privileged upbringing by a doting relative with household slaves was said to leave her selfish and demanding. Her Japanese coworkers would come to regard her as beautiful and highly literate but self-willed and high-strung. Maggie attended Oakland Institute in Norristown, Pennsylvania, where she graduated with honors and committed her life to missionary work. James, a Yankee nine years her senior, was spouse-hunting when he preached in Brownsburg's New Providence Presbyterian Church as guest minister. He discovered Maggie, "a fine specimen of a woman" and "the right one."[4]

At Kanagawa the newly arrived Ballaghs needed the best servants they could procure. In contrast to the well-appointed *Kathay,* the ship that had brought them as far as Shanghai, the little brig they boarded for Japan was marked by "filth that is quite perceptible, ants, cock-roaches and rats scampering over and into every thing; a little low dark cabin, no deck, a corpse on board, inefficient and small crew." Even worse, they had encountered gales and monstrous waves en route. Maggie, pregnant and seasick, had been tossed about in her bunk for days, her moaning drowned out by the groaning of the ship's wooden hull. She survived this bruising ordeal only to fall into what is now called culture shock. Her new home was "this old temple, rocking and creaking with the wind, dark and gloomy within, the rafters filled with mosquitoes and bats." Nights were "hideous" because of "the noises and smells that assail us." Days were overshadowed by "heathenism with all its revolting practices."[5]

In this oppressive environment Maggie gave birth to Carrie Elizabeth, attended by Dr. Hepburn. "The last five months have been ones very trying to me," she wrote in July, a month after the delivery. Especially burdensome was a stream of visitors who kept the Hepburn house filled to capacity.[6] Among them was an Episcopal missionary couple who had taken in the Ballaghs at Shanghai and pampered them as family. They came to Kanagawa to restore the wife's failing health, which declined instead. She often complained of a lack of comfortable accommodations and palatable foods despite Maggie's best efforts to repay kindness to these "dyspeptics." After three stressful months the couple sailed on to California, where the wife died two days after their arrival. Her husband embarked for New York with her remains, only to perish in a steamer fire that consumed his wife's corpse as well. This weird and tragic tale weighed heavily on Maggie's mind.[7]

Maggie continued to entertain guests while dealing with sore eyes from lacquer poison and studying the language with "a frisky little baldheaded priest at the back of the house." Her husband and Dr. Hepburn met with their respective teachers at the front and the center of the house. To acquire the language, Maggie "would say over the i-ro-ha, write it, screw my face, wiggle my body, beat my forehead to make the new words stick."[8]

Learning Japanese was strain enough for any alien, but Maggie was also learning to care for an infant whose demands were greater than those of her pony and pussy cat at the temple home. Carrie needed protection from the oppressive summer heat, irritating fleas, and swarming mosquitoes. Maggie had expected relief from the mosquitoes by September, when she expressed "consternation to find them coming thicker and larger and more venomous in their bite!" Feeding Carrie was also a problem, since milk could not be had. Maggie gave the child "tea and ricewater" while searching for a wet nurse. Reflecting on her spiritual calling, she concluded that "babies make sad havoc of missionary aspirations."[9]

Margaret Ballagh

James Ballagh

In the spring of 1862, before Carrie's birth, Jonathan and Eliza Goble gave up their little house at Jōbutsuji and moved to rented quarters in Yokohama. At year's end Dr. Hepburn, his wife not yet returned from abroad, likewise moved to the settlement, occupying a spacious Western-style house with an adjoining clinic he had designed. This left only two missionary families on the compound, the Browns in the priests' house and the Ballaghs in the temple proper. Since Hepburn had taken his own servants with him, the Ballaghs were thrown back on servants that they or the Browns had trained. With no cooking stove and three young men to board, they needed good help. It is possible that Sam began helping the Ballaghs at this time, perhaps while still in the Browns' employ.[10]

During the latter half of the year the Browns went through a crisis so severe that they almost quit Japan in their embarrassment and despair. Their daughter Julia was with child. The father was a frequent visitor to the compound, James Frederick Lowder, soon-to-be stepson of Sir Rutherford Alcock, the British minister to Japan. The young lovers wished to marry, but Lowder's mother opposed a union beyond the circle of aristocracy. The agonizing dilemma weighed heavily on Robbins Brown as Julie's father and pastor of the foreigners' church. "In his own language," Ballagh wrote, "he has felt as though all his bones were broken." To Brown's relief, the couple married forty-eight hours before their baby was born and later were restored to communion after making public confession of their sin. Efforts were made to hide the scandal from the Japanese, but Sam Patch would have known about it as a member of the Yokohama church if not as a resident of the temple compound.[11]

James Ballagh, soon after his arrival in Japan, had reported Sam's presence in the Sunday services held in the parlor of the English consulate in Yokohama. Among those attending, he noted, were "black men looking as respectable as any, and one Japanese, Mr. Brown's servant." A year later Brown reported that the church's Japanese member was working in Ballagh's home. Sam's transfer from one household to the other could have occurred anytime after Hepburn's move to Yokohama. It was in 1863, after Brown's report, that Sam's affiliation with this nondenominational congregation became known to the Baptist church in Hamilton, New York. The Hamilton church dismissed him from its membership December 7, an infamous date for Japan-America relations in the century ahead.[12]

Sam cooked for the Ballaghs as he had for the Gobles and Browns. Food was conveniently available from vendors who came to the compound entrance. They offered eggs, wild boar meat, hares, pigeons, and a fine variety of fish, but the missionaries had to send to Yokohama for "passable beef." Maggie wrote of one vendor who had "spinach, but not very tender; turnips, squashes and potatoes—both Irish and sweet." The same vender had persimmons, oranges, and grapes; chestnuts and walnuts. "These are only the winter vegetables and fruits," Maggie added.[13]

There was much more indeed. Among the other fruits cultivated in the district surrounding Kanagawa were apples, pears, plums, peaches, nectarines, figs, lemons, and watermelons. The vegetables also included carrots, lettuce, tomatoes, egg plant, cucumbers, mushrooms, bamboo shoots, daikon, and several varieties of peas and beans.[14] As for grains, farmers in the region grew rice, wheat, buckwheat, corn, and five kinds of millet. Japan had an abundance of farmland and was fully self-sufficient in food production, unlike today when it is the world's largest importer of foodstuffs, a nation so urbanized that it produces less than half the calories its people consume.

Removal under Protest

After Dr. Hepburn moved from Jōbutsuji, government officials informed Brown and Ballagh that they could not rent the temple for another year because the lease had expired. They refused to leave. Their adamancy frustrated the authorities and infuriated Hepburn, who had signed the contract as the temple's first foreign resident and expected his colleagues to honor it. The defiant squatters prevailed until a crisis arose in the spring of 1863, the threat of war between England and Japan growing

On the Tōkaidō

out of the 1862 murder of the English merchant C. L. Richardson. Americans in Japan were no less apprehensive than the British, knowing that a war would affect all foreigners alike. Many were panicky after the U.S. legation at Edo was destroyed May 25. Fire started at one end of the two-hundred-foot temple building at two o'clock in the morning, and within fifteen minutes had spread to the other end, devouring nearly everything within. Careful investigation would show that the blaze was accidental, but many foreigners jumped to the conclusion that it was arson and a portent of woes to come.[15]

The gathering war clouds had drawn the American screw sloop *Wyoming* to Japan, detouring it from its primary mission of hunting down the CSS *Alabama*. Robbins Brown for one wanted that Confederate raider pursued because it sank the American ship *Contest* to the bottom of the ocean and with it five hundred dollars worth of photographs and books he was sending home.[16] But he welcomed the *Wyoming* to Japan. The danger of war between England and Japan caused Americans to put aside their differences over the Civil War at home and join ranks with pro-Confederacy British for mutual survival.

On the last Sunday in May 1863 a hundred Japanese soldiers despatched from Edo stood guard in the temple grounds at Jōbutsuji amid rumors that the foreign residents might be attacked. That same day the U.S. minister in Edo, Robert H. Pruyn, was frightened into fleeing to Yokohama on the *Kanrin-maru*. U.S. consul George S. Fisher, the only consul still in Kanagawa, was also pressured into moving. As a precaution Fisher placed the women of his household on the *Wyoming*. The ship's captain, Commander David S. McDougal, offered to take Elizabeth Brown, Maggie Ballagh, and their children aboard also, but these women declined to move on the Sabbath day. Robbins Brown, who had preached in Yokohama that morning, likewise took a firm stand against violating the Sabbath. The diplomats yielded. Early the next morning a contingent of American marines from the *Wyoming* appeared, as well as Consul Fisher and Minister Pruyn, to escort the missionaries to safety in Yokohama. The Sabbath over, they offered no resistance.[17]

"The Japanese soldiers head the procession," Maggie wrote, "we in the center, and the American marines following. Mrs. Brown was escorted by the Commodore and Captain of the ship; I walked between the Minister and the Consul; and Miss Hattie B. between her father and my husband. We walked very solemnly to the wharf, and were put hastily into the boats and quickly rowed over the bay, then left to find a home where we could."[18]

Maggie also revealed that eleven-month-old Carrie was on a rice and tea diet since Sunday morning because her wet-nurse had left at that time. She did not say who carried the child in the procession Monday morning, but likely it was her servant Sam. Rutherford Alcock once pointed out that it was common to see a Japanese man walking about with a small child in his arms.[19]

From Pillar to Post

Yokohama was in turmoil, with foreigners arming and barricading themselves and Japanese fleeing the town with their futons and other possessions. The Ballaghs stayed for a while with the Hepburns (Clara had returned from America) and then reluctantly accepted the offer of two rooms in the American consulate, a small cluster of Japanese houses joined by a veranda and surrounded by a high black fence. The rooms were dirty and living conditions repugnant. "The Consul did the dwellers in the consulate building an offense," James griped, "in proposing to bring the wounded into the court and chapel room knowing that others must give place to them." Sam probably dwelt in the consulate also. The Browns occupied a hastily rented house that was sparsely furnished.[20]

War was averted when the Japanese government gave in to British demands and paid an indemnity of $440,000, roughly one-third of the government's annual income. Twenty chests filled with coins were brought by hand carts to the British consulate.[21] Life in the settlement returned to a semblance of normalcy, though hardly for the missionary evacuees from Kanagawa. They were sorely discontent.

Ballagh and Brown quietly arranged to have their furniture hauled to the jetty for shipment across the inlet to their former temple home. When their move was reported to the governor, he requested Consul Fisher to stop them on grounds that lawless *rōnin* were still on the prowl in the region. Fisher countered that the missionaries found Yokohama inconvenient and expensive. The governor then offered to help the two missionaries financially by granting them a more favorable exchange rate if the consul would intervene and block their move. Fisher complied. Keeping the Ballaghs in Yokohama meant keeping Sam there too.[22]

The Ballaghs felt no safer in Yokohama than in Kanagawa. A Japanese guard at the British legation, Itō Gumpei, had murdered two English marines. Thieves had broken into the Ballaghs' own house at the U.S. consulate, giving them quite a fright. And there were problems with the settlement other than insecurity. "The climate was uncertain and disease was rife," said one report. "Smallpox was a frequent visitor; there were epidemics of cholera and dysentery as well as measles. Malaria was commonplace and deaths frequent." The dreaded cholera had struck even the Goble household, claiming the life of four-year-old Dorinda.[23]

In late August Ballagh complained that he had been forced to move four times during the previous two months. He was tired of "shifting about" and "disheartened with cleaning of old Japanese houses to live in." Good accommodations were indeed hard to come by. Francis Hall wrote of "English, Americans, Dutch, French, Prussians, Swiss, Portuguese, and nondescript, four hundred souls, already stifling for room." Lots were scarce and their prices soaring. These taxing months could only have exasperated Sam as well. He too must have pined for the more settled life of his former temple home.[24]

Later in the year Ballagh learned that his current landlord would return from China in January, displacing him yet again. That was the last straw. He told Minister Pruyn he would return to his home in Kanagawa the first of the year and "respectfully but firmly said nothing could stop me." Pruyn, who had already warned that Japanese obstinacy would "justly give great offence to the President of the United States," passed on the ultimatum. "Unless suitable buildings are immediately provided for Mr. Brown and Mr. Ballagh and their families," he warned the Shogun's Council, "I shall send them to Kanagawa next week and they shall not leave there again when once there." Ballagh's stubborn antics paid off handsomely. The governor granted him and Brown a Yokohama lot to be divided between them, one worth far more than the Kanagawa homes they had abandoned under duress.[25]

The lot, number 167, was a spacious 200 by 114 feet, more than half an acre. It faced a busy thoroughfare near the customhouse and adjoined the camphor tree under which Perry had signed the Treaty of Kanagawa. This piece of ground was so coveted that Ballagh ran into a brick wall trying to obtain the deed for his mission board. Asserting that "possession is ownership in Japan," he was soon "engaged in tearing out partitions in one of the little houses, getting over doors and windows from K. [Kanagawa] and in seeing the fences removed to have them in readiness to enclose the lot where marked off today."[26] The Browns remained where they were, so the Ballaghs had more than ample room for their servant Sam.

Jōbutsuji had not lacked for weird noises. The Ballaghs well remembered the scampering rats and cawing crows, the daily gongs, bells, and chants. The complex had not lacked for wafting odors. But the busy thoroughfare near the Yokohama wharf was more irritating still. Maggie grumbled about "Jacks' drunken sprees, coolies' cries, and songs, the prayers of mendicant priests, the beggars' wail of sorrow, the stench of the filthy ditch just outside the lot, and under my window, also of decaying fish, eggs and vegetables from the market close by." Nevertheless, after the pillar-to-post life they had endured the preceding months, a place they could call their own was "an oasis in the wilderness of discouragement."[27]

Sam too began to feel at home in Yokohama. The foreign portion had English signs that he could read better than the Japanese signs in Kanagawa. Church services were held conveniently nearby, in the court room of the American consulate. Thus a gold "spread eagle" adorned the back of the platform that served as a pulpit. Curious Japanese who peered through the doors and saw the eagle above the preacher's head spread the word that Americans worshiped this stately bird.[28] Sam attended the Christian services with the same impunity as the foreigners, dressing and behaving as one of them.

Two years after the move to Yokohama, Ballagh administered baptism to his Japanese language teacher. Yano Mototaka (Ryūzan), a shaven-headed Buddhist acupuncturist from Edo, had come to Kanagawa to teach Robbins Brown. When the Ballaghs arrived in Japan, Brown passed him on to James, who not only studied under Yano but tried to convert the "quack doctor." Ballagh had him translate the Gospels of Mark and John in hopes that the message would win its way into Yano's heart. As the teacher became increasingly ill with a lung disease, he began to respond to his pupil's fervent prayers. When at last he asked for baptism, Ballagh warned him of the legal consequences and for a time declined to administer the rite. At last, when Hepburn advised that Yano's end was near, Ballagh consented.[29]

The historic baptism, the first conducted by a Protestant in Japan, took place in a back room of Yano's Kanagawa home the first Sunday in November 1865. Hepburn assisted Ballagh with the ceremony, and Yano's wife, son, and daughter witnessed it. The son, a businessman and the one most likely to suffer if the "crime" became known, had given his consent to the private affair. Yano was elated. When James and Maggie called on him Thanksgiving Day, he thanked them for their kindness and told them "he was going to Jesus' side and he would make mention of us to Jesus." The convert died one month after his baptism and was buried at Jōbutsuji, with Buddhist rites conducted as required by law despite the son's efforts to buy off the priests.[30]

For five years prior to Yano's baptism, so far as is known, Sam Patch had been the only baptized Japanese Protestant in the country. After Yano's death December 4, Sam was again the only one. Three baptisms would take place in Nagasaki the following year, and others would follow in Nagasaki and Yokohama, but not until 1872 would the total number exceed ten.[31]

In 1866, a few months after Yano's baptism and subsequent death, Maggie Ballagh decided to return to the United States. Nearly five years had passed since leaving her home in Brownsburg, Virginia—five anxious years of bloody battles, social upheaval, and broken communication. Now that the Civil War had ended, Maggie longed to see family and friends, hear their tales of horror, and learn whether they had received the many letters she had sent. She wanted to inspect her property and take stock of her finances in the aftermath of a devastating war.

But there were more compelling reasons for her trip home. As her mission board reported later, Maggie returned to the States for "sanitary reasons." "The experience of life in Japan," her husband explained, " . . . has had a very injurious effect on her nervous system & in peculiar state of mothers is much more affected." Maggie was pregnant and neurotic. She had obtained first-class medical care under Dr. Hepburn, who had delivered not only Carrie but her second child aptly named Anna Hepburn. But Maggie was increasingly reticent to presume on her "beloved physician" now that his dispensary was flooded with Japanese patients and medical students, whom he preferred to serve over the expatriate community. Dr. Hepburn would still give ungrudging time to a long-time patient like Maggie, but his skills and compassion were no substitute for a prolonged break from the anxieties of life in Japan.[32]

Thus Maggie would seek medical help in the United States. And to make the long journey in her condition, she needed the services, however imperfect, of faithful Sam Patch. Why could not her faithful husband satisfy her needs? James was still engaged in the battle with government authorities to gain clear title to lot number 167. He dared not jeopardize his advantage by an extended absence from the scene. As a compromise, he agreed to accompany Maggie and the children as far as San Francisco, seeing them safely across the Pacific to American soil.

Ironically, they traveled on the two-hundred-ton *Ida D. Rogers,* the "filthy brig," the "frail little craft" that had brought them from Shanghai to Yokohama in 1861. Perhaps they had no other option at the time. Perhaps this ship was cheaper than any alternative. Whatever the reason for their choice, the "A 1 extreme clipper brig," as it was touted, made the voyage in thirty-one days with a load of tea and nine passengers, including Sam and the four Ballaghs. Their first Sunday night in San Francisco James preached at the United Presbyterian Church.[33] Doubtless Sam attended this church also, not the First Baptist Church as when he was under Goble's wing.

The Great Disappearing Act

After three weeks in the bustling port Maggie and the children sailed on the steamship *Golden City* and transferred at Panama to the steamer *New York*. When they arrived in New York City, Theodore Ferris, the Reformed board secretary, attempted to meet Maggie but was frustrated in his efforts. "Her feelings & state of health I presume led her friends to keep her secluded," James wrote in apology.[34] Maggie spent some time with her in-laws in Tenafly, New Jersey, across the Hudson River from the Bronx. Then she proceeded to her beloved Brownsburg, Virginia.

Japanese nurse, summer and winter

Was Sam still with Maggie and her girls when they reached her home? Japanese scholarship has assumed without question that he was. But a lacuna in the records makes his whereabouts after reaching San Francisco a matter of speculation. The passenger list of the *Golden City* as published named only cabin passengers, including "Mrs. M. K. Ballagh and 2 children."[35] The words "with servant" do not follow, although they appear with other names in the passenger list and had been added to the Ballaghs' name on the manifest of the *Ida D. Rogers*. Did Sam remain in San Francisco, where his footprints disappear? Assuming that he did accompany Maggie to New York, did she discharge him there or in Tenafly, where family and friends were available to help meet her needs?

The questions need to be raised because Brownsburg has no tradition of a Japanese accompanying Maggie. There seems to be no mention of Sam in the Rockbridge County newspapers, the records of Maggie's church, or other documents that have been combed for clues. D. L. Kinnear, a family historian and genealogist who read an avalanche of Maggie's personal letters sent to her relatives, found no reference to Sam in his extensive research. Maggie's return aroused much talk of her children, Kinnear noted, since the relatives had not previously known she had borne any.

There would have been talk also of a Japanese servant if Sam had come with her, he was convinced, and the story would have been passed down to subsequent generations. Sam's appearance would have caused a sensation, a talked-about, unforgettable event.[36]

Whatever Sam was about during this hiatus in the records, it is certain he did not return to Japan with Maggie's husband. Nearly two weeks after seeing his family off from San Francisco, James sailed on the *Ida D. Rogers* as one of five passengers listed by name. Sam was not among them.[37]

Having returned to Yokohama, James charged his mission board three hundred dollars for his wife's passage to America. "I spent much more," he wrote in justification, "for the stay at San Francisco, freight on her baggage, and nurse to wait on the children home."[38] This nurse who added to his personal expense presumably was Sam Patch. The implication is that Sam was expected to accompany Maggie, Carrie, and Anna all the way to Brownsburg. And the fact that Maggie called him "faithful" implies that he did not quit on the way. But it is equally true that Maggie called him "inefficient." She might well have dismissed him before reaching home.

In early 1869 James Ballagh returned to the United States and rejoined his family in Brownsburg. When they set out for Japan in the fall of 1870, the Ballaghs left eight-year-old Carrie with Susan Withrow, who had raised Maggie. Taking the younger children Anna and James Curtis, they crossed the continent by rail and boarded the *America* in San Francisco. Neither the train's passenger list nor the steamer's includes Sam Patch. Four unnamed passengers in the ship's steerage disembarked at Yokohama, but there is no hint that Sam was among them. The Ballaghs spent a week in a hotel and three weeks with the Verbecks in Tokyo, then moved into Goble's house on the Yokohama Bluff.[39]

The Ballaghs were still renting the Goble house three years later when Edward Warren Clark arrived in Yokohama and hired Sam to be his cook. Likely he was working for the Ballaghs at this time, but when he had returned to Yokohama is unclear. From 1866, when he went to America with the Ballaghs, until 1871, when Clark stepped into his life, Sam Patch was working, eating, sleeping—but where? Probably his trail will come to light in the future, but for now those are hidden years except for a sliver of light emanating from Hawaii.

During the 1860s, after Hawaii's native population had declined in number over several decades, the government sought to alleviate the labor shortage by importing agricultural workers from abroad. In 1868 the chartered ship *Scioto* arrived from Yokohama with 148 Japanese recruited

as contract laborers in the cane fields or the sugar houses on the planta-
tions, and a few as domestics. The motley group of "coolies" included six
women and one child. All the men but two had cut off their topknots as a
token of gratitude to the gods who had delivered them from a fierce storm
en route. One of the men, Ishii Sentarō. was destined to become the oldest
Japanese in Hawaii before his death in 1936 at the age of 102.[40]

The new arrivals were pleased to find three Japanese in Honolulu, but
two of these left immediately for the United States. The third, known
simply as Sentarō, aided his countrymen in their sightseeing and helped
alleviate their homesickness. Makino Tomisaburō, the laborers' supervisor,
reported in a letter to Japan that Sentarō was an able interpreter and had
provided valuable assistance to the group. Others among the immigrants
expressed gratitude for the interpreter's kind deeds. They described Sentarō
as over thirty years old, and Makino identified him as a native of Kanagawa.[41]

Was this ministering angel Sam Patch? He was about thirty-four at the
time and a native of Kanagawa in the sense that he had lived there three
years with missionary families. Or was he an unreported castaway named
Sentarō who had arrived in Hawaii and remained? Apparently no one by
that name was mentioned in the Hawaiian newspapers, and conclusive
proof of his identity has not yet come to light. As of now, Sam Patch is a
candidate. By the end of 1869, when the Ueno Keihan embassy arrived in
Honolulu to investigate alleged maltreatment of the Japanese laborers,
Sentarō had vanished from the scene.[42]

The most plausible theory for these uncertain years may be that Sam
accompanied Maggie Ballagh as far as New York City but not to Brownsburg, where his presence would have left a lasting mark. Maggie's friends
and relatives in New York may have convinced her that she no longer
needed the Japanese servant to help with the children. She may not have
needed any convincing, having grown weary of his presence. It was feasible
to dismiss Sam because he knew his way around in the States and was fully
capable of looking after himself. He could have returned to San Francisco
alone and moved on to Honolulu before eventually returning to Yokohama. There a challenging new job lay ahead.

Chapter 8

Rice Cakes and the Fatted Duck

He became the chief of my kitchen department. He baked the bread, roasted the ducks, made pies and puddings, and his rice cakes were everywhere famous.
—Edward Warren Clark[1]

THE booming of a cannon at the Yokohama wharf signaled the arrival of a steamer from abroad. Sam Patch ignored the sound, all too familiar in this boom-boom port where warships frequently saluted men of rank with plaster-cracking barrages. But the arrival of the *Great Republic* on that bright autumn day—October 25, 1871—was to be of enormous consequence to forty-year-old Sam. One of the passengers sculled ashore was Edward Warren Clark, a twenty-two-year-old science teacher who would hire Sam as his cook within a month and oversee his life to its tragic end.[2]

Like James Ballagh, Warren Clark was a Rutgers graduate imbued with missionary zeal. After college he toured Europe with classmate William Elliot Griffis and Willie's sister Margaret, then tarried in Geneva to study theology at the École de Théologie.[3] Though steeped in physics and chemistry and demonstrably qualified to teach these subjects to the brainy men and boys who would crowd his classes in Japan, Clark's true aim in life was to be a man of the cloth.

This lofty aim came as naturally as his intellectual pursuits. Warren's mother Eliza was a minister's daughter, and his Yale-trained father Rufus was pastor of the prestigious First Dutch Reformed Church of Albany, New York. His father's four brothers likewise were clergymen, among them Thomas Clark, formerly Protestant Episcopal bishop of Rhode Island and later presiding bishop of the United States. So it is hardly remarkable—though it might be today—that all four sons of Rufus and Eliza followed the same calling, Warren as an Episcopal rector after his stint in Japan.[4]

Not only science and theology, but journalism came naturally to Warren Clark. His parents were both writers, his father credited with 130 publications. His more prolific uncle Thomas was honored with an LL.D. degree from Cambridge University. Warren did not rise to that stratospheric level, nor was he a match for William Griffis, who distinguished himself as the most widely read of the nineteenth-century writers on Japan. But he published voluminous reports of his travels in Europe and Asia, with some fifty of his letters from Japan appearing in the *New York Evangelist* and at least fifteen in the *Albany Evening Journal*. One of his four noteworthy books, *Life and Adventure in Japan*, though dismissed by Nitobe Inazō as "of passing interest," was translated into Japanese nearly a century later and continues to throw light on the life and times of Sam Patch.[5]

As an impressionable eleven-year-old in New York City, Warren Clark saw the pioneering Japanese Embassy of 1860 ride up Broadway in a dazzling procession with seven thousand welcoming troops.[6] While at Rutgers he gained the lasting friendship of several Japanese students who were the sons of prominent government officials. Some of these students and other Japanese visited his home in Albany and attended his father's church. These contacts aroused in Clark a desire to follow in the footsteps of Griffis, who sailed to Japan in late 1870 to teach natural science in the castle town of Fukui.

William Griffis stood in the vanguard of hundreds of foreigners employed by the Japanese government to help the long-secluded nation catch up with the West in science and technology and other crucial fields. The new Meiji regime was so determined to attain equality with the Western powers that it was willing to pay handsomely for instruction in the political, economic, and military systems of those countries. Thus the proliferation of *yatoi,* literally "employees," who taught in schools or held key positions in various government agencies while helping to train their Japanese replacements. While some *yatoi* were vagrants and ne'er-do-wells, frauds with little or no qualification other than being in Japan at the right time, many were highly competent and well worth the generous salaries they commanded. This was true of Griffis and Clark.

The Meiji regime represented the imperialists who had overthrown the Tokugawa shogunate in 1868. Keiki, the fifteenth and last in this line of shoguns, had retired to Shizuoka, the Tokugawas' ancestral home about ninety miles southwest of Yokohama. So many of his former retainers had followed him into exile that some six thousand ex-Tokugawa samurai were now living in Shizuoka or its environs. According to the 1870 census, the castle town had a total population of 20,725 in 4,565 households.[7]

In this "St. Helena of Tycoonism," as Clark called it, the progressive authorities had established a school of higher learning called Gakumonjo. It was here that Clark, recommended by Griffis, was to teach. A case can be made that Gakumonjo was the best school in Japan, for many teachers in the leading Tokugawa institutions had followed Keiki to Shizuoka. There were strong departments of Japanese studies, Chinese studies, and Western studies. Clark would be surprised to find that a great many books in European languages had been brought here, even a four-volume *History of the Christian Church*. Shizuoka was a scholar's paradise.[8]

The *Yatoi* Hires a Cook

After disembarking from the *Great Republic* at Yokohama, Warren Clark passed through the clean but lively streets of the town, crossed a wooden bridge, and climbed the shaded path to the Bluff, the wind-cooled elevation where scores of foreign residents lived in princely style. He found his way to number 48, an imposing house set on a choice lot of two-thirds an acre. Though owned by James and Maggie Ballagh, it was occupied by three representatives of the Woman's Union Missionary Society who had come to Japan in response to the Ballaghs' appeal for women who could educate and train Japanese girls. They had established the Yokohama Mission Home, with fifty-year-old Mary Pruyn as director.[9]

A former Albany resident and longtime friend of the Clark family, Mrs. Pruyn settled Warren in a comfortable room and lavished on him her motherly love. He found that half a dozen Japanese children—boys as well as girls—were residents and that others came regularly for instruction in Bible and hymn-singing. Wednesday night prayer meetings in English attracted soldiers, sailors, and other foreigners as well as curious Japanese. Wide-eyed with excitement, Clark thanked God for the good fortune of lodging in the Mission Home.[10]

Taking a steamer to Tokyo, Clark called at the official residence of the Suruga clan, in whose province Shizuoka was located. Clan officials welcomed the new teacher and honored him with a "big dinner." Among those present were Ōkubo Ichio and Katsu Kaishū, towering statesmen whom Sam Patch also would come to know and admire. Governor Ōkubo was to leave Shizuoka the following spring to assume new duties as governor of Tokyo. Admiral Katsu had been minister of the navy in the

Tokugawa regime and would hold the same position in the Meiji govern-
ment. These two statesmen had boldly negotiated the settlement with Saigō
Takamori and the imperial army that enabled Tokugawa Keiki to surrender
Edo without a fight.[11]

Clark was especially drawn to Katsu, who had arranged his employment.
He was pleased to find that the admiral had a great smile, loved jokes, and
lived as a paragon of virtue. In a later biography he praised Katsu as
"possessing more of the essential human characteristics of the lowly
Nazarene than I have elsewhere seen in a world which I have thrice
girdled."[12]

While in Tokyo Clark also called at the residence of Iwakura Tomomi,
the powerful *udaijin* ("minister of the right"), who in December would leave
for America as head of a much larger embassy than the one Clark had seen
in 1860. Iwakura, his head adorned with a miter-like hat, received Clark
with a warm handshake and thanked him for befriending his son Asahi at
Rutgers and bringing a letter from him. Clark had also brought letters from
other Japanese friends of note, including Governor Ōkubo's son. So from
the outset the new teacher had connections in Japan far more powerful
than those of Sam's earlier employers. He would prove to be, in the words
of A. Hamish Ion, "one American whose influence far surpassed that
normally wielded by so young a man."[13]

Katsu notified Shizuoka of Clark's arrival, and two school representatives came to Yokohama to meet him. Hitomi Katsutarō, who had survived
a bullet in the chest, was an able administrator with whom Clark would
have frequent dealings. Nakamura Masanao was a Chinese scholar and
Confucian humanist who would become his "warmest friend and most
intimate companion." Nakamura would also play a highly significant role
in Sam's life. The thirty-nine-year-old scholar had spent a year in England
as one of the supervisors of a dozen Japanese students and was now
teaching English at Gakumonjo. He had declined Iwakura's invitation to
accompany his embassy abroad because, he told Clark, he preferred to
"stay home and study." His childlike humility and broken English betrayed
his recent achievement as translator of Samuel Smiles's *Self Help*, a
phenomenally popular work that Japanese scholars have called "the Bible
of the Meiji era."[14]

During a visit with Clark at the Mission Home, Nakamura was
entertained by the children and their singing. Deeply moved, he asked
permission to lodge there "to see how foreigners lived, and to learn about
the Christian religion." With Mrs. Pruyn's consent, he remained nearly two

weeks, while Hitomi apparently stayed elsewhere. Nakamura spent much of the time working on a translation of John Stuart Mill's *On Liberty,* taking advantage of the help with English available there. He paid Mrs. Pruyn twenty-five dollars when he and Clark departed for Shizuoka.[15]

By then Clark had engaged Sam Patch to accompany him to a place where "a beef-steak or a mutton-chop are unknown, a loaf of bread is a myth, and milk, butter and cheese are fairy tales." Sam's knowledge of American-style cooking and his experience in missionary homes would be indispensable. Likewise his grasp of English. Clark worried that learning Japanese would be a daunting task, even though he had attained proficiency in French. "With me," he told Griffis, "languages come by hard work alone, & it's no joke for me to attempt one."A good cook who transcended both the culinary and language barriers would be a godsend to the bachelor from abroad. For Sam, moving into the new job was like slipping into a tailor-made suit.[16]

It is generally assumed, and probably true, that Clark hired Sam away from the Ballaghs. Katsu's diary mentions that the day following his meeting with Clark, the new teacher was to visit Ballagh in Yokohama.[17] Whether James and Maggie gave him up with reluctance is unclear. Perhaps it was a noble sacrifice on their part, in recognition of the stressful isolation Clark would face in the interior. But it is no less likely that they welcomed the opportunity to shift responsibility for Sam's keep to someone else. Like Jonathan Goble a decade earlier, James was pouting over his financial woes.

The Ballaghs' annual salary at the time was one thousand dollars plus a hundred dollars each for the two children living with them. "My household expenses last month," James wrote in March, "were $130, $30 above my salary. This arose from entertaining missionary brethren." Griffis, a future cleric, had stayed with the Ballaghs his first two-and-a-half weeks in Japan, and a total of four missionaries had imposed on them in February alone. Some beneficiaries of Ballagh hospitality paid or offered to pay for their keep, but others were freeloaders. So the parade of guests that made Sam's help more essential also made it less affordable.[18]

Ballagh had purchased Bluff lot 48 in his wife's name, using Maggie's inheritance money, and had engaged Jonathan Goble to build them a house at a cost of about four thousand dollars. He complained that Goble's ill-treatment of the workmen increased expenditures by five hundred to a thousand dollars. "It cost me so much," Ballagh wrote in December, "that tho I built it for a comfortable house for my family against their return to

Japan I have not been able to live in it to this day and will not for a year or two to come."[19]

The Ballaghs were paying seventy-five dollars a month to rent Goble's house at Bluff 75A. Presumably they were collecting a larger amount from Mrs. Pruyn, who had declined the Ballaghs' offer to sell her the house at cost. Goble had sent his wife and children home to America and was living in a room above his print shop behind the main house. Probably Sam was living on the property with the Ballaghs and aware of the growing tension between them and their landlord.

James Ballagh faced an acrimonious lawsuit from Goble, who claimed that he was still owed three hundred dollars for the construction of the house at Bluff 48. The lawsuit was a terrible distraction at the very time James wanted to give Warren Clark the attention he deserved as a newcomer with significant college and church ties. As for Sam, it must have been dismaying to see his two long-time patrons lashing out at one another as though strangers to the Christian brotherhood. The infamous trial of Goble versus Ballagh in the U.S. consular court commenced ten days before Sam left Yokohama with Clark and was reported daily in the English press. At trial's end in December, Ballagh was ordered to pay Goble $143 as well as half of the court costs of $100.20. Then if not before, he must have been thankful to have dropped Sam from his household ledger.[20]

In contrast to Ballagh, Clark had money to spare. His *yatoi* salary was a lucrative $3,600, six times what he would have been paid as a single missionary under Ballagh's mission board. In addition, he was provided with suitable housing and the use of a riding horse. And unlike Griffis, who helped support family members back home who were in "the slough of poverty," Clark had his full pay to himself. He could afford to hire Sam with the enticement of a raise and still maintain a lavish lifestyle that Griffis could only envy.[21]

While in Yokohama Clark hired Japanese carpenters to make the furniture he would need in Shizuoka—tables, chairs, sideboard, wardrobes, bureaus, cane sofas, high-post bedstead, writing desk, and book rack. With advice and assistance from Mrs. Pruyn, he "lay in a store of cans and provisions, such as flour, yeast-powder, sugar, butter, condensed milk, canned tomatoes, oysters, fruits of various kinds, etc." Most of the provisions he shipped to Shizuoka by sea along with his furniture, boxes of chemicals and apparatus, and personal baggage. A servant he employed named Ginzō also went on the little steamer, accompanied by his wife. Sam traveled overland with his boss.[22]

Clark set out for Shizuoka by horseback Monday, November 27, 1871. Besides Sam, his retinue included Nakamura, Hitomi, couriers, porters, interpreters, and—no less essential—mounted guards. Early that year two foreign teachers who had dismissed their assigned bodyguards had been attacked by sword-wielding *rōnin* on the road. Both had sustained deep slashes. Xenophobia remained strong after a dozen years of foreign presence and a revolutionary change of government.[23]

The Clark party took a leisurely five days for the ninety-mile journey. The first day was memorable for a side trip to the Kamakura *daibutsu*, a thirty-eight-foot bronze statue of Amida Buddha. Clark climbed up into the Buddha's spacious lap, sat on one of the two touching thumbs, and belted out the doxology. This stunt must have enlivened what was likely Sam's first visit to the Great Buddha. If he had not learned it already, he now realized that his new master loved to clown. Audacious and uninhibited, Clark possessed an exuberance that was infectious even in staid Japan.

The newcomer, and possibly his servant, spent nights tossing on the flea-swarming floors of rat-infested inns along the way. Sleep was elusive also because of the incessant, often excruciating noises that penetrated the paper sliding screens. There were the "shrill whistles" blown by blind persons passing in front of the inn after dark, the "coarse laughter and yelps" of the watchmen and porters thronging the kitchen most of the night, and the "talk and jabber" of other guests in nearby rooms.[24]

To cross the rugged Hakone mountains, where the road was paved with huge stones like those of the Appian Way, the party switched from horses to *kago*s. A legless bamboo chair slung from thick poles and carried on men's shoulders, the *kago* was to Clark "a kind of living coffin, made especially to break backs!" After six hours of bouncing uphill in these confining chairs, the travelers arrived at charming Lake Hakone and put up at an inn. "My cook prepared supper from the preserved provisions brought with us in tin cans," Clark reported. He had followed the advice that Griffis was to publish in his *Yokohama Guide*, that a foreigner traveling in Japan take "one's own eatables." Clark had done even better, also taking his own cook.[25]

Ernest Satow, an earlier traveler on this famous trunk road, reported having to "taste various local delicacies, among which was a horribly tenacious kind of gruel, resembling bird-lime in appearance, made from the powdered root of the Dioscorea japonica, a species of wild potato." Similarly, Clark expressed his revulsion at the "unsavory odors . . . of unmentionable Japanese dishes." Sam's cooking spared his master "digestive tribulation."[26]

The next morning the Clark party set out before daylight and descended a portion of the way by foot, the road illuminated by huge dried-reed torches carried by the porters. After stopping at another inn for breakfast, the party switched to jinrikishas, the two-wheeled carriages pulled by brawny human horses whose naked bodies displayed elegant tattoos. Jinrikishas—rickshas for short—were swifter and more comfortable than kagos and thus were preferred where road conditions permitted their use. Jonathan Goble had designed a prototype of this vehicle in 1869, mass production had commenced in 1870, and already its popularity was revolutionizing the travel industry throughout the land. The inauguration of ricksha service in Shizuoka coincided with Clark's arrival there.[27]

Never had Sam traveled with so important a personage as Clark. They were met at the entrance of each city or large village by local officers "who in flowing robes and having long swords, knelt politely before us, placing their faces to the earth, and heaving a deep sign of welcome which resembled a miniature typhoon. Themselves on foot, they escorted us through the whole length of the district under their jurisdiction, picking up any stray straw or stone that lay in the way, and finally bowing again and bidding us a safe journey." The courtesy was no less apparent than the intense curiosity. As they passed through towns whole neighborhoods were thrown into agitation by the arrival of the "chalky creature" from abroad, and "long lines of awe-struck faces presented themselves at every window and door and crevice."[28]

A Temple Home in Shizuoka

When the party arrived at an inn four miles from Shizuoka, Clark was welcomed by Yatabori, the chief officer of the school, and then by local officials. Dismissing the jinrikishas, the group mounted jet black ponies for the grand entry into town. The procession crossed a deep moat into the old castle grounds—the castle itself had burned—and halted before the governor's residence, where some twenty men of obvious rank were standing on the porch. After an exchange of bows, Clark removed his boots and was ushered inside for conversations with the local officials through English and French interpreters.

The reception completed, Clark and Sam were led to Ren'eiji, a Buddhist temple in Chiyoda-mura—some two and a half miles to the east—where Katsu had arranged for them to live. There a table was already spread with a good dinner to refresh them. Clark was amazed at the amount of attention and respect everyone bestowed on him. "Even the carpenters and workmen about the house," he wrote, "never permit me to pass them without a polite and graceful obeisance on their part, and even the watch-dog also wags his tail when I approach." It was a case of being "killed with kindness."[29]

The temple grounds, entered through massive gates, covered several acres nestled against a high hill from which one could glimpse Suruga Bay five miles away and hear the roar of the waves breaking on the beach. On the terraced hillside was a cemetery whose thickly scattered headstones seemed at the mercy of growing trees. Katsu's mother was buried there, having died the previous year. Nearly a dozen buildings of various sizes were scattered over the grounds amid bamboo groves and colossal pines. The building assigned to Clark was a central complex used as a reception hall. Workmen were still in the process of removing the Buddhist gods and other paraphernalia, replacing tatami with wooden floors, installing glass windows, and otherwise adapting the structure to the needs of the foreign guest.[30]

With the delivery of Clark's freight from the port of Shimizu, six miles to the north, his crude dwelling was transformed into a semi-Western home with carpets, tables, chairs, beds, pictures, and books, a place where Clark could live comfortably and entertain guests with aplomb. As seen in a ground plan he drew, there were outside halls and balconies in typical Japanese style, overlooking a Japanese garden on one side of the house and a fish pond on the other. The servants' house in back stood close to an entrance that led directly into the centrally located kitchen, which was separated from the dining room by a short hallway. As kitchen chief, Sam had access to a Western cooking stove (probably the only one in the province), familiar kitchen utensils, and well-stocked pantries.[31]

Two interpreters lived in the main house with Clark. Shimojō, the more gifted, could interpret specialized lectures in chemistry and other fields with astonishing ease, especially if Clark went over material with him in advance. His being the same age as Clark and a devout Christian also enhanced their relationship. William Griffis later praised Shimojō as "one of the sweetest and gentlest spirits that ever quitted or tenanted a human form." Sam was nearly twice their age and even further removed from them intellectually.

Even so he often amused the younger men of the household, as Clark noted, "with his droll style and strange stories."[32] Everyone could appreciate a raconteur.

Life at Ren'eiji was little different from life at Jōbutsuji in Kanagawa where Sam had spent three years. Buddhist worship was conducted in an adjoining open structure three times a week, and funerals, memorial services, and lively preaching missions drew bustling crowds from time to time. The great bronze bell in a high tower tolled at sundown each day. Drums and gongs sounded all too frequently, and the priests chanted loud prayers well into the night. Most important for Sam, the American bachelor living at this noisy temple seemed to entertain more guests than all the missionary families at Jōbutsuji combined.[33]

In mid-December Sam prepared a noon meal for the local governing council, his first major opportunity to show off his culinary skills. What Clark referred to as "lunch" included oyster soup, ducks, chickens, ham, sardines, bread, biscuits, jellies, preserves, and apples, all downed with tea, coffee, and chocolate. Even so, he received more than he gave. In advance of their visit the officials had dispatched messengers with a costly present of bronze. In the following days and weeks gifts continued to arrive. Ōkubo Ichio sent two dozen fresh eggs and three loaves of sponge cake. A student brought a dozen nice quails. A friend sent a pair of pigeons. The locals seemed to vie with one another in showing appreciation to Clark for his enthusiastic teaching and neighborly spirit.[34]

The frequent gifts of food helped keep Sam's larder well stocked, supplementing what Clark ordered from Yokohama. The local markets were not very appealing except for the fresh fish, which Sam prepared daily. Fowl were best obtained alive since there was no guarantee they had not died of disease. Anything received as a gift was generally superior to ordinary market goods.[35]

Two days after the lunch for the governors Clark conducted the first Sunday Bible class at his home. A group of young men showed a lively and sparkling interest while Clark, using Nakamura as interpreter, expounded the Christian way for two and a half hours. Sam too would have listened intently, even if from an adjacent room. Clark sent the students off each one with a Bible under his arm. Soon they were conducting their own Bible class each Sunday afternoon, meeting at one of their own houses.

Before coming to Shizuoka Clark had signed his three-year teaching contract only after removal of a stipulation that would have barred him from teaching Christianity, which was still proscribed by law. He was the

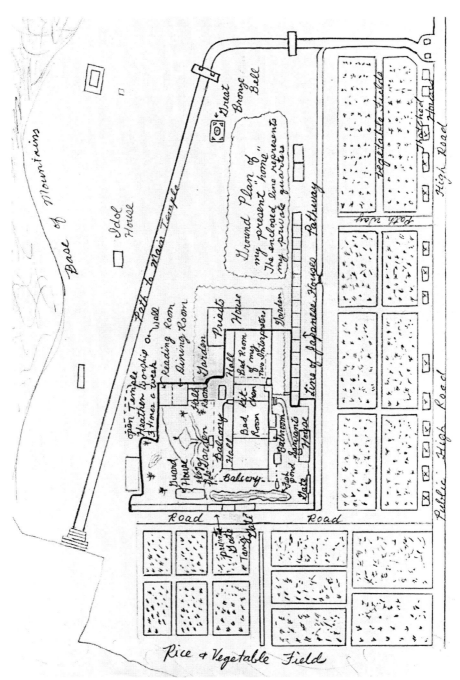

Clark's sketch of his temple home. Redrawn by Andrew Parker

first *yatoi* allowed to work in the interior without pledging to keep his faith to himself. "You are a conqueror," said an influential leader. "You have broken down a strong Japanese wall. Now, you can teach us the Bible and Christianity."[36] How did he pull it off? Clark believed, no doubt correctly, that his rapport with Iwakura Tomomi had worked in his favor. It was truly a ground-breaking feat.

Like Leroy Janes and William Clark, dynamic *yatoi* teachers who later produced the famous Christian groups known as Kumamoto Band and Sapporo Band, Clark was no less enthusiastic for evangelism than were Goble, Ballagh, and other professional missionaries. He used textbooks that were rich in Christian content, among them Francis Wayland's *Elements of Moral Science* and *Elements of Political Economy*. Clark also kept a good supply of English Bibles for distribution as well as copies of the Gospel of Mark in Japanese, translated and recently published by missionaries J. C. Hepburn and S. R. Brown.[37]

Even though Clark's contract did not forbid such activities, he doubtless would have encountered local opposition had not Nakamura and Katsu given their support. Nakamura took an active part in Clark's Bible classes and sought personal instruction in matters of faith. He also sent a daughter to Mrs. Pruyn's school in Yokohama, as did his partner Kihira, who formed a company with Nakamura for publishing the latter's works. Katsu advised local officials that "inasmuch as religion pertained to a man's own conscience alone, it should be left to the individual, and not meddled with by the Government."[38] Religious toleration in Shizuoka was advanced for the time.

Classes formally began at Gakumonjo Monday, December 25, 1871, after Clark had heard examinations and appointed his assistants and interpreters. Having won a concession on the weekly Sabbath as a holiday from classes, he made no issue of Christmas or other religious holidays. From the outset the foreign teacher was a phenomenon. Despite the formidable language barrier, he successfully taught and demonstrated the marvels of Western science to nearly a thousand students and supervised fifty assistants. His courses were English, French, geometry, chemistry, and natural philosophy (physics). Classes met daily except Sunday.[39]

Clark usually arose at six. After the breakfast Sam prepared, he walked the one and a half miles to the school in the southwest corner of the old castle grounds, giving his guards a brisk workout by covering the distance in twenty-five minutes. He could have traveled by horseback or jinrikisha, but Clark preferred walking for the exercise, making the round trip twice a day. Each morning from nine to twelve he taught languages, and each afternoon from two to five he taught the other subjects through interpreters in both English and French. He also demonstrated scientific experiments in a new laboratory erected for this purpose.[40]

Clark had brought scientific apparatus from America to enhance his classroom instruction. In addition, he had access to a large store of useful items the Tokugawa rulers had brought from Tokyo. These included old-fashioned instruments obtained through the Dutch, such as weighing machines, spectroscope, sewing machine, and terrestrial globe. Also available were gifts brought with the Perry expedition, which were hidden over one of the castle gates. There were maps of the United States, which Clark put on the wall of his laboratory, air pumps, electric machines, model locomotive and steam engine, horseshoe magnet, barometer, standard measures, and specimens of American marbles.[41]

Sam and Clark were soon shocked by a violent crime at the school. The twenty-year-old gatekeeper, bent on thievery, sneaked into a room where some money had been left. Finding another guard sleeping there, he dispatched the hapless fellow with his sword and fled with the loot. The villain was caught in a neighboring province and brought back to Shizuoka. Clark was told that he was immediately tried and beheaded but eventually learned that the execution was delayed more than a year.[42]

After a few months Clark was commuting to school on a jet black Japanese pony he called "my young Bucephalus" after the spirited horse of Alexander the Great. This cut travel time to ten minutes. A half-naked, splendidly tattooed *bettō* (groom) ran ahead like a deer and uttered cries to clear the road and make everyone get out of the way. Clark grew tired of the pony, especially after being launched on "an aërial voyage ten feet over his head," and started using a four-wheeled foreign carriage that the Dutch had presented to the shogun. Keiki had brought it to Shizuoka, but having no need of it, lent it to Clark. The governor ordered the whole length of the road from the temple to the school widened and improved to accommodate the carriage. This meant new embankments and bridges, a construction project that tacitly bestowed on the *yatoi* the status of daimyo if not emperor (roads were being built and improved for Emperor Meiji's inspection tours of the country beginning that year). Clark played the part. He drove as furiously as the biblical Jehu with the sad result that his horse soon expired. However he traveled, upon returning home from a hard day at school he would find Sam awaiting with "hot rice-cakes and honey, and plenty of nice things."[43]

Parties and Guests Galore

Sam cooked not only for special dinner parties and frequent visitors like Katsu and Nakamura but for at least eight people full time. Clark kept several of his best students in addition to the interpreters, among them Ōkubo's twelve-year-old son. A notable student who did not live with Clark but visited often was Matsudaira Mikawa, an ex-daimyo. Sam's cooking helped nourish the cream of Japan.[44]

He served the first foreign guest in Shizuoka the last two days of January. William Griffis, en route from Fukui to a new teaching assignment at the Imperial College in Tokyo, arrived for a long anticipated reunion with his dear friend Ed. "Griff" was accompanied by his servant Saki and an officer named Inoue. Sam cooked for the guests in lavish style, drawing on a fresh supply of well-timed provisions received from Yokohama only the day before. After offering them dinner and supper (both Griffis and Clark used these terms for the noon and evening meals respectively), the next morning he served what Griffis called "a plentiful breakfast."[45]

The climax of the Griffis visit was a one o'clock dinner attended by Clark's VIP friends. Sam served the best of available American food to twelve men seated in the improvised dining room that was separated from the kitchen by a long hall. "The fatted duck was killed," Clark gloated. Yatabori, Nakamura and Shimojō partook of the feast, as did Hattori Ayao, who had succeeded Ōkubo as governor and like him was gifted in poetry and literature. Ōkubo, ill at home, sent his regrets and a poetry-inscribed fan. Katsu was in Tokyo, where he now spent most of his time as minister of the Navy. Tokugawa Keiki did not come, nor did he ever visit Clark's home, but rather declined the invitations in the politest manner possible. The deposed shogun, who stuck to falcon hunting and prudently avoided controversial issues such as the foreign presence in Japan, would send a perfumed note written in his own hand, explaining that it would not be politically wise for him to make the visit. Or as Griffis once put it, Keiki was "politically dead, and does not wish to get out of his coffin."[46]

After dinner the local guests presented Griffis with a variety of gifts in appreciation of his recommending so competent a teacher as Clark. As was often the case in Japan (and still is), the traveler could not carry all the presents with him. A good part of the edibles, including the sponge cake, confectionary, ducks, and eggs from Hattori, were left behind, presumably for Sam to dispense as needed. Having been delayed on his journey earlier by snowstorms, Griffis had to rush away at three that afternoon, after sleeping only one night in the extra long bed constructed especially for his visit. "He came like a star," Clark wrote, "he went like a comet."[47]

"Ed lives very luxuriantly and dresses very finely," Griffis reported after returning to Tokyo. He appraised Ginzō and Sam Patch as "two very good and expensive servants from Yokohama." His later account of this visit in *The Mikado's Empire* pictures Sam as a bit proud and smug in his privileged life. "Sammy's notoriety has somewhat spoiled his pristine modesty," Griffis wrote, "and his head, having never been ballasted with over two-thirds the average quantum of wit, is occasionally turned, to the annoyance of his master." This widely read portrayal of an inattentive dimwit needs to be balanced with the earlier "very good servant."[48]

After Griffis's cometlike departure, Clark invited Ren'eiji's head priest to dinner. The pleasant old gentleman, apparently in his sixties, showed up in his priestly robes of elegant blue silk and satin. He was accompanied by a younger cleric. The meal Sam prepared featured a roast duck, which Clark carved ostentatiously before his vegetarian guests. The priests declined the meat politely but otherwise struggled valiantly to accommodate themselves to the new experience. "The spoons they almost swallowed," Clark wrote, "and the knives and forks they handled upside down." The final course was a volcanic plum pudding that frightened the guests and made the host look like a "fire eater." The priests left a box of eggs and a supply of sponge cake when they bowed themselves away.[49]

Sam's impulsive master was no more hesitant to tout his American citizenship than his Christian faith. Japanese carpenters worked two weeks to erect a large flag pole close to the guardhouse at the main entrance to his temple home. Then Clark invited several friends to join him in raising the stars and stripes at five A.M. New Year's Day (February 9 by the Western calendar). The private sunrise ceremony turned public—if not zany—when those gathered saluted the colors with sixty gun and pistol shots, awakening the whole countryside.

During that special day the Clark house was besieged with visitors dressed in their finest apparel. Some wore ceremonial garments that spread out at the shoulders, giving Clark the impression of a flock of spread eagles. Aided by Sam, the teacher served lunch to one of his classes of younger boys. They made "an onslaught on my stock of provisions," Clark wrote, and left with their stomachs and sleeves filled to capacity.[50]

From that time on the big "flower flag" waved over the temple each day, and smaller American and Japanese flags decorated the gate posts. It was as if Sam was once again "under the protection of the flag." But there was more immediate and tangible protection. Half a dozen guards and their watchdog remained day and night at the temple gate. Clark kept his revolver and gun handy and even slept with Katsu's short sword under his pillow. These precautions were not excessive in a country where the majority of foreigners were said to be armed, and in a town where Clark sensed danger in his frequent encounters with swaggering samurai. "The impudent looks which they throw at you from their black eyes," he wrote, "are not calculated to comfort you in the presence of those barbarous looking swords, whose edges are kept sharp as razors."[51] No doubt Sam was grateful for the protection afforded him as the servant of a foreigner revered by those eager to learn from the West but despised by many a xenophobic on the prowl. He must have been haunted at times by memories of Dankichi's chilling fate.

That spring Clark laid out an American garden on a vacant plot of ground at his temple home and planted seeds provided by Horace Capron, agricultural advisor to the Japanese government. He expected to enhance his food supply and satisfy his own appetite for fresh and nutritious vegetables. With the exception of potatoes and spinach, those in the Japanese markets were said to be rather coarse and tasteless to foreigners. Clark's plants thrived and gave much promise, the corn, beans, melons, and pumpkins doing especially well. But at summer's end, to Sam's disappointment as well as Clark's, a typhoon laid waste everything in the garden.[52]

In May Clark made an emergency trip to Yokohama to have an aching tooth extracted after self-medication failed to assuage the pain. Accompanied by a guard and an interpreter, he raced his fancy carriage to Numazu, as far as road conditions permitted, then switched to conventional carriers for the rest of the journey. After recovering at Mrs. Pruyn's from the dentist's forceps and chloroform, he returned to Shizuoka by the steam-yacht *Emperor* with a delegation of Americans who wanted to inspect the tea cultivation in Suruga province. The delegation included Consul Charles O. Shepard, a few businessmen, and several officers from the flagship *Colorado*. It was a time when the United States was consuming nine-tenths of Japan's exported tea.

Putting in at Shimizu, Clark and his fellow Americans boarded rickshas for the six-mile trip to Shizuoka. The presence in the region of nearly a dozen foreigners, some in bright uniforms, caused quite a stir. Clark housed the visitors at his temple residence, filling the four beds and some of the floor space. "It kept us pretty busy," he reported, "especially in the kitchen department."[53] Sam had to hustle. Besides satisfying the voracious appetites of the huge foreigners, he had to cook for Hitomi and other officials who twice joined the visitors for dinner.

Sam continued to cook for visitors from near and far, but he found a diminishing number of eaters at the table on a daily basis. Clark's live-in companions and others who visited most often were nearly all summoned to Tokyo. Clark complained about "the policy of the Government in calling off a large number of my best friends, my best students, and my best assistants, to place them in positions of trust in Yedo." He appealed for "the upholding and upbuilding of education throughout the Provinces, and against the idea of centralizing everything at Tokeio."[54] But his words fell on deaf ears. The new Meiji regime sought the best and the brightest to staff its various departments, and the Tokugawa exile community in Shizuoka offered a vast pool of experience and talent.

Statesmen Katsu and Ōkubo, scholars Nakamura and Kihira, English interpreter Shimojō, French interpreters Itō and Ari—these and others on whom Clark relied so heavily for their expertise and friendship were taken away in this "brain drain" to the capital. By October he was lamenting that "all my friends & best students & all that have any brains or push have gone . . . Things are getting pretty lonely here now-a-days."[55]

Even the twelve-year-old Ōkubo boy was no longer with Clark. At his father's request he had remained even after the family's move to Tokyo in June. But later that summer Clark had returned the boy to his parents after treating him to the charming sights of Kamakura, the caves and divers in Enoshima, his first church service in Yokohama, and his first train ride on the British-built railway line up to the capital. Clark missed the boy, but probably not as much as he missed Nakamura and Shimojō on whom he had depended so heavily.[56]

Although Clark's protests against the brain drain were ineffectual, the Ministry of Education made a minor concession to accommodate him. It allowed Gakumonjo to suffer a lingering rather than immediate demise. Hitomi was appointed head of the shrunken, dying school.[57]

Mansion on the Moat

One ray of sunshine that pierced the gloom hanging over Clark was the promise of better living quarters. Katsu and Ōkubo, worried that the rat-infested temple home was too unprotected and inconvenient for the foreign teacher, had decided to build him a Western-style house that would provide maximum security and comfort. They agreed to build it at Katsu's expense in the name of Tokugawa Iesato, the nine-year-old prince of the province who was under Katsu's care. The house would be available to Clark as long as he remained as teacher. At their request he selected the site, designed the house, and—with varying degrees of success—supervised the hundreds of stonecutters and carpenters engaged to put up a structure radically different from any they had ever built before. The workers balked at the idea of chimneys, for instance, but Clark persisted in having them built.

Some of the stone for the project was brought from a neighboring

Clark's house. Sam Patch is standing in front of the servants' quarters

province, but most of it came from the ruins of the ancient castle just across the inner moat, the castle once occupied by Ieyasu, founder of the Tokugawa shogunate. Once again, as when the road between his temple home and the school was improved, Clark was being treated as though of daimyo rank. When the work was finished in December after six months' work, he boasted "a costly and substantial stone house on the corner of the castle-moat."[58]

The two-story structure had about twenty-seven hundred square feet of floor space. James Ballagh described it as "a perfect gem of beauty and durability." Architects have continued to study it with intense interest, and an urban planning study group made a scale model of the house.[59]

The mansion stood at the northwest corner of the castle grounds, at the highest part of the great stone embankment that skirted the thirty-foot-deep outer moat. The spot today is occupied by the Shizuoka family court, but Clark would be hard pressed to find it, so drastically has the topography been altered. The site in Clark's day commanded a charming view of the surrounding town and countryside. From the front, which faced north, one could see peerless Mount Fuji and waving fields of grain. Although the house overlooked public roads and rows of Japanese homes, it was secluded and secure, reachable only by going a quarter of a mile in either direction to one of the bridges crossing the moat.[60]

The house was partially shaded by four giant pine trees, from two of which were suspended American and Japanese flags. Behind it stood the servants' quarters, a Japanese-style bungalow with about four hundred square feet of floor space. The contrast between the two structures was conspicuous. "My cook 'Sammy' sleeps in his little Jap kennel," Clark jested, "a few feet from the house."[61] In the courtyard was a well and a stone furnace where Sam heated water for baths.

Clark's house was lavishly furnished. In the eyes of cultured Japanese it was cluttered, with Japanese treasures crudely displayed in dissonant environments. The parlor, or sitting room, showcased the elegant gifts he had received, among them a bronze crane from the Daisanji (local governing officials), a sword rack from a former governor, a long heirloom sword Ōkubo had presented him in his son's name, a short harakiri sword Katsu had worn as an admiral in the Tokugawa navy. This room also contained a harmonium, or reed organ, which Clark played for Christian worship in the home and with which he often entertained and astonished his guests.[62]

A photograph Clark took of the parlor shows a placard that reads, "Glory to God in the highest, and on earth peace, good will toward men." Ballagh reported after his visit that "hymns, texts, and daily promises" were hung in every room. The pious placards bore such messages as "Faith, Hope, and Charity," "God is my salvation," "None that ever put their trust in him shall be ashamed." These devotional decorations were intended to bear a Christian witness to visitors as well as nourish Clark's own soul. Also on display a few months after the house was built was a board tablet bearing the infamous edict against Christianity. Clark obtained it from Ōkubo after the Meiji government, under pressure from the Western powers, ordered such tablets removed from public display.[63]

Sam took special pride in the new kitchen of which he was chief. The doors and windows were made of an unidentified wood that resembled mahogany, and the walls were of smooth stone. The cooking stove, sink, and other equipment were "all in orderly and clean condition," Clark boasted, "and the floor is well scrubbed." Just off the kitchen was a cupboard and store cellar, and provisions were also kept in an upstairs room. Sam could draw from "dozens upon dozens of freshly-canned fruits and vegetables of all kinds which line the shelves."[64]

The dining room where Sam served up his famed cuisine was by far the largest room in the house. It was well carpeted, and its walls and ceiling were covered with a light and cheery paper. The long dining table, a globe lamp in its center, was covered with a heavy velvet cloth decorated with flowers. Over the sideboard was suspended a plate glass mirror that Nakamura had sent from Tokyo. Beyond the sideboard was a marble mantelpiece with a clock above it. The room was decorated with a map of the world and various pictures and ornaments.

After moving into the new house, Clark hosted more than a dozen dinner parties the first few weeks, usually with ten to twenty persons present. His hospitality was most spectacular on Christmas day, the first anniversary of his teaching in Shizuoka. In the early evening several hundred persons, guided by appointed ushers, walked through the only Western home in the region and doubtless the first that most of the people had seen. Even the palatial exterior had hardly prepared them for the luxurious interior. The women were especially fascinated by the gleaming American kitchen over which Sam presided. They had never seen a cooking stove with an oven, or various appliances for baking, roasting, and other culinary operations. Their kitchens, primitive in comparison, centered in a stone box with ashes, on which coals were placed and over which rice was cooked. The smoke would find its way out through an opening in the roof.

After the open-house tour the Christmas crowd gathered on benches and mats set up in the courtyard enclosure to see a show as novel and spectacular as the house they had traipsed through. The night was pleasant and mild. Clark used a magnesium stereopticon and picture-slides he had ordered from Philadelphia earlier in the year "as a personal gift for the benefit of this province." He showed the capitol at Washington, the suspension bridge at Niagara, the Fairmount Water works at Philadelphia, Broadway in New York, and other views of America. His interpreter explained each picture. Then he moved on to Mont Blanc and other scenes from Europe. The show, billed as a "trip in imagination through foreign countries and the starry heavens," concluded with revolving astronomical diagrams including the Little Bear and other constellations. This last part of the performance was designed to prove that the earth was round, but some of the viewers were unconvinced.[65]

While hundreds of dazzled guests drifted back to their homes, forty chosen elite—the maximum number Clark could accommodate in his carpeted dining room—remained for dinner. They sat at two long tables instead of the usual one. The tables were lit up with three large lamps and numerous candles, and the glittering lights were reflected in the large mirror that hung on one side of the room. The tables were spread with a prodigious quantity of food: "ducks and chickens in abundance, cakes and pies (mince, pumpkin, and quince), plenty of corn, peas, beans, succotash, tomatoes, white potatoes . . . luscious bowls of jellies and sweetmeats . . . oranges and fresh apples, as well as other fruits."[66]

As a climax to the sumptuous dinner, Clark carved a large turkey he had fattened up for Christmas. It was "well stuffed and plump, with oyster-sauce accompaniment." His rationale for serving the bird last was that the guests would be so full by then as to leave a slice of meat—perhaps even a drumstick—for Clark's own plate and enjoyment. But they consumed the turkey ravenously as though it was the first course of a long delayed meal. "Not a vestige remained," Clark moaned, "save a few stuffing-crumbs, and that unmentionable appendage which goes over the fence last."[67]

Eating ravenously was one way the guests showed their appreciation for Clark's efforts to show his appreciation for the new house. He had indeed gone all out for the occasion. Many of the foods were expensive imports from London and San Francisco that he had ordered from Yokohama.[68] Sam too had given his best in cooking the meal and getting it together while Clark was showing his stereoptican slides.

Nine days later William Griffis paid his second visit to Shizuoka and his first to the stone mansion beside the moat. He was accompanied by Marion M. Scott, a distinguished professor at Tokyo Normal School who introduced American methods in elementary education to Japan. Griffis had telegraphed from Numazu, utilizing the newly installed wire that farmers would watch for hours in hopes of seeing a message go by. So when the two men reached the well-illuminated house at six P.M., Sam had their supper prepared. He also became one of the topics of conversation; Griffis noted in his diary that Clark told the "story of Sammy."[69]

The next day, a rainy, dreary Saturday, Sam cooked for a dinner party that Clark hosted in honor of his out-of-town guests. Among those present were the school's first officer, Hitomi, and the fat and jolly second officer. Once again the entertainment was a stereoptican show. On Sunday, after

Clark's three-hour Bible class, the three Americans visited Clark's old temple home and found that all traces of Clark having lived there had been obliterated save for the glass windows he had installed. After a three-o'clock dinner, Griffis and Scott left for home.[70]

Griffis afterwards wrote that Clark's house was not as large as the one he had occupied in Fukui but more finely finished. Its doors and windows, he told his sister Martha in Philadelphia, "would grace Chestnut St." Griffis applauded the luxurious furnishings, the bountifully supplied larder, and the "trained cook and servant from Yokohama (Sam Patch)."[71]

In late April Clark rolled out the carpet for Mary Pruyn. "As I am a sort of mother to him now," she wrote, "I came here to see how nice he lives." She made the grueling journey from Yokohama in three days, bravely enduring the relentless bounce of rickshas and kagos ("those barbarous vehicles"), often in pouring rain. Her journey, "the very hardest thing of the kind I could even imagine," was a precursor of the more extensive travels in Japan of the adventurous Englishwoman, Isabella Bird. On her tours around Shizuoka, Mrs. Pruyn aroused great attention and astonishment "as the first foreign lady who had ever been in that city."[72]

The mansion by the moat, Pruyn reported, offered "all the comfort and luxury of an Albany home." Sam served up his best cooking those weeks, and Clark rolled out all the stops with his organ playing, singing, and stereoptican slides. He also brought in dancers and musicians worthy of a queen, treating his surrogate mother to performances with samisen, koto, and *biwa* (a four-stringed lute). "Singular and rude as their instruments were," the guest acknowledged, "there was true music in them, and I enjoyed it exceedingly." For weeks the big stone house reverberated to laughter and applause. It was a fitting replay of Clark's exciting first weeks in Japan at the American Home, when Mary Pruyn was host and he was guest.[73]

Chapter 9

Faithful in Life, Peaceful in Death

Though an associate of humble capacity, Sam was faithful in his own little sphere, and he was the only individual who remained uninterruptedly with me during my sojourn in the country . . . Sam's face, when raised, was calm and natural.

—E. Warren Clark[1]

SHORTLY before Mary Pruyn's visit, Clark was awakened by an earthquake that "shook me out of the house in my night-flaps." Following her visit he reported a shock of a different kind: "Lost my faithful servant 'Ginzo' – gone away to be small yaconin [official] of small village." Like Sam Patch, Ginzō had worked for Clark since the start of his tenure in Shizuoka and had proven worthy of his hire. In May, after a year and a half of service, Ginzō was summoned to his home north of Tokyo to succeed his father as a village official and inherit the family's rice fields and thatched-roof house. This was his right and duty as eldest son. His foreign employer, bowing to Japanese custom, sent him off with a generous bonus and fervent benediction.[2]

The loss was profound. "He has been around me so constantly," Clark mused, "that it almost seems like missing one of my own members, not to have him near, to light the fire or the lamp, post letters, serve the table, and pour out tea." But with Ginzō out of the picture, Clark took a deeper interest in his one remaining servant, peppering him with questions he had never asked before. He learned that Sam's "by-gone experiences have been as varied and romantic as some modern Marco Polo." The longtime cook was now essential in a different and deeper sense, for solitude breeds a craving for companionship with almost any warm body. Except for Sam Patch, Clark lamented, "not a person is near."[3]

Clark's closest friends and companions had migrated to Tokyo while he was still in his temple home, leaving him lonely even then. His live-ins had dwindled from eight or so to zero. The upstairs bedroom where Clark slept in the spacious new house had originally been meant for his interpreter Shimojō. This room, with four windows facing east, was well furnished with camphor-wood furniture and pictures of famous European scenes. But not even the welcome sunshine that roused Clark on fair mornings that spring could alleviate his nostalgia for Shimojō and other close friends. In January Shimojō had entered a Tokyo hospital with terminal consumption brought on by "overstudy." "He died with the hope and comfort and faith of a Christian," wrote Nakamura for his gravestone inscription.[4]

Clark's chief interpreter now was Sugiyama Magoroku, who had been baptized by James Ballagh in Yokohama the previous year. Sugiyama was proficient, but he had once fainted while interpreting at Clark's house during a concert given by a team of Japanese musicians. "The Japs are a weakly set, there's no mistake," Clark wrote; "and how they are going to get physically better, on the strength of rice & slops, is more than I can see."[5] He feared that Sugiyama might go the way of Shimojō. His servant Sam was eating enough Western food not to be a concern.

Although Sam had fewer mouths to cook for than in earlier months, Ginzō's exodus left him with more tasks to perform. Even without live-ins, Clark required an efficiently run house, one in top condition anytime guests arrived whether expected or not. He believed in laws "written in black and white, covering every imaginable condition." Tacked up in his kitchen was a double sheet of "household regulations" for Sam to follow. On one side were listed the set times for washing, sweeping, cleaning, cooking, killing (ducks especially), bathing, scrubbing, making beds, baking bread, polishing stoves, polishing shoes, and "everything you can think of." On the other side were listed fines for violating these regulations,"either as to time or thoroughness." These rules had to be "closely observed."[6]

"His pay is four times as much as is usually given in such a place," Clark wrote of Sam, "and his board of foreign food and little extras leads him to exert himself like a good fellow to fulfil every iota of the big programme which continually stares him in the face, well knowing that if he fails in the least I will cut down his 'loose change.' So my household affairs run on smoothly and regularly." Apparently this carrot-and-stick policy worked well, though mortal Sam had his failings. Clark once asked William Griffis to tell Maggie (Willie's sister) that he wished for some of her "celestial"custard. "Poor Sam Patch," Clark explained, "has made several futile attempts to imitate it, & he gets it half omelet & half custard!"[7]

In July Griffis showed up for the third time, accompanied by Maggie and an assistant named Yamada. Sam had supper ready for the guests when they arrived Sunday night at 9:15, after three-days' travel by train, horse, kago, and ricksha, with precious little sleep along the way. Maggie had been "nearly devoured by fleas" during the night spent at Hakone, but she rested well in Shizuoka despite the hot weather and "mosquitoes plenty." She and Willie observed Monday as their delayed Sabbath, singing hymns, listening to the melodeon, reading, writing, strolling about the town. Tuesday morning they were up at 4:15 for Sam's early but substantial breakfast and were off at 5:10. Maggie left with praise for Clark's "excellent cook."[8]

Clark seized upon the visit as an opportunity to vent his feelings. Willie Griffis listened with sympathy, himself irked at the country's educational policies. "With delays, vexations and disappointments," he noted, "and the

Sam Patch (?) sitting on veranda with Clark

school gone to ruin . . . Clarkie is disgusted and mortified beyond measure at all things Japanese." Clark's plans at the time were to finish out the year as best he could, return home, attend an Episcopalian theological seminary, and settle down as a "humble minister in some quiet place."[9] Often his playful spirit had masked the seriousness with which he carried out his teaching duties. Now there was no place for levity, and his buoyancy was diminished. At such low ebb Clark was fortunate to have Sam still with him as solace and support.

Pigeons, Pork, and Pests

Sam often stewed pigeons that Clark shot in a wooded area between the school and his house. He baked roasts from the big game his master bagged on hunting expeditions. After one hunt, supported and expedited by clan officials, Clark came home with two deer and three wild boars, the largest boar weighing nearly two hundred pounds. Clark shared the meat with the officials, but there was plenty Sam had to cook.[10]

Clark craved good pork, but even this monied foreigner refused to buy it at the going rate. A Japanese farmer who kept a dozen or more pigs near his old temple home offered a small one for fifty dollars and a large one for two hundred dollars. Toward the end of 1873, however, pork became available in the city markets, and Clark obtained a fine roast "at the considerate price of half a 'boo' (i.e. twelve cents!)."[11]

Clark used his weapons for other than hunting and target practice. One day Sam discovered an enormous snake coiling and squirming in the front yard. The frightened cook ran upstairs screaming for Clark, who came out with his shotgun and killed the intruder. A few days later a large black snake lay at the kitchen door. Clark fired at it with his revolver several times but missed, then brought his shotgun to finish off the job. "Both of these snakes," he claimed, "were fully as long as my body." And he saw others almost daily as he walked along the bank of the moat.[12]

The area around the mansion was also infested by wild dogs. "I am engaged in a canine warfare at present," Clark reported; "but Jap yelpers are absolutely susceptible of nothing except bullets. For I have used up 'heaps' of Arsenic, Farton-Emetic, Cyanide of Potassium, Oxalic Acid, & lots of other stuff, & these un-killable dogs have swallowed all, & yet they live! I am going to try lead now!"[13] Clark did not submit a follow-up report on the dogs, but it is clear that his guns were ineffective against another kind of pest: centipedes. These hideous, dirty-brown creatures were more fearful than the snakes. Their sting caused swelling and excruciating pain, as Clark learned one night when he jumped out of bed with his leg on fire and found his tormentor between the sheets. So pervasive were these venomous crawlers that Sam must have been a victim as well.

Another annoyance Clark had to live with was the many false rumors about him that circulated among the common people. Some of these rumors must have reached Sam's ears. It was said that Clark could change his shape and appear and reappear at pleasure. He could work miracles, as evidenced by his inexplicable laboratory feats, especially his manufacture of explosives such as nitroglycerin and dynamite. It was further said that the ghosts of the Tokugawa family paid the foreigner a visit each night and killed him "by inches" for desecrating the ancient castle with his presence. Because the presence of foreigners in Japan had led to the Tokugawa collapse, Clark bore part of the blame for the pitiful plight of Keiki and hundreds of his vassals and retainers who lived in exile in Shizuoka, many with a drastically reduced standard of living.[14]

In August Clark used his vacation time to visit Yokohama and obtain a new stock of provisions. His shopping done, he sent his interpreter Sugiyama directly to Shizuoka on the Tōkaidō with ten boxes of goods. Then he and James Ballagh set out by another route to Mount Fuji. After climbing the famous peak, they both came to Shizuoka, providing Sam his first opportunity in nearly two years to see his former employer. Probably they talked at length, for Ballagh had a genuine interest in ordinary folks like Sam.[15]

By September Clark was teaching a mere three hours a day, almost frittering away his time. A plaque over his laboratory door read, "God bless our school," and he daily led his students in singing hymns such as "Joyfully, joyfully." But Gakumonjo had become "Ichabod." The glory had departed, and so had the joy. "I have reached the lowest point possible," Clark moaned. Things had gone downhill ever since the Griffis visit. He was tired of pounding his head against the wall of Meiji centralization. Having hit rock bottom, he was resigned to following his friends to Tokyo and teaching at the Imperial College, Kaisei Gakkō, though it meant being "under the direct flap of the Mombusho's [Ministry of Education's] diabolical wings."[16]

In October, Clark entertained two more distinguished guests, George Cochran and Henry Loomis. To Sam's chagrin, perhaps, their visit lasted two weeks rather than the customary two or three days. Irish-born Cochran impressed his host as "a man of ability and good sense" who was also "very pleasant and jolly." He and his wife Catherine had recently left the pastorate of a prominent Toronto church to establish the Canadian Methodist Mission in Japan. Henry Loomis, who with his wife Jennie had come to Japan the previous year, had just founded the first Presbyterian church in Yokohama at Dr. Hepburn's dispensary and was the eighteen-member congregation's first pastor. Already proficient in Japanese, Loomis talked about religion to several gatherings in Clark's house, probably to Sam's edification.[17]

Moving up to the Capital

In December Clark wound down his affairs in Shizuoka and struck out for his new teaching post in Tokyo. He entrusted his household goods to a swarm of packers who wrapped them in sheets of rice straw and bound them securely with straw rope. A long train of hand carts, each pulled by a man in front and pushed by a woman behind, ferried the bundles and bales to the port of Shimizu. There the goods were loaded onto a clumsy fifty-foot-long junk to be transported around treacherous Cape Irō at the southern end of the Izu Peninsula and on to the capital. Clark was worried. Many a junk had been wrecked off that cape so dreaded by sailors, and a few months later the French steamer *Nil* would suffer the same fate with a heavy loss of life.[18]

If Clark wondered about the safety of his custom-made furniture, cherished books, and hundreds of personal gifts from Japanese officials and friends, Sam Patch had all the more reason to be concerned. His very life was at stake, for he accompanied Clark's freight, just as Ginzō had accompanied it in the opposite direction two years before. Probably for the first time since abandoning the crippled *Eiriki-maru* two decades earlier, Sam experienced life on a cargo junk.

Rapidly modernizing Japan now had thirty-two Western-style sailing vessels. It boasted a fleet of steamships, twenty in its navy and two hundred in its mercantile marine. But there were also 22,670 registered junks engaged in the coastal trade, and these vulnerable ships, like the *Eiriki-maru* of the previous generation, were still haunted by contrary winds. Sailors were still being blown out to sea. It could happen to Sam again. Though a passenger rather than a crew member, he felt the old-time thrill and danger as the junk edged up the rugged coast he knew so well.[19]

Clark traveled overland. He squirmed in *kago*s and rickshas as far as Yokohama, then boarded a train at the fancy stone depot. At Shimbashi Station, the end of the line, Clark switched to a ricksha once again for the final sprint to the Griffis home where he was to live. He arrived December 24 at the very time Willie Griffis and his sister Maggie were leaving for Yokohama to spend the Christmas holidays.[20]

As noted in the previous chapter, Griffis had moved from Fukui to Tokyo two years earlier, visiting Clark en route. He had occupied a new two-story house, considerably smaller than his Fukui mansion, until Maggie had come to Japan in August 1872. Then the two had moved into a new and larger one-story house, with Maggie "in charge." They had purchased a gorgeous ricksha for $22.50 and hired a puller who doubled as a weed puller for the garden. Maggie, usually referred to in Clark's letters as Mademoiselle Maggie or Her Majesty Maggie, was now teaching full time at Tokyo Jogakkō, Japan's first government school for girls.[21]

Their eight-room bungalow, with shuttered windows and a tile roof, was one of twelve houses in a walled compound adjoining the Imperial College. Most of the professors lived in the compound, in what is now Kandanishiki, Chiyoda Ward. Willie and Maggie were conveniently located near the entrance gate, with ready access to the nearby moat and high stone walls of the imperial castle (they saw the castle burn to the ground in May 1873). The Ministry of Education and the college's new director, Hatakeyama Yoshinari, had asked the Griffises to allow Clark to live with them because their house was the largest on the compound and no other suitable house was available. To accommodate Clark the Griffises evicted the several Japanese students they were keeping under their roof. The students' room became their dining room, and the former dining room, where Maggie had also conducted her Sunday school, became Clark's private space.[22]

Clark's new one-year teaching contract increased his salary from 300 dollars per month to 320 yen.[23] The yen, minted only since 1871, was roughly equivalent to one American dollar or one Mexican dollar. With this level of income Clark could afford the luxuries enjoyed by Tokyo's European quarter and continue to support Sam Patch without straining his budget.

Clark had been in Tokyo three weeks when Sam arrived with the freight. Not only had Sam traveled by junk for the first time in more than two decades, he probably walked on Tokyo streets for the first time in as long. In some ways the city had not changed. Clark described it as "simply a vast wilderness of houses . . . an endless succession of tiled and shingled roofs."[24] Yet it had undergone a major transformation from Edo, the shogunal capital, to Tokyo, the imperial capital (literally, "eastern capital"). Emperor Meiji had been installed in the vast castle grounds at the center. The population of a million or more at the time of Sam's first visit had declined to 520,000 in 1872, because the daimyo and dispossessed samurai had returned to their provinces. But it would rise to a million again by 1880.

The populous part of the city east of the castle grounds, ravaged by fire in 1872, had been rebuilt with wider and straighter streets enhanced with sidewalks and gas lamps. The main street, the local portion of the Tōkaidō, had been widened to more than ninety feet. Japanese called it Tōri, while foreigners sometimes called it Broadway or Fifth Avenue (today it is Ginza). The street ran from the railway station to Nihonbashi, the famous bridge from which all distances in Japan were measured, and was lined with two-story houses half foreign and half Japanese. North of Nihonbashi the houses were traditional Japanese style. Many Tokyo streets were congested with rickshas, carriages, pedestrians, chickens, dogs, and cats.[25]

Western merchants and missionaries lived in Tsukiji, the foreigners' concession on reclaimed land near the mouth of the Sumida River. Tokyo's wholesale fish market is located there today. The only foreigners allowed to live outside the concession were the *yatoi* such as Griffis and Clark. Life was safer than in the early years when Sam's junk mate Iwakichi was among those murdered. But on the evening of January 15, just two days before Sam's arrival, Tosa swordsmen attacked Iwakura Tomomi as he returned from the palace in his carriage. Iwakura received three wounds but managed to flee in the darkness, accidentally falling into the cold but safe waters of the moat.[26]

Sam probably lived in the servants' room of the Griffis bungalow, one of eight rooms (nine including the bathroom) Maggie listed in her description of the house. Soon after Sam's arrival, Maggie wrote to her sisters: "Clarkie is established with us and has his servant with him. In disgust at Japanese cooks we have hired an American black man and turned over the house into his hands paying him so much a month & he furnishes everything." Since she was teaching, Maggie explained, she and Willie had to have dependable help and especially a good cook. They were going to try him one month. "Our new cook seems very good, she wrote after one week. "He gives us elaborate meals, all well cooked." But Willie told his journal three days later that "Clark returned from his chase after the *kuronbō* [black person]," as though something were amiss. How long the cook stayed and how well Sam got along with this counterpart would be interesting to know.[27]

It would also be interesting to know how Sam got along with Maggie. She and her brother were arguing over when and by what route to return to America, and she suffered "falling of the womb" and "severe dragging pains." Maggie was far from her best during the six months Sam was about.[28]

Willie had negotiated a six-month extension to his contract, even though Clark had been hired to succeed him. So until he and Maggie left Japan in July, the school had two chemistry teachers to fill one slot. Both men taught several subjects each in addition to chemistry. During those months

Griffis spent a great deal of time writing articles and tourist guides, and he began work on *The Mikado's Empire,* his magnum opus.[29]

Clark was no less busy. Despite a full teaching schedule six days a week at the college, he taught three Bible classes on what was supposed to be his Sabbath day of rest. He rose each Sunday at six-thirty, ate the breakfast Sam had prepared, and readied his room for the first class that met at eight. Students from the scientific department came to this class, and those from the legal department came to the evening class Clark taught in the same room. During the day Clark attended church and conducted a three o'clock class for former Shizuoka students in the home of Nakamura Masanao.[30]

Nakamura lived at 17 Edogawa-chō, Koishikawa-ku, about two miles from the school and near a hill known as Kirishitan-zaka or "Christian Slope." Here a steep lane ran beside the prison that had housed European Jesuits, Jean Baptiste Sidotti among them, and other Christians who had apostatized after long and fiendish torture. At this historic location Nakamura had established a school of English and Chinese, called Dōjinsha. In January 1874 George Cochran started coming up from Yokohama to preach at the school, often staying with Clark and assisting with his Sunday classes. In April Cochran and his family moved into a Western-style house built for them on the school grounds, and Clark turned the Sunday afternoon class over to him entirely. On Christmas morning, 1874, Cochran would have the honor of baptizing Nakamura as well as his adopted son Kazuyoshi, claiming them as the first Methodist converts in the capital.[31]

In Clark's Tokyo home, as in Shizuoka, Sam served many a notable guest. One was ten-year-old Iesato, or "Sami san," the Tokugawa prince who would have ruled Japan as shogun had his family not been toppled from power. As consolation he would eventually be chosen president of the House of Peers. It was in Iesato's name that Clark had been provided with a new house and valuable laboratory equipment in Shizuoka. The vivacious little prince was accompanied by several retainers and Governor Ōkubo's thirteen-year-old son who had lived with Clark. Both boys were elegantly dressed in Western suits, with diminutive swallowtail coats and light pants.[32] Clark entertained the little chaps with the steam engines and electrical machines in his classroom, then brought them back home for the dinner Sam had prepared for these teenage elite.

Among the foreign visitors to the Clark home were two of Sam's former employers, James Ballagh and Robbins Brown ("a sweet singer and understands music thoroughly," Maggie told her diary). Nakamura and his family came nearly every week. Other frequent visitors were Governor Ōkubo, Katsu Kaishū, and Hatakeyama, the school's director. Ōkubo was so sympathetic toward Christianity that he tolerated the blatant missionary activity at Nakamura's school and elsewhere that he as governor could have repressed. Katsu was to make a confession of personal faith in Christ prior to his death in 1899. Hatakeyama had become a Christian at Rutgers. He would die in his early thirties of tuberculosis, like Shimojō a victim of "overstudy."[33]

Clark heard that Katsuki Kegorō, a student he had known in Albany, had returned to Japan and was staying near Nihonbashi. Prior to Clark's leaving for Japan in 1871, Katsuki had entrusted him with some letters and had given him an elegant dressing case furnished with razors and other travel needs. Katsuki had even offered to lend him—Clark had declined—his precious copy of Dr. Hepburn's English-Japanese dictionary, which actually belonged to the college at Saga, Katsuki's home town. And what fears this Saga connection evoked!

A Saga militarist, Etō Shimpei, had resigned from the Council of State in protest against the council's decision not to wage war against Korea. The Hermit Kingdom had broken off relations with the pro-Western Meiji government, accusing it, in Griffis's words, of "slavish truckling to the foreign barbarians."[34] Etō was infuriated that his nation did not punish the brash neighbor for its insults and taunts. He had returned home, joined forces with a faction of dissatisfied samurai, and launched a revolt against the Tokyo regime. Clark recalled that Katsuki had regaled him with dreadful harakiri stories back in Albany, and he feared that the warlike youth would join in the rebellion and get himself killed. Perhaps Katsuki could be persuaded not to return to his native province at so dangerous a time.

So Clark sent Sam Patch on a life-and-death mission to find his friend. Sam returned from Nihonbashi with the disappointing news that Katsuki had already left to join his comrades in Saga. Not only was Clark too late, but the result was no less terrible than he had feared. A punitive expedition under Home Minister Ōkubo Toshimichi crushed the rebellion in a mere ten days, and Katsuki, like Etō, was among the dozen ringleaders who were beheaded.[35]

Sam was blameless in this misfortune, but soon after the fruitless search he was guilty of a whopping blunder. In Shizuoka Clark had received from Tokugawa Keiki a present "which would have rejoiced the heart of a Baptist, a large porphyry bathing tub!" He later described it as "an immense aquarium bowl made of the finest Chinaware, and carried by four men. The bowl was beautifully ornamented with blue waves, fishes, and turtles, and was so large that I sat in it and had my photograph taken!" When Clark moved to Tokyo, the bowl followed by junk with his other household goods. One day Sam poured several gallons of hot water into the bowl, attempting to use it as a bathtub. The bowl "exploded with a terrific noise, frightening the wits out of poor Sam, and leaving me only fragments of my present from the tycoon!" Clark estimated his loss at one thousand dollars.[36]

The Scourge of *Kakke*

July brought a welcome summer break from his daily teaching duties. Clark saw Willie and Maggie Griffis off to America, sent Sam to the hospital ill, and left on a month-long trip with an American friend and a fourteen-year-old Japanese, Kawamura Isami. Kawamura had just returned from America with a remarkable command of idiomatic English, having accompanied the Iwakura embassy and remained in the United States to study at Ann Arbor, Michigan.[37] The Clark party of three sailed to Kobe on the steamer *Oregonian* and, after visiting Osaka and Kyoto, returned to Tokyo via the Tōkaidō. Clark met former students in several towns along the way but especially in nostalgic Shizuoka, where he stopped for two days.

Soaking wet from rain and floods, the travelers first went to Clark's former mansion on the moat, which they found deserted. Then they visited the little house occupied by Davidson MacDonald, a Canadian medical missionary, and his wife Annie. The MacDonalds were away at the time, on vacation in Hakone. But Clark and his companions were allowed to dry their clothes beside the kitchen stove. This was the very stove on which Sam had cooked so proudly before moving to Tokyo, for Hitomi Fujitarō, who provided the house for the McDonalds, had bought Clark's stove for use by his successor. Clark afterwards visited his old school campus, now devoted to Japanese and Chinese studies at a less prestigious level than before. His beloved lecture room was empty and bare.[38]

At cool Hakone, a summer resort for foreigners and Japanese alike, Clark was delighted to see the MacDonalds. They told him they would move into his mansion on the moat immediately after their return to Shizuoka. Clark was pleased to have so eminent a successor as Davidson MacDonald, one who would make a deep and lasting impression on the town and its environs. The Canadian would educate his students with competence, minister freely as a physician, and establish a strong Methodist church on the Christian foundation Clark had laid.[39]

After about two weeks in Hakone, where he basked in the company of friends escaping Yokohama's oppressive heat, Clark completed his journey back to Tokyo. Faithful Sam was waiting for him, though unwell. "He was imprudent in leaving the hospital too soon," Clark wrote, "so as to have my house in good order on my return." Clark sent him back to "the Tokio hospital" for further treatment. According to a newspaper report of Sam's illness in *Chōya shimbun*, this hospital was in Shiba Sannai, a name used for the temple grounds of Zōjōji, the great family temple of the Tokugawa shoguns. Early in the year the main structure and the bell tower had been destroyed by fire, the work of arsonists. But on the extensive grounds were a Navy-built residence and a number of subordinate temples that were being used as housing for foreigner employees, including firemen,

Clark in the aquarium Sam broke

carpenters, blacksmiths, and others. The little hospital on the premises that met their medical needs was afterwards called Tokyo General Hospital and later became Tokyo Charity Medical University Hospital, which occupies the site today.[40]

Sam's physician was an American, the newspaper said. A missionary friend called him an "English doctor." Perhaps he was Dr. Ashmead, whom Maggie Griffis identified as "the physician at Tokei Fu" (the hospital was the Tōkei-fu [Tokyo] Byōin). There was also a foreign doctor whose katakana name was Sabachū. But however competent the physician, however advanced the hospital care, Sam was doomed. He was suffering from *kakke*, which Clark described as "a kind of dropsy peculiar to the Japanese." It was later identified as beriberi. *Kakke* was claiming twenty thousand Japanese lives a year in the wake of a widespread dietary change from unpolished to polished rice. No one knew at the time that the strange and dreaded disease was caused by a deficiency of vitamin B_1 (thiamine), for which many peoples of eastern and southern Asia were dependent on rice hulls. Its Asiatic importance is seen in its name: *beri* is a Sinhalese word for weakness.[41]

The Japanese who later proved the connection between *kakke* and a diet of unpolished rice was Takagi Kenkan, a physician trained in London. Takagi served on the government's Beriberi Investigation Committee after becoming medical inspector general of the navy in 1885. It is a noteworthy coincidence that he was also the chief founder of the Charity Medical University that stands on the site where Sam was treated for *kakke* before its cause was known.[42]

In Sam's time the disease was puzzling indeed. In 1873 the British physician William Willis reported that Japan had a kind of beriberi he did not recollect seeing in his home country. The same year American physician Duane B. Simmons performed an autopsy in Yokohama on a policeman who had succumbed to *kakke*. "Generally it is mistaken for heart trouble," Simmons reported. "The cause is restriction of the circulation of blood." His conclusion encouraged patients to drink sake.[43]

When William Griffis had his students write an essay in English on *kakke*, they pointed out that the malady affected city dwellers, particularly those in Tokyo, not those in rural parts, and that doctors often prescribed with success removal to another part of the country. Some noted that victims usually fell ill at the beginning of summer. Several emphasized the ideographic meaning of *kakke*, which is written with two Chinese characters, one meaning feet or legs, the other meaning temper or feeling. The patients usually suffered swelling in their legs and the inability to feel even mosquito bites. Harafuchi, a student who was recovering from the disease, reported that he could now walk but was still "devoid of sensation on my legs." Griffis himself defined *kakke* as "leg-humor."[44]

Clark's reference to Sam's disease as "a kind of dropsy" (now called hydrops) suggests the cardiac or wet type of beriberi, as opposed to the neuritic or dry type. The wet type is distinguished by the collection of fluids in the abdomen and other parts of the body and eventually by heart failure. Whatever the type, the cause was a deficiency of thiamine or an inability to assimilate it.

Why would Sam have this problem? He had long been nourished by the foods he prepared for his master's palate. His diet was chiefly Western as late as May 1873, when Clark referred to his "board of foreign food." But some time after that date, it is quite possible that Sam reverted to the native fare whose staple was white polished rice. As Clark revealed at the time of his death, Sam had a wife.[45] Her name, age, background, religion—all are veiled in obscurity. Probably she was regarded as the mistress of a foreigner—Sam was not considered a Japanese—and no record was made of the marriage. If a wedding was conducted, it would have been a Christian ceremony. Researchers have usually assumed that the couple were united in Shizuoka, possibly in the fall of 1873, and that they shared the servants' house at Clark's mansion. It is also conceivable that the relationship began after the move to Tokyo. If Sam switched from a Western diet to his wife's native cooking, he could have developed beriberi fairly soon, for the body excretes thiamine within days and does not store it well.

J. Hope Arthur and his wife Clara, of the American Baptist Missionary Union, found Sam in the hospital and began visiting him often. Perhaps they had first seen him at the Griffis house, having been there for tea on at least two occasions.[46] As shadows lengthened across the landscape of his life, Clara wrote, Sam "begged that we would take him to die in a Christian home." Perhaps he disliked the atmosphere in the hospital, whose patients included rough seamen. The Arthurs removed the furniture from one room of their two-story brick house and accommodated Sam and his wife in Japanese style.[47]

The house belonged to Mori Arinori, Japan's minister of education and a cherished friend of the Arthurs. Upon arriving in Japan the previous year, they had been appalled to find the missionaries in Yokohama living in the foreign community on the Bluff and isolated from the Japanese people they had come to serve. They were resolved to avoid this isolation when they moved to Tokyo in March 1874. Since foreigners were not allowed to live outside the Concession without special permission and a patron to assume responsibility for them, they turned to Mori, who made them nominal guests in a house he owned. They were a mile away from any English or American neighbor, and the same distance from the hospital where they found Sam.[48]

"It is in the very heart of the business portion of the city," Arthur said of his home, "convenient to the markets, and within three minutes' walk of the railroad station. We have a room on the first floor, capable of seating fifty persons, which opens on the Tōkaidō, the great highway through which flows the travel of the empire." It was the fulfillment of their dreams. As Clara Arthur reported, each morning about a dozen of their "back-door neighbors . . . men, women, and children of the lower classes"

J. Hope and Clara Arthur

came for prayers and Bible study.[49]

Yet this location had its negative side. All day long the Japanese who passed by in great numbers on that busy road would look in at the front windows. Nameless odors drifted in from the stagnant moat nearby. The well in their yard from which they drew their water was half-covered in grass and near open drainage ditches that carried waste from a dozen native houses. The environment was more conducive to chills and fever than to healthy living. It was especially hard on Arthur. Afflicted with tuberculosis, he would return to the United States within three years and die at the age of thirty-five.

The environment was of no concern to Sam. All that mattered now was being in a Christian home, and that the Arthurs could offer. So it was here, in Mori Arinori's Western-style house on the Tōkaidō, now Ginza, that Sam Patch died October 8, 1874. As was customary, his limp body was folded into a little box scarcely three feet square, "with head bowed and knees doubled up and crossed in front." Probably he was folded in before rigor mortis had set in, making it unnecessary to cut ligaments under the knees and big toes, as was often done. The surgical procedure was said to spoil the dream of the land of bliss. Cremation, preferred by Buddhists, was not an option at the time. The government had prohibited its practice in July 1873, thinking it incompatible with Westernization, but would rescind the prohibition in May 1875.[50]

When Clark called late that evening, he opened the lid of the box for a final look at his trustworthy servant by the light of a flickering candle. He raised Sam's face and saw that it was "calm and natural." The childlike Christian had died in peace. An English New Testament Clark had given him the year before lay in his hand. Sam's wife had placed it there to be buried with him, perhaps in keeping with his own request.[51]

Clark had telegraphed James Ballagh to come from Yokohama and conduct the funeral service. Although he had not returned to the United States with his family, Ballagh was out of town and missed the telegram. So Clark asked David Thompson to officiate. Thompson was pastor of the Shin Sakae Presbyterian Church in Tokyo and interpreter to the United States Legation under Minister John A. Bingham.[52] He conducted the service in Japanese at the Arthur home, in the downstairs room that could accommodate fifty people. Probably some of the local residents who had been attending Christian services in the home were present, along with the curious who might wander in from the busy street.

As reported in *Chōya shimbun*, Thompson traced the course of Sam's life, then closed his message with an admonition:

> It is not necessary for you to entreat God the Heavenly Father for Sammy to enter the next life. Neither is it necessary for you to worship his spirit. Sammy's spirit has already entered God's eternal rest. Nor is there any benefit in ceremonies to comfort the spirit of the dead. Today, for your own sake, you need to believe sincerely in the true God. If you pray to the true God, you will be richly blessed in accordance with his will.[53]

After the service the box containing the corpse was lifted into a hearse cart about five feet high and shaped like a temple. Its sides and roof were removed for the loading and then reassembled. An odd funeral procession then made its way up the Tōkaidō to its terminus at Nihonbashi and on through Ochanomizu and Suidōbashi to Hondenji, a temple in Ōtsuka Naka-machi. Leading the cortege was the hearse drawn by two old men. It was followed by three rickshas. The first carried Sam's wife and another woman; the second, the Arthurs; the third, Clark and Nakamura. En route they passed by Kirishitan-zaka, or Christian Slope, a reminder that Sam was fortunate indeed to have lived out his Christian life without persecution.

With two and a half miles to cover, the trip seemed interminably long, and Clark urged the two old men in the lead to speed up the procession. When they did, he wrote, the jolting pace "nearly shook the hearse and its contents to pieces." Despite the speed-up, the sun had gone down when the cortege arrived at Hondenji. Clark stumbled through the twilight to Nakamura's grave plot to make sure the hole had been dug as he had directed. It was in order. Returning to the temple proper, Clark was surprised to find that Buddhist funeral rites for Sam had begun. Rather than interrupt the solemnity of the occasion, he endured the pagan rites without complaint, thinking that the priests were trying to give a good return on the money he had given them in advance for the trouble of the burial there. Actually the priests had a more compelling incentive, for until 1874 Japanese law required that all burials be conducted with Shinto or Buddhist rites. As was customary, they honored Sam with a *kaimyō* or posthumous Buddhist name—Shinjuin Ichijō Shinshi—and duly entered it in the temple register.[54]

Clark watched the square box lowered into the grave, which was lit up by the glare of torches and lanterns. Then he saw a man strike the top of the box with a shovel. He was trying to break it in and fill it with earth. Clark told him to disregard this custom and simply fill up the grave, which he did.

Clark had planned to bury Sam beside his interpreter Shimojō, who probably rested in the city cemetery at Zōshigaya. But this cemetery, opened in 1869, was restricted to registered Japanese citizens, and Sam had not registered as required by the Meiji government. Probably he knew about the law but disregarded it, having lived the greater half of his life as more an American than a Japanese.[55] Nakamura, true to his nature, graciously offered to share his ancestral grave with the stateless servant.

Conspicuously absent from the funeral and burial rites was the man who had taken Sam under his wing in America and brought him back to Japan: Jonathan Goble. Alienated from the other missionaries, probably he was late in learning of Sam's terminal illness and death. Clark naturally tried to contact Ballagh, whom he admired, and not Goble whom Ballagh detested. A Madison University professor, John James Lewis, who was visiting in Japan at the time and learned of the funeral from the Arthurs, probably shared the information with the Gobles while in their home. It was too late then for Jonathan to pay due respects to his former protégé.[56]

Sam may be compared to Francis Xavier's first convert Yajirō, whose baptismal name was Paul. As Christian firstfruits and potential evangelists to their own people, both Paul and Sam proved to be broken reeds, arousing hopes that were never realized. Both came to a sad end in very different ways. Paul's death is shrouded in obscurity. He is said to have died as a pirate or at the hands of pirates, and it can only be conjectured that he died a Christian. There is no doubt that Sam's simplistic faith endured to the end.[57]

But even Sam never became an evangelist to his own people as Goble had hoped. His shipmate Heco, who not only converted to Catholicism but took American citizenship, wrote in his 1863 autobiography, "Japan being the land of my parents, it is not to my liking to end my days as a foreigner. It is my hope to learn to read and write in Japanese, to become a Japanese as time goes by."[58] To a considerable extent Heco fulfilled this ambition, even though the removal of the anti-Christian signboards in 1873 did not change the prevailing opinion that Japanese nationality and Christian faith were incompatible or, at best, strange bedfellows. Sam never even made the effort to regain his Japanese heritage. He secluded himself from his people, living as a foreigner in the service of foreigners.

It was and is a Japanese custom to place in the casket something that was important to the deceased. By placing a New Testament in his lifeless hand, Sam's widow acknowledged that he treasured its message and found in it a source of comfort and strength. Probably she was not a Christian herself. Clark later reported that she had requested money from him to buy incense to burn before her husband's tomb.

Epilogue

HONDENJI stands on a busy thoroughfare in Bunkyō Ward within a five-minute walk of Ochanomizu Women's University. The seven-hundred-year-old Buddhist temple is affiliated with the Nichiren sect, having switched from Zen in the early seventeenth century. Its three main buildings survived the great earthquake of September 1923 and the incendiary bombings of March 1945, both of which left vast stretches of Tokyo in ruins. Passing through the temple's roofed portal from the traffic-clogged street is like stepping into the remote past.

The burial ground stretches across the rear half of the temple precincts. Against the backdrop of a concrete-slab fence stands a cluster of old stones inscribed with weather-worn Chinese characters. Here, in the family plot of Nakamura Masanao, is the grave of Sam Patch.

"Over Sam's remains," wrote Warren Clark, "I caused a stone cross to be raised, upon which were inscribed the simple words, SAM PATCH."[1] If his instructions were carried out, the stone cross was tolerated only for a time. The surviving stone marker is a squarish slab five inches thick and about eighteen inches high and wide. It bears the name Sam Patch, but in a form that must have puzzled many a reader of graveyard inscriptions. There are four Chinese characters in a vertical line: *san* (three), *hachi* (eight), *kun* (mister), and *haka* (grave). The first two, when read together, are pronounced *sam-pachi*, the Japanese rendering of the Western name Sam Patch. So the inscription can be translated "The Grave of Mr. Sam Patch." Smaller characters give the date of death: October 8, 1874.

In 1982, when the Nakamura plot was renovated, Sam's marker was moved a little forward and to the left. A stone tablet, taller but narrower than the old marker, was set next to it. The inscription translates as follows:

Mr. Sam Patch / Born in Aki/ Real name: Sentarō / American name: Sam Patch.

In the closing period of the shogunate *[bakumatsu]* he was ship-wrecked with Joseph Heco and others and rescued by an American vessel. Later he visited Japan with Commodore Perry as interpreter and sailor.

After returning to America he became the first Japanese to receive Baptist immersion. He again came to Japan with Pastor Goble and cooperated with him in translating the Gospel of Matthew (entirely in hiragana) devoting himself fully to its completion. Later he served Teacher Clark [*Kuraaku kyōshi*], and at the end of his life was a coach-man for Professor Keiu [*Keiu sensei*].[2]

Died October 8, 1874, at age 41. The gravestone inscription is brush writing by Professor Keiu. This inscription by Nakamura Katsuhiko, March 1982.

This inscription, in contrast to the shorter one on the plaque at the American Sam Patch's grave in Rochester, New York, focuses on the subject's life rather than his death. But like the chiseled inscription on the Rochester stone that gives a wrong year of birth, this inscription is flawed. Even though it was provided by Nakamura Katsuhiko, a grandson of Masanao, this summary of Sam's life requires a few clarifications and corrections.

Aki, Sam's birthplace, was an ancient province—also called Geishū—that is now a part of Hiroshima Prefecture. His shipwreck and rescue with Heco and others in 1850–51 occurred shortly before, not during, the historical period known as *bakumatsu*, or end of the shogunate. This period is usually dated 1853–68. We should note further that Sam came to Japan with the Perry expedition as a sailor—a landsman—but not as an interpreter. His intellect was too meager for the latter role, although his ability to speak Japanese did prove useful to the Americans on at least one occasion.

A more serious error in the inscription perpetuates the old but groundless notion, widespread in Japan, that Sam had a part in Jonathan Goble's translation of the Gospel of Matthew ("devoting himself fully to its completion"). Goble learned some spoken Japanese from Sam when the castaway was under his wing, as Samuel Damon noted, but he employed better qualified teachers after arriving in Japan. Moreover, Goble and Sam Patch were permanently separated long before the missionary began work on the translation. Kawashima Daijirō, Japan's leading authority on Goble's version of Matthew, has demonstrated that Sam Patch's contribution was nil.[3]

It is also incorrect to say that Goble's Matthew was entirely in the hiragana syllabary. The translation contains no less than fifty-six different Chinese characters. Goble kept them at a minimum for the sake of the common reader, but where clarity or accuracy required kanji, he used them in his text.

The inscription concludes with references to E. Warren Clark and Nakamura Masanao, whose pen name was Nakamura Keiu. That Sam was Nakamura's coachman (*gyosha*) has not been documented, but Nakamura Katsuhiko explained that he was told this by his mother. The work as coachman was probably part-time and temporary, for Sam was in Clark's employ at the time. Probably the grandson included this intelligence on the tablet because he wanted to show a connection between the lowly Sam Patch and the great Professor Keiu and thus justify Sam's intrusion into the Nakamura family plot. The inscription will instruct his descendants for generations to come.

Despite the good intentions, the inscription fails to note the decisive

Sam Patch's grave, Hondenji, Tokyo

reason for Sam's presence. As stated before, Nakamura Masanao offered to share his plot out of compassion for Sam, who was disqualified for burial in the city cemetery, and as a personal favor to Warren Clark, who assumed major responsibility for his servant's burial. Also involved was Nakamura's growing commitment to Sam's and Clark's Christian faith. As noted before, Nakamura was baptized on Christmas Day following Sam's death, becoming the first prominent Meiji figure to profess the Christian faith openly.

Nakamura's actual grave is not in this family plot at Hondenji. It is in Yanaka Cemetery, where he is interred with his Christian wife and their Christian descendants. Only his umbilical cord rests in the company of his non-Christian ancestors and descendants at Hondenji.[4] That makes Sam Patch all the more conspicuous as a desecrater of that Buddhist soil. Perhaps there is irony in the plaque's reference to him as a Baptist and not as a Christian. Unlike the term "Christian," which would be conspicuous and glaring, "Baptist" is little known in Japan.

Appendix

Crew of the *Eiriki-maru*

The crew members are listed from the oldest to the youngest, with their approximate ages when rescued at sea in 1850. Their multiple names make an alphabetical arrangement rather awkward. This material is adapted from Murakami, "Kurobune no Nihonjin suifu," 14; and Inoue, *Dotō o koeta otokotachi*, 221–23.

Manzō, Sauemon. 60. Captain. Died aboard *St. Mary's* near Hawaii.
Chōsuke, Chōnosuke. 50. First mate, navigator, helmsman.
Jimpachi. 38. Second mate (?).
Ikumatsu. 38.
Kiyozō, Sukebee. 32.
Kyōsuke. 32. Died at Nagasaki during confinement.
Tokubee. 29.
Jisaku, Tora. 27.
Seitarō, Seibee, Honjō Zenjirō. 27. Elevated to samurai rank.
Bunta, Rishichi, Yotarō. 26.
Yasutarō. 25. Died at sea when approaching Nagasaki.
Tamizō, Ōkichi. 24.
Asagorō, Asauemon, Genjirō, Yamaguchi Asagorō. 23. Mate responsible for supplies. Elevated to samurai rank.
Kamezō, Kame, Kamegorō. 22. Returned to Japan on *Niagara*.
Iwakichi, Gankichi, Denkichi, Dankichi, Dan Ketch, Dan. 21. Murdered in Edo.
Sentarō, Santarō, Kurajirō, Kurazō, Kurasuke, Unosuke, Matō (?), Sam Patch, Samuel Sentharo, Sammy. 19. Cook. Became a Baptist.
Hikotarō, Hikozō, Joseph Heco, Hamada Hikozō. 14. Cook. Became a U.S. citizen and a Roman Catholic.

Following are the crewmen as named and identified in *Illustrated News,* January 22, 1853. Each name is followed by the current spelling and by the person's name listed above if different and identifiable.

1. Tametho. Tamizō
2. Hecotho (Cabin Boy). Hikozō. Hikotarō

3. Montho (The Captain). Manzō
4. Geesahkoo. Jisaku
5. Simpay. Sempei. Unidentified
6. Ewatho. Iwazō. Iwakichi (?)
7. Simpatch (Cook). Sempachi. Sentarō
8. Drehecho (?). Unidentified
9. Keotho. Kiyozō
10. Commetho. Kamezō
11. Kechetho. Kichizō. Unidentified
12. Ahsahgodro. Asagorō
13. Same as 10
14. Saypatch. Seipachi. Seitarō (?)
15. Ekotho. Ikuzō. Ikumatsu (?)
16. Jimpatch (2d Mate). Jimpachi
17. Yasatahro. Yasutarō
18. Chonowski (Mate). Chōnosuke. Chōsuke

Chronology

1831?

SP born on Ikuchijima and named Sentarō.

1842

His mother dies.

1843

His father Kumazō dies.

1850

Oct. 20   Leaves Ōsaka for Edo as cook on cargo junk *Eiriki-maru*.

Oct. 27   Junk puts in at Kumano, where Hikozō joins the crew.

Nov. 10   Junk leaves Kumano with 17 men aboard.

Nov. 18   Stops at Uraga for inspection of crew and cargo.

Nov. 19   Sails up Edo Bay.

Nov. 21   Arrives at Edo, begins discharging cargo.

Nov. 25   Leaves Edo with small cargo.

Nov. 26   Stops at Uraga for additional cargo.

Nov. 30   Sets out for Ōsaka.

Dec. 2   Blown off course by storm in Enshū-nada.

1851

Jan. 22   SP and 16 crewmates rescued by American bark *Auckland*.

Mar. 4   *Auckland* arrives at San Francisco.

Mar. 9   SP and crewmates pitch in to help discharge cargo.

Mar. 16   They go sightseeing; *Alta California* editor visits Japanese aboard ship.

Mar. 19   SP and crewmates taken to masquerade ball at San Francisco Exchange.

Mar. 21   Go shopping on Long Wharf.

Mar. 22   Transferred to USR *Polk,* looked after by Thomas Troy.

Apr. 6   Visit Plaza.

May 4   Witness Fifth Great Fire of San Francisco.

June 22   Witness Sixth Great Fire.

Oct. 25   Attend agricultural exhibition.

1852

Feb. 27   SP and crewmates transfer to USS *St. Mary's.*

Mar. 1   Leave San Francisco, accompanied by Thomas Troy.

Mar. 21   Sight island of Hawaii; Captain Manzō dies.

Mar. 22   Ship anchors at Hilo, where Manzō is buried.

May 1   *St. Mary's* arrives at Hong Kong.

May 3   Sails to Macao.

May 8   Troy and 16 Japanese transferred to USS *Susquehanna.*

May 22   *Susquehanna* moves to Hong Kong.

May 25   Troy and 12 Japanese granted shore leave.

May 29   Ship sails for Amoy.
June 4   Returns to Hong Kong.
June 21   Leaves Hong Kong for Whampoa.
June 26   Returns to Hong Kong.
?   Japanese visit Rikimatsu; 9 make thwarted attempt to go to Chapu.
July 14   *Susquehanna* leaves Hong Kong for Whampoa.
Aug. 11   Moves to Cum Sing Moon.
Aug. 20   Troy, Hikozō, Kamezō, and Jisaku leave ship to return to San Francisco. 13 Japanese remain aboard.
Oct. 20   *Susquehanna* steams to Macao.
Nov. 6   Returns to Hong Kong.
Nov. 30   Moves to Macao.
Dec. 7   Returns to Hong Kong.
Dec. 19   Leaves Hong Kong for Manila.
Dec. 27   Arrives at Manila.

1853
Jan. 10   Two Japanese are allowed ashore at Manila.
Jan. 14   Spanish officers and ladies spend day on ship.
Jan. 20   *Susquehanna* leaves Manila.
Jan. 31   Arrives Hong Kong.
Feb. 5   Shore leave granted to 5 Japanese.
Feb. 24   Ship leaves for Whampoa.
Mar. 6   Returns to Hong Kong.
Mar. 20   Moves to Macao.
Mar. 21   Takes on board Commissioner Humphries, leaves for Shanghai.
Mar. 22   13 Japanese presented to Commissioner Humphries.
Mar. 26   Request second interview with Humphries, ask to leave ship at Shanghai.
Mar. 27   *Susquehanna* arrives at Shanghai.
Apr. 1   Captain Buchanan permits 4 Japanese to leave ship, as requested by Otokichi.
Apr. 7   Buchanan permits 8 Japanese to leave ship, keeping only SP aboard. Commodore Perry arrives at Macao and Hong Kong on USS *Mississippi.*
Apr. 9   SP shipped as landsman on *Susquehanna,* first called Sam Patch in ship's log.
May 4   Perry arrives at Shanghai.
May 9   *Susquehanna* becomes flagship.
May 17   Leaves Shanghai with SP aboard.
May 26   Arrives Naha, Okinawa.
July 2   Leaves Naha.
July 8   *Susquehanna* and 3 other warships anchor off Uraga.
July 10   First worship service in Japanese waters conducted on *Susquehanna.*
July 13   Perry delivers President Fillmore's letter to Japanese officials.
July 14   Perry and SP transfer to *Mississippi,* steam up to Shinagawa, return to *Susquehanna.*
July 17   *Susquehanna* leaves Edo Bay with SP aboard.
July 25   Arrives at Naha.
Aug. 2   Leaves Naha.
Aug. 7   Arrives at Hong Kong.

1854

Jan. 14   *Susquehanna* leaves Hong Kong.
Jan. 24   Arrives Naha
Feb. 1   Kamata Nōju (Jack Canoe) becomes SP's shipmate.
Feb. 4   *Susquehanna* leaves Naha.
Feb. 13   Enters Edo Bay.
Feb. 18   *Powhatan* becomes flagship.
Feb. 24   SP transferred to *Powhatan,* which moves up to Kanagawa.
Mar. 6   Interviewed by Kayama Eizaemon on *Powhatan* deck, declines repatriation.
Mar. 31   Treaty of Kanagawa signed.
Apr. 10   *Powhatan* approaches Edo.
Apr. 18   Arrives at Shimoda.
May 13   Leaves for Hakodate.
May 17   Arrives at Hakodate.
June 7   Returns to Shimoda.
June 18   SP transfers to *Mississippi* with Perry.
June 22   Has final encounter with Japanese officials, declines repatriation.
June 25   *Mississippi* leaves Shimoda.
June 29   SP interprets for inspection of Amami Ōshima.
July 1   *Mississippi* arrives at Naha.
July 17   Leaves Naha for Hong Kong.
July 21   Iwakichi (Dankichi) enlists as landsman on *Susquehanna* at Shanghai.
July 22   *Mississippi* arrives at Hong Kong with SP.
July 24   Steams up river from Hong Kong to Whampoa.
Aug. 5   11 *Eiriki-maru* crewmen leave Chapu on Chinese junk.
Aug. 15   *Mississippi* returns to Hong Kong.
Aug. 19   Yasutarō dies at sea on Chinese junk.
Aug. 20   10 *Eiriki-maru* crewmen arrive safely at Nagasaki.
Sept 12   *Mississippi* leaves Hong Kong.
Sept 21   Arrives at Shimoda; *Susquehanna* is in port.
Oct. 1   Leaves Shimoda.
Oct. 23   Arrives at Honolulu; *Susquehanna* and *St. Mary's* are in port.
Oct. 26   Kyōsuke dies of illness in Nagasaki.
Oct. 30   Hikozō is baptized a Catholic in Baltimore, becomes Joseph Heco.
Nov. 9   *Mississippi* leaves Honolulu with SP aboard.
Nov. 21   Arrives San Francisco.
Dec. 16   Departs San Francisco for New York via Valparaiso and Rio de Janeiro.

1855

Apr. 22   *Mississippi* arrives at New York.
Apr. 23   Commodore Perry visits *Mississippi.*
May 8   Jonathan Goble leaves Marine Corps and takes charge of SP.
May 17   Goble and SP enroll in academy of Madison University in Hamilton, N.Y., but soon withdraw.
June 4   Registered in Wayne census as boarders in home of Gilbert Ganong.
Oct. 11   Enter Madison Academy again and room together, but SP soon transfers to public grammar school.

1856

Apr. 14   Goble marries Eliza Weeks. Afterwards, SP lives with them in Hamilton.

1858

Mar. 6   SP confesses his Christian faith at Hamilton Baptist Church.

Mar. 7   Baptized by Hezekiah Harvey in Chenango Creek.

1859

Nov. 3   SP gives testimony and sings Japanese song at Goble's ordination service in New York City.

Nov. 5   Leaves New York on *Baltic* with Gobles.

Nov. 13   Crosses Panama Isthmus by train.

Nov. 27   Arrives at San Francisco.

1860

Jan. 29   Iwakichi murdered in Edo outside English legation.

Feb. 2   SP sails for Honolulu on bark *Frances Palmer* with Gobles and Thomas Troy.

Feb. 17   Arrives at Honolulu, stays in Sailor's Home courtesy of Samuel Damon.

Feb. 19   Attends Kaumakapili Church with Gobles.

Feb. 25   Presented to Queen Emma by U.S. Commissioner.

Feb. 27   Testifies at missionary gathering in Fort Street Church.

Feb. 29   Sails for Japan in bark *Zoe* with Gobles and Troy.

Apr. 1   Arrives at Kanagawa, remains aboard vessel for security.

Apr. 15?   Goes ashore under protection of American flag, joins Gobles and S. R. Browns at Jōbutsuji.

Apr. 24   Writes thank-you note in English to Samuel Damon.

May   Gobles move into their own house in Kanagawa.

Nov. 23   S. R. Brown claims SP as family cook.

1861

Nov. 11   James and Margaret Ballagh arrive in Kanagawa, live with J. C. Hepburn.

1862

Spring   Gobles move to Yokohama.

Dec. 29   Dr. Hepburn moves to Yokohama; Ballaghs perhaps employ SP at this time.

1863

Feb. 18   Yokohama Union Church is organized with SP as a member.

Mar. 2   Brown reports that SP is working in Ballagh's home.

June 1   SP moves to Yokohama with Ballaghs.

Dec. 7   Dismissed by Hamilton Baptist Church.

1866

Mar. 23   Leaves Yokohama with Ballaghs on bark *Ida D. Rogers*.

Apr. 26   Arrives at San Francisco.

May 19   Maggie Ballagh and children leave San Francisco for New York on SS *Golden City*.

June 1   Ballagh leaves San Francisco on bark *Ida D. Rogers*. Maggie and children leave Aspinwall on SS *New York*.

June 9   Maggie and children arrive at New York.

June 17   Ballagh arrives at Koloa in Sandwich Islands.

July 30   Ballagh arrives at Yokohama.

Nov. 26   Ballagh loses possessions in Yokohama fire.

1868

June 19 *Scioto* brings 148 Japanese laborers to Hawaii. Sentarō (SP?) assists them as interpreter and guide.

1869

Feb. 13 Ballagh arrives at New York for furlough and reunion with his family.

1870

Nov. 25 Ballaghs arrive at Yokohama on SS *America.*

1871

Oct. 25 E. W. Clark arrives at Yokohama on SS *Great Republic.*

Nov. 27 Clark leaves for Shizuoka with SP as his cook.

Dec. 2 Clark and SP arrive at Shizuoka, take up residence in Ren'eiji.

1872

Jan. 30–31 W. E. Griffis visits Clark en route from Fukui to Tōkyō.

Dec. Clark moves into new Western-style house with servants' quarters for SP.

1873

Jan. 3–5 Griffis and Marion Scott visit Clark.

May Mary Pruyn visits Clark. Servant Ginzō and wife depart, leaving SP as only person living with Clark.

July 20–22 Griffis and sister Margaret visit Clark.

Aug. Ballagh visits Clark.

Oct. George Cochran and Henry Loomis visit Clark.

Dec. 21 Clark leaves for new position in Tōkyō, traveling overland. SP travels by junk with freight.

Dec. 24 Clark arrives in Tōkyō, shares house with Griffis and his sister Margaret.

1874

Jan. 17 SP arrives at Tōkyō aboard cargo junk.

Feb. 14 S. R. Brown spends night at Griffis-Clark home.

Mar. 7 J. H. and Clara Arthur move to Tōkyō from Yokohama.

Mar. 21 Ballagh visits Griffis-Clark home.

Apr. 1 Mrs. Pruyn spends night.

Apr. 11 Tokugawa Iesato comes for dinner with Clark.

May 21 Brown visits Griffis-Clark home.

June 24 Arthurs visit home.

July 9 Ballagh visits again.

July 18 W. E. and Margaret Griffis leave for America.

July 23 Clark sails for Kyōto after putting SP in hospital ill.

Aug. 9–10 Clark stops in Shizuoka.

Aug. Clark returns home after monthlong absence, puts SP in hospital again.

Oct. 8 SP dies of beriberi in home of Hope and Clara Arthur.

Oct. 9 After funeral service in Arthur home, SP is buried in Nakamura family grave at Hondenji.

Notes

Introduction

1. The author visited Sam Patch's grave and copied the inscription in May 1999.

2. Log Book, USS *Susquehanna*, 9 April 1853, National Archives.

3. Matthew C. Perry, *Narrative of the Expedition of an American Squadron to the China Seas and Japan, Performed in the Years 1852, 1853, and 1854, under the Command of Commodore M. C. Perry, United States Navy, by Order of the Government of the United States*, comp. Francis L. Hawks (Washington: Beverley Tucker, Senate Printer, 1856), 1:485–86.

4. Commoners often used family names privately, and some wealthy farmers and favored merchants were permitted to use them publicly. Others were awarded a family name in recognition of their outstanding achievements. Mukōyama Hiro, "Names and Lineages in Japan," part 1, *East* 13 (November 1977): 12; Kobayashi Motoki, "Diversity from 'Double Desire': Why are there so many Japanese family names?" *East* 35, no. 6 (March/April 2000): 50.

5. Donald L. Canney, *U.S. Coast Guard and Revenue Cutters, 1790–1935* (Annapolis: Naval Institute Press, 1995), 17.

6. Clara Arthur Mason, *Etchings from Two Lands* (Boston, 1886), 132–33. See also John Jas. Lewis, "Sundown to Palestine," *Democratic Republican* (Hamilton, N.Y.), 7 January 1875.

7. E. Warren Clark, letter, 26 May 1873, *New York Evangelist*, 14 August 1873.

8. Margaret Tate Kinnear Ballagh, *Glimpses of Old Japan* (Tokyo: Methodist Publishing House, 1908), 123.

9. E. Warren Clark, *Life and Adventure in Japan* (New York: American Tract Society, 1878), 232; *Encyclopedia Britannica* (1968 ed.), s.v. "Japan, the People" (12:882); William Elliot Griffis, *The Mikado's Empire*, 9th ed. (New York: Harper & Brothers, 1900), 570.

10. F. C. Pollay, "Japan in 1852," transcribed by Herbert A. Wisbey Jr., *Crooked Lake Review*, no. 27 (June 1990): 5; anonymous writer in *American Baptist*, 17 April 1860.

11. Mason, *Etchings from Two Lands*, 133; Clark, *Life and Adventure*, 232; Griffis, *Mikado's Empire*, 548.

12. Inazo Nitobe, *The Intercourse between the United States and Japan: An Historical Sketch* (1891; reprint, Wilmington, Del.: Scholarly Resources, 1973), 158.

13. Frederick Wells Williams, *The Life and Letters of Samuel Wells Williams, LLD.: Missionary, Diplomatist, Sinologue* (New York, 1889), 226; S. Wells Williams, "A Journal of the Perry Expedition to Japan (1853–1854)," ed. F. W. Williams, in *Transactions of the Asiatic Society of Japan*, vol. 37, part 2 (1910), 122n; Harry Emerson Wildes, "The Kuroshiwo's Toll," in *Transactions of the Asiatic Society of Japan*, 2d ser., vol. 17 (1938), 218, 228. On Sam as a hostage, see chapter 4.

14. On Sam's grave inscription, see Epilogue. His biography is Miyachi Yasunobu, *Sentarō* (Tokyo: Kyōkai Shimpōsha, 1982). It was refuted as highly imaginative by

Kawashima Daijirō in "Sentarō no hyōka ni tsuite" (Concerning an appraisal of Sentarō), *Tō no hikari*, no. 285 (February 1983): 1–2.

15. Internet, www.virtualjapan.org/BSS; Tony Bennett and Sebastian Dobson, "The Sentaro Daguerreotype: A New Episode in Japanese Photo-History Discovered," Internet, www.old-japan.co.uk/Sentarō.article.html, based on article in *PhotoHistorian: Quarterly of the Historical Group of the Royal Photographic Society* 116 (summer 1997).

16. Clark, *Life and Adventure*, 40.

Chapter 1. Gods and Demons at Sea

1. George Elison, *Deus Destroyed: The Image of Christianity in Early Modern Japan* (Cambridge, Mass.: Harvard University Press, 1973), 321. The work includes Elison's complete translation of *Kirishitan Monogatari* (Tales of Christians), an anonymous chapbook dated 1639. This chapbook and others like it were widely read and highly influential throughout the Edo period (1603–1868).

2. The exact date of Sam's birth is unknown. On 6 March 1854, Sentarō told a Japanese official he was twenty-three years old. On 4 June 1855, he told a New York census taker he was twenty-four. Assuming that he reckoned his age by the Western method and answered correctly on both occasions, Sentarō was born between 5 June 1830, and 6 March 1831. But it is possible that he used the Japanese method of reckoning one's age, by which a child was one year old at birth and two years old on the first New Year's following birth. If so, Sentarō was born in 1832 or, allowing for the later Japanese New Year's, early 1833. It is possible that Unosuke, the name he used upon returning to Japan in 1860, is based on his birth year. If so, he was born in 1831, the year of the Hare (U). The association is possible even though a different kanji is used.

3. Murakami Mitsugi, "Kurobune no Nihonjin suifu" (Japanese sailor on a black ship), *Kaiji shi kenkyū* (Studies in maritime history), no. 7 (1 March 1982), 14.

4. *Chūgoku shimbun*, 27 June 1982, article reproduced in *Shu no ashiato* (Footprints of the Master), no. 20 (29 October 1982). Miyachi Yasunobu kindly sent me copies of the Kōfukuji records. On Manjirō, see Emily V. Warriner, *Voyager to Destiny* (New York: Bobbs-Merrill Co., 1956), 251; and Peter Duus, *The Japanese Discovery of America: A Brief History with Documents* (Boston: Bedford Books, 1997), 82.

5. Edwin O. Reischauer and Albert M. Craig, *Japan: Tradition and Transformation* (Tokyo: Charles E. Tuttle Co., 1978), 104.

6. *Kodansha Encyclopedia of Japan,* s.v. "kaisen"; Charles J. Dunn, *Everyday Life in Traditional Japan* (Tokyo: Charles E. Tuttle Co., 1972), 111–12; Haruna Akira, *Hyōryū: Josefu Hiko to nakamatachi* (Drifting: Joseph Heco and his companions) (Tokyo: Kadokawa Shoten, 1982), 9–11. *Higaki* literally means diamond-shaped fence or railing.

7. Haruna, *Hyōryū*, 19.

8. Inoue Tomoyoshi, Higashine Buichi, and Nakajima Yoshine, *Dotō o koeta otokotachi: Hyōryū shiryō kenkyū* (Men who overcame the raging sea: Studies of historical materials on sea drifting) (Harima, Hyōgo Prefecture: Harima Education Committee, Town of Harima, 1997), 224–26.

9. Matthew C. Perry, *The Japan Expedition, 1852–54: The Personal Journal of Commodore Matthew C. Perry* (Washington: Smithsonian Institution, 1968), 155.

10. Masayoshi Sugimoto and David L. Swain, *Science and Culture in Traditional Japan, A.D. 600–1854* (Cambridge, Mass.: MIT Press, 1978), 176–78, 232–23; Katherine

Plummer, *The Shogun's Reluctant Ambassadors: Sea Drifters* (Tokyo: Lotus Press, 1984), 33; *Kodansha Encyclopedia of Japan,* s.v. "Kaigai Tokō Kinshi Rei," "National Seclusion," "Ships."

11. Sir Rutherford Alcock, *The Capital of the Tycoon: A Narrative of a Three Years' Residence in Japan,* 2 vols. (1863; reprint, New York: Greenwood Press, 1969), 2:99. See also Perry, *Narrative of the Expedition,* 1: 448–49.

12. Plummer, *Shogun's Reluctant Ambassadors,* 36.

13. H. S. K. Yamaguchi et al, *We Japanese,* combined edition of 3 books (Miyanoshita: Fujiya Hotel, ca. 1951), 475; *Kodansha Encyclopedia of Japan,* s.v. "Kotohira Shrine." See also Joseph Heco, *The Narrative of a Japanese,* ed. James Murdoch, 2 vols. in 1 (Yokohama, n.d.), 1:6–11, in which Heco describes his visit to the Kotohira Shrine.

14. Murakami, "Kurobune no Nihonjin suifu," 14; Inoue, *Dotō o koeta otokotachi,* 221–23. See also Appendix: Crew of the *Eiriki-maru.*

15. *American Baptist,* 17 April 1860; *Kodansha Encyclopedia of Japan,* s.v. "Japanese people, physical characteristics of" (4:35).

16. Heco, *Narrative of a Japanese,* 1:26–27; Hikozo (Joseph Heco), *Floating on the Pacific Ocean,* trans. Tosh Motofuji (Los Angeles: Glen Dawson, 1955), 1. The remainder of this chapter makes extensive use of these two works.

17. Yazaki Takeo, *Social Change and the City in Japan: From earliest times through the Industrial Revolution,* trans. David L. Swain (Tokyo: Japan Publications, 1968), 134.

18. Inoue, *Dotō o koeta otokotachi,* 226–27.

19. Hikozo, *Floating on the Pacific Ocean,* 7.

20. For their temple affiliations, see Inoue, *Dotō o koeta otokotachi,* 221–22.

21. Inoue, *Dotō o koeta otokotachi,* 173–76, 290.

22. E. W. Clark, letter, 26 May 1873, *New York Evangelist,* 14 August 1873; Haruna, *Hyōryū,* 37.

23. Ogasa Yoshinori, "Kurobune ni notta Hiroshimajin" (Hiroshiman on a black ship), part 1, no. 4, *Chūgoku shimbun* (3 February 1994), quoting from "Nagase murabito hyōryū dan," 1855.

24. Haruna, *Hyōryū,* 44.

25. Heco, *Narrative of a Japanese,* 1:56; Duus, *Japanese Discovery of America,* 14–15, 25; William Elliot Griffis, Fukui Journal 1871–1877, 111, W. E. Griffis Collection, Rutgers University.

26. *Alta California,* 22 March 1851. The newspaper gave the exact location as 31°54" N, 105°14" E. The latitude runs through Kagoshima Prefecture and indicates that the *Eiriki-maru* had drifted in a southerly as well as easterly direction. The reported longitude runs through interior China! Obviously the figure 105 is a typographical error. If corrected to 150, the position is in general agreement with Jennings' estimate of five hundred miles from Japan and a later report that the rescue took place six hundred miles from Japan. But in light of the fifty-two days of drifting and the known course of other wrecked junks, Chikamori Haruyoshi has suggested that the 105 might be corrected to 165, giving credence to a very different estimate—given in Bunta's deposition—of 650 *ri* (1,586 miles) southeast of the mainland. This is unlikely, as Jennings' chronometer gives him the edge over Bunta's estimate recorded nearly four years later. Chikamori Haruyoshi in *Josefu Hiko kinenkaishi,* no. 27 (28 June 1990): 1–7; Haruna, *Hyōryū,* 51–52; *Hutchings' California Magazine* 3, no. 8 (February 1859), as reproduced in *Josefu Hiko kinenkaishi,* no. 28 (12 December 1990): 17.

27. *American Baptist,* 16 March 1858; Heco, *Narrative of a Japanese,* 1:67–69.

28. Heco, *Narrative of a Japanese*, 1:68.

29. Masao Miyoshi, *As We Saw Them: The First Japanese Embassy to the United States (1860)* (Berkeley: University of California Press, 1979), 111.

30. Alcock, *Capital of the Tycoon*, 2:478.

31. Miyoshi, *As We Saw Them*, 32–33; Donald R. Bernard, *The Life and Times of John Manjiro* (New York: McGraw-Hill, 1992), 193, 196.

Chapter 2. Pampered Ward of Uncle Sam

1. Heco, *Narrative of a Japanese,* 103.

2. *Alta California*, 5 March 1851.

3. Heco, *Narrative of a Japanese*, 1:83–85.

4. Heco, *Narrative of a Japanese*, 1:85–87.

5. *Alta California*, 5 March 1851; Heco, *Narrative of a Japanese*, 1:91–92. The storeship was probably the *Apollo* or *General Harrison*.

6. *Alta California*, 17 March 1851.

7. Heco, *Narrative of a Japanese*, 1:90.

8. *Alta California*, 13 March 1851; Lewis Francis Byington, ed. *The History of San Francisco*, vol. 1 (Chicago: S. J. Clarke Publishing Co., 1931), 163.

9. *Alta California*, 19 August 1851, 17 February 1852.

10. One indication is that alien pupils greatly outnumbered Americans in the public school conducted at the First Baptist Church on Washington Street as well as the free school in Happy Valley, an area just below Market Street into which the fast-growing city had spilled. The ratios were 102 foreigners to 72 Americans at the school in the Baptist church and 75 to 38 in Happy Valley. *Alta California*, 1, 4 March 1851.

11. *Alta California*, 17 March 1851.

12. *Alta California*, 5, 17, 23 March, 5 April 1851; *Scientific American* 7 (20 December 1851): 106.

13. *Sailor's Magazine*, December 1859, as copied in *Friend* 9 (1 March 1860): 22. Macy's full name is given in *Alta California*, 18 September 1850.

14. *Alta California*, 18, 19 March 1851. For Japanese accounts of the ball, see Hikozo, *Floating on the Pacific Ocean*, 27–29; Heco, *Narrative of a Japanese*, 1:92–97; and Haruna, *Hyōryū*, 82–86.

15. Etsu Inagaki Sugimoto, *A Daughter of the Samurai* (1926; Tokyo: Charles E. Tuttle Co., 1966), 154.

16. Nitobe, *United States and Japan,* 155; Henry F. Graff, ed., *Bluejackets with Perry in Japan* (New York: New York Public Library, 1952), 26.

17. Miyoshi, *As We Saw Them*, 76.

18. *Alta California*, 20 March 1851.

19. Chikamori Haruyoshi, *Kurisuchan Josefu Hiko* (Tokyo: Amurita Shobō, 1985), 53, 63. In two of the three instances Chikamori, probably unintentionally, uses the singular form "barbarian."

20. *Alta California*, 26 March 1851.

21. *Alta California*, 22 March 1851.

22. Katherine H. Chandler, "San Francisco at Statehood," Internet, www.sfmuseum.org/hist5/oldsf.html, p. 6 of 10; William Martin Camp, *San Francisco: Port of Gold* (Garden City, N.Y.: Doubleday & Co., 1947), 87.

23. *Illustrated News*, 22 January 1853, reproduced in *Josefu Hiko kinenkaishi*, no. 39 (28 June 1996), 3; Bennett and Dobson, "Sentaro Daguerreotype." Surprisingly, there are eighteen numbered sketches for a crew of seventeen. Figures 10 and 13 are both captioned with the name Commetho (Kamezō), and they have look-alike features. The first is wearing a kimono, while the second appears in an undershirt and is wearing a headband. Apparently the artist who made the sketches from the daguerreotypes failed to notice that one man appeared twice in different apparel.

24. Kaneko Hisakazu, *Manjirō, the Man Who Discovered America* (Tokyo: Hokuseido Press, 1954), 116.

25. *Evening Star* (Washington, D.C.), 3 November 1857, and *Hutchings' California Magazine* 3, no. 8 (February 1859), as reproduced in *Josefu Hiko kinenkaishi*, 12 December 1990; *Dictionary of American Naval Fighting Ships*, vol. 5, 340; *Alta California*, 19 September 1850; Hikozo, *Floating*, 33–34; Donald L. Canney, *U.S. Coast Guard and Revenue Cutters, 1790–1935* (Annapolis: Naval Institute Press, 1995), 20–21. The *Polk* was sold in 1854 for $3,350.

26. Heco, *Narrative of a Japanese*, 97–99.

27. Hikozo, *Floating*, 34–35; Canney, *Revenue Cutters*, 20–21.

28. *Alta California*, 17 March 1851.

29. Treasury Department *Regulations*, 1 November 1841, quoted in Scott Price (Historian, U.S. Coast Guard) to author, 24 April 2000; Muster and Pay Roll of the U.S. Revenue Cutter Polk, March 1851 to February 1852, National Archives; Hikozo, *Floating*, 34 (Japanese text in Inoue, *Dotō o koeta otokotachi*, 60); Heco, *Narrative of a Japanese*, 102. The *Polk*'s Captain Hunter drew $100, and First Lieutenant John M. Gowan drew $80, the designated compensation for these officer ranks. But the cook and the steward, being in the enlisted ranks, drew $70 each instead of the designated $16.

30. Heco, *Narrative of a Japanese*, 104; Haruna, *Hyōryū*, 92.

31. *Alta California*, 7, 25, 27 April 1851.

32. Chandler, "San Francisco at Statehood," 3–4; Byington, *History of San Francisco*, 162–63.

33. *Alta California*, 11 March 1851.

34. *Alta California*, 18 August 1851; Haruna, *Hyōryū*, 93.

35. *Alta California.*, 30 April 1851.

36. *Alta California*, 6 May 1851. See also issues of 5, 7, 11, 15 May 1851.

37. *Alta California*, 6 May 1851.

38. *Alta California*, 5 May 1851.

39. *Alta California*, 20 July, 26 May 1857.

40. *Alta California*, 20 July, 26 May 1857; Museum of the City of San Francisco, Internet, www.sfmuseum.org/hist5/churches.html.

41. Inoue, *Dotō o koeta otokotachi*, 21.

42. *Alta California*, 23 June 1851.

43. *Alta California*, 30 July, 9 October 1851.

44. *Alta California*, 13 March, 11 September 1851.

45. Heco, *Narrative of a Japanese*, 90; *Alta California*, 27 February 1851.

46. *Alta California*, 12 July 1851.

47. *Alta California*, 18, 19 August 1851.

48. *Alta California*, 4, 6 July 1851.

49. *Alta California*, 24, 25 October 1851.

50. *Alta California*, 4 January 1851.

51. *Alta California*, 24 February 1852.

52. Julia Cooley Altrocchi, "Paradox Town: San Francisco in 1871," in *California Historical Society Quarterly* 28 (1949): 43.

Chapter 3. Voyage from Paradise to Hell

1. Hikozo (Joseph Heco), *Floating on the Pacific Ocean*, 37.

2. *Alta California*, 5 March 1851.

3. William Elliot Griffis, *Matthew Calbraith Perry: A Typical American Naval Officer* (Boston, 1887), 290; Robert Erwin Johnson, *Far China Station: The U.S. Navy in Asian Waters, 1800–1898* (Annapolis: Naval Institute Press, 1979), 50–51.

4. *Alta California*, 29 March, 2, 5 April 1851.

5. *Alta California*, 18 February 1852; Heco, *Narrative of a Japanese*, 106–7.

6. *Dictionary of American Naval Fighting Ships*, vol. 6, 250.

7. Heco, *Narrative of a Japanese*, 168.

8. *Alta California*, 2 March 1852; Heco, *Narrative of a Japanese*, 110.

9. *American Baptist*, 1 July 1852. The *St. Mary's* arrived at the port of Hilo March 22. *Polynesian*, 3 April 1852.

10. *American Baptist*, 1 July 1852; *Hutchings' California Magazine* 3, no. 8 (February 1859), as reproduced in *Josefu Hiko kinenkaishi*, no. 28 (12 December 1990): 16; Inoue, *Dotō o koeta otokotachi*, 22.

11. Heco, *Narrative of a Japanese*, 111-12; Haruna, *Hyōryū*, 106–7.

12. Inoue, *Dotō o koeta otokotachi*, 22; Haruna, *Hyōryū*, 107; Haruyoshi Chikamori, "Following the Footsteps of Heco in America," *Josefu Hiko kinenkai shi*, No. 10 (12 December 1977), 10; Ogasa, "Kurobune ni notta Hiroshimajin," part 2, no. 2 (14 February 1994).

13. Hikozo, *Floating*, 36.

14. Johnson, *Far China Station*, 51–52.

15. Log Book, *Susquehanna*, 8 May 1852; Johnson, *Far China Station*, 55.

16. Heco, *Narrative of a Japanese*, 114-16; *Dictionary of American Naval Fighting Ships*, vol. 6, 685; Donald L. Canney, *Frigates, Sloops, and Gunboats, 1815–1885*, vol. 1 of *The Old Steam Navy* (Annapolis: Naval Institute Press, 1990), 32–35, 173.

17. Heco, *Narrative of a Japanese*, 115.

18. Haruna, *Hyōryū*, 112.

19. Quoted in Peter Booth Wiley with Ichiro Korogi, *Yankees in the Land of the Gods: Commodore Perry and the Opening of Japan* (New York: Penguin Books, 1991), 37.

20. *Nihon Kirisutokyō rekishi daijiten* (Dictionary of Japanese Christian history) (Tokyo: Kyōbunkan, 1988), s.v. "Amakusa hyōmin," "Harada Shōzō"; Plummer, *Shogun's Reluctant Ambassadors*, 168–69.

21. Jessie G. Lutz, "Karl F. A. Gützlaff: Missionary Entrepreneur," in *Christianity in China: Early Protestant Missionary Writings* (Cambridge: Committee on American-East Asian Relations of the Department of History in collaboration with the Council on East Asian Studies / Harvard University, 1985), 61–67.

22. Stephen W. Kohl, "Strangers in a Strange Land: Japanese Castaways and the Opening of Japan," *Pacific Northwest Quarterly* 73 (1982): 23.

23. Williams, *Life and Letters*, 100, 99.

24. William G. Beasley, *Great Britain and the Opening of Japan, 1834–1858* (London: Luzac and Co., 1951), 120; Haruna, *Hyōryū*, 113–15; Howard F. Van Zandt, *Pioneer American Merchants in Japan* (Tokyo: Lotus Press, 1980), 134.

25. Log Book, *Susquehanna*, 25 May 1852.

26. Heco, *Narrative of a Japanese*, 117–18; Haruna, *Hyōryū*, 119. The nine who went were Genjirō, Seitarō, Yotarō, Tamizō, Kamezō, Iwakichi, Tokubee, Kyōsuke, and Yasutarō. The seven who stayed were Chōsuke, Kimpachi, Ikumatsu, Kiyozō, Jisaku, Hikotarō (Heco), and Sentarō (Sam Patch). This episode probably occurred during the *Susquehanna's* extended stay in Hong Kong June 26 to July 13. The Japanese had been aboard two months, which is close enough to Heco's recollection of three months. Earlier in June the ship had gone to Amoy and then to Whampoa and Blenheim Reach. When it left Hong Kong in July, it moved up toward Canton yet again and remained in the area until August 11, when it anchored at Cum Sing Moon.

27. *Alta California*, 17, 22 March 1851.

28. Muster Roll, *Susquehanna*, 31 July 1852.

29. Ogasa, "Kurobune ni notta Hiroshimajin," part 2, no. 5 (17 February 1994).

30. Log Book, *Susquehanna*, 19, 20 August 1852; Heco, *Narrative of a Japanese*, 122; Muster Roll, *Susquehanna*, 31 July, 30 September 1852.

31. Ogasa, "Kurobune ni notta Hiroshimajin," part 2, no. 5 (17 February 1994); Heco, *Narrative of a Japanese*, 123–34.

32. Log Book, *Susquehanna*, 10 January 1853.

33. Johnson, *Far China Station*, 57.

34. Log Book, *Susquehanna*, 5 February 1853.

35. Bayard Taylor, *A Visit to India, China, and Japan, in the Year 1853* (New York, 1855), 290.

36. Taylor, *Visit to India*, 290.

37. Taylor, *Visit to India*, 292. Chapu is now a part of the Zhapu Economic Development Zone, which also includes the ports of Dushan and Haiyan.

38. Taylor, *Visit to India*, 322.

39. J. W. Spalding, *The Japan Expedition: Japan and Around the World* (New York, 1855), 95.

40. Beasley, *Opening of Japan*, 115–16. Otokichi's story is well told in Kohl, "Strangers in a Strange Land," 20–28.

41. Haruna, *Hyōryū*, 148–49.

42. Williams, *Life and Letters*, 84.

43. Quoted in Kohl, "Strangers in a Strange Land," 21.

44. The signatures are reproduced in *Shu no ashibito*, no. 23 (29 October 1986).

45. Ebisawa Arimichi, *Nihon no seisho: seisho wayaku no rekishi* (The Japanese Bible: History of Japanese translations) (Tokyo: Nihon Kirisuto Kyōdan Shuppankyoku, 1981), 105–9; Bernardin Schneider, "Japan's Encounter with the Bible," *Japan Christian Quarterly* 48 (no. 2, spring 1982): 72–73; *Nihon Kirisutokyō rekishi daijiten* (Dictionary of Japanese Christian history) (Tokyo: Kyōbunkan, 1988), s.v. "Owari hyōmin."

46. D. B. McCartee, *A Missionary Pioneer in the Far East: A Memorial of Divie Bethune McCartee*, ed. Robert E. Speer (New York: Fleming H. Revell Co., 1922), 144–45; Beasley, *Opening of Japan*, 115–16.

47. Log Book, *Susquehanna*, 1 April 1853; Stuart Creighton Miller, "Ends and Means: Missionary Justification of Force in Nineteenth Century China," in John K. Fairbank, ed.,

The Missionary Enterprise in China and America (Cambridge: Harvard University Press, 1974); Taylor, *Visit to India,* 298; Samuel Elliot Morison, *"Old Bruin": Commodore Matthew C. Perry 1794–1858* (Boston: Little, Brown, and Co., 1967), 403.

48. Log Book, *Susquehanna,* 7 April 1853.

Chapter 4. Conscript and Volunteer

1. Bunta (Rishichi, Yotarō) as quoted in Haruna, *Hyōryū,* 150–51.

2. Log Book, USS *Susquehanna,* 9 April 1853.

3. Perry, *Narrative of the Expedition,* 1:340.

4. Arthur Walworth, *Black Ships off Japan: The Story of Commodore Perry's Expedition* (New York: Alfred A. Knoff, 1946; reprint, Hamden, Conn.: Archon Books, 1966), 33–34.

5. Inoue, *Dotō o koeta otokotachi,* 22; Ogasa, "Kurobune ni notta Hiroshimajin," part 2, no. 7 (19 February 1994); Haruna, *Hyōryū,* 153–59.

6. Perry, *Narrative of the Expedition,* 1:486.

7. Log Book, *Susquehanna,* 17 May 1853, 13 January 1854; Muster Roll, *Susquehanna,* 1855, 11 February 1855.

8. Williams, "Journal," 2, 28.

9. Williams, "Journal," 6.

10. John S. Sewell, "With Perry in Japan," *Century Magazine* 70 (1905): 353; Otis Cary, *A History of Christianity in Japan: Roman Catholic, Greek Orthodox, and Protestant Missions* (2 vols., 1909; reprint [2 vol. in 1], Tokyo: Charles E. Tuttle Co., 1976), 2:31; Morison, *"Old Bruin,"* 327–28.

11. Taylor, *Visit to India,* 434.

12. Williams, "Journal," 65; Daniel Crosby Greene, "The Japanese Version of the New Testament," *Japan Evangelist* 13 (August 1906): 262. William Elliot Griffis wrote that Williams "was remembered as *Keredomo San* (Mr. Keredomo, or Sir Nevertheless)." Griffis, *Hepburn of Japan* (Philadelphia: Westminster Press, 1913), 92.

13. Williams, "Journal," 65–66; Perry, *Narrative of the Expedition,* 1:267–68.

14. B. J. Bettelheim diary, entries of 30, 31 January, 1 February 1854, Church Missionary Society Archives, London.

15. Bettelheim diary, 30 January 1854.

16. Bettelheim diary, 1 February 1854; Muster Roll, *Susquehanna,* 11 February 1855. Canoe's term of enlistment was 1 February 1854 to 31 January 1856.

17. Log Book, *Susquehanna,* 15, 24 February 1854; Williams, "Journal," 83, 96.

18. Edward Yorke McCauley, *With Perry in Japan: The Diary of Edward Yorke McCauley,* ed. Allan B. Cole (Princeton: Princeton University Press, 1942), 91.

19. Perry, *Narrative of the Expedition,* 1:340, 71.

20. Haruna, *Hyōryū,* 164-65.

21. McCauley, *With Perry in Japan,* 103–4.

22. McCauley, *With Perry in Japan,* 91–92; Perry, *Narrative of the Expedition,* 1:342; Williams, "Journal," 122.

23. Murakami, "Kurobune no Nihonjin suifu," 12; Haruna, *Hyōryū,* 191; McCauley, *With Perry in Japan,* 91.

24. See chapter 1, note 1.

25. Inazō Nitobe, *The Intercourse between the United States and Japan: An Historical Sketch* (1891; reprint, Wilmington, Del.: Scholarly Resources, 1973), 158; Perry, *Narrative of the*

Expedition, 1:450. The ambivalent sentence in the *Narrative* occurs in a paragraph that compiler Francis Hawks probably meant to attribute to Perry even though it is not in quotes.

26. McCauley, *With Perry in Japan,* 91; Haruna, *Hyōryū,* 192–94; Perry, *Narrative of the Expedition,* 1:342.

27. McCauley, *With Perry in Japan,* 92.

28. Morison, *"Old Bruin,"* 362; F. Calvin Parker, *Jonathan Goble of Japan: Marine, Missionary, Maverick* (Lanham, Md.: University Press of America, 1990), 246–49.

29. Murakami, "Kurobune no Nihonjin suifu," 13.

30. Sewall, "With Perry in Japan," 357; Wiley, *Land of the Gods,* 392.

31. Log Book, USS *Mississippi,* 1852–54, no. 9, 18 June 1854, National Archives. Log Book, *Susquehanna,* same date, mentions Sam Patch and Jack Canoe but not the two Chinese.

32. Perry, *Narrative of the Expedition, 1:*450, 485.

33. Haruna, *Hyōryū,* 195.

34. Haruna, *Hyōryū,* 196.

35. Perry, *Narrative of the Expedition, 1:*485–86; Haruna, *Hyōryū,* 196; Kawashima Daijirō, *Jonasan Gōburu kenkyū* (Jonathan Goble studies) (Tokyo: Shinkyō Shuppansha, 1988), 63.

36. Haruna, *Hyōryū,* 196.

37. Williams, "Journal," 182; Oliver Statler, *The Black Ship Scroll* (Tokyo: Charles E. Tuttle Co., 1963), 41.

38. For Matō as he appears in the Japan Society of Northern California scroll, see Statler, *Black Ship Scroll,* 38.

39. For the Matō sketch identified as Otokichi, see Haruna, *Hyōryū,* 196. A variation of the sketch appears on the cover of a lecture outline, "Saisho no hōyaku seisho—Yohane fukuinsho no shomondai," which Haruna delivered 15 October 1983 at the Yokohama Archives of History.

40. Log Book, *Mississippi,* 29 June 1854; Williams, *Journal,* 227; Keith Seat, ed., "Jonathan Goble's Book," in *Transactions of the Asiatic Society of Japan,* 3d ser., 16 (1981): 138.

41. Pollay, "Japan in 1852."

42. Haruna, *Hyōryū,* 171–77, 217; Inoue, *Dotō o koeta otokotachi,* 282; *Shu no ashiato,* no. 23 (29 October 1986); Ogasa, "Kurobune ni notta Hiroshimajin," part 5, no. 4 (7 April 1994).

43. Muster Roll, *Susquehanna,* 11 February 1855, entry no. 707; Muster Roll, *Susquehanna,* 1855, entry on page following no. 738 (numbers on this page do not show in microfilm); Perry, *Narrative of the Expedition,* 1:486.

44. William Speiden Jr., "Journal of a Cruise in the U.S. Steam Frigate Mississippi" (manuscript journal in 2 vols., Naval Historical Foundation, Washington, D.C.; issued in microfilm by Scholarly Resources, Wilmington, Del.), entry of 1 October 1854; Pollay, "Japan in 1852."

45. *American Baptist,* 22 March 1855. See also note 41. Morison (*"Old Bruin,"* 411) states incorrectly that the *Susquehanna* returned via the Indian Ocean and the Cape of Good Hope.

46. *Daily Alta California,* 26 November 1854; *Friend,* 3, no. 10 (1 November 1854): 77; *Friend* 9, no 3 (1 March 1860): 20.

47. *Polynesian,* 28 October, 11 November 1854; Speiden journal, 8 November 1854.

48. *New American Cyclopaedia*, vol. 14 (New York, 1862), 317–19; Byington, *History of San Francisco*, 271, 177

49. Heco, *Narrative of a Japanese*, 146–47.

50. E. W. Clark, letter, 26 May 1873, *New York Evangelist*, 14 August 1873; Log Book, *Mississippi*, 27 January–26 April 1855; *New York Daily Tribune*, 23 April 1855; Morison, *"Old Bruin,"* 416.

51. K. Jack Bauer, *The New American State Papers, Naval Affairs*, vol. 7, Personnel (Wilmington, Del.: Scholarly Resources, 1981), 219; *New York Times*, 7, 8 May 1866.

52. Griffis, *Matthew Calbraith Perry*, 404–5.

53. Clark, letter, 26 May 1873, *New York Evangelist*, 14 August 1873; Perry, *Narrative of the Expedition*, 1:486.

Chapter 5. Immersion in an Icy Creek

1. *American Baptist*, 16 March 1858.

2. Clark, *Life and Adventure*, 40–41; Clark, letter, 26 May 1873, *New York Evangelist*, 14 August 1873.

3. Jonathan Goble, "The Baptist Mission in Japan," *Freeman* (London), 2 August 1872, 377; Philetus Olney obituary in *Thirty-Sixth Annual Meeting of the Baptist Convention of the State of Michigan, 1871* (Detroit, 1872).

4. Madison University Student Register, 1818–1856, entry of 17 May 1855, Colgate University Archives; Perry, *Narrative of the* Expedition, 1:6; *New American Cyclopaedia*, vol. 9 (New York, 1860), 720.

5. Madison University Student Register, 1818–1856, entry of 17 May 1855.

6. Madison University Student Register, 17 May 1855; Steuben County census records, 1855.

7. *Catalogue of the Officers and Students of Madison University for the Academic Year 1855–6* (Hamilton, N.Y., 1856), 19, 23; Howard D. Williams to author, 4 April 1979.

8. *Catalogue of Madison University, 1855–56,* 30–31.

9. *American Baptist*, 4 October 1855.

10. *The First Half Century of Madison University (1819–1869)* (Hamilton, N.Y., 1872), 470.

11. Clement, "Jonathan Goble," 182.

12. Parker, *Jonathan Goble of Japan*, 74.

13. Ernest W. Clement, "Jonathan Goble and his Japanese Protégé," *Japan Evangelist* 20 (April 1913): 182; Theodore B. Knox to author, 13 July 1979; George W. Eaton obituary in *The New York Baptist Annual for 1873* (New York, 1873), 58–60.

14. Clement, "Jonathan Goble," 183. Clement's notes of the interview with Samuel Joseph Douglas are in the Goble file, American Baptist Historical Library, Atlanta. On Douglas, see *The New York Baptist Annual for 1915* (New York, 1915), 90.

15. *American Baptist Memorial* 15 (April 1856): 119; *Baptist Family Magazine*, May 1858, 121; Perry, *Narrative of the* Expedition, 1:557.

16. *New York Times*, 22 May 1860.

17. *American Baptist*, 16 March 1858.

18. *American Baptist*, 16 March 1858; Haruna, *Hyōryū*, 206.

19. *American Baptist*, 16 March 1858.

20. *American Baptist*, 16 March 1858; Hezekiah Harvey obituary in *The New York Baptist Annual for 1894* (New York, 1894), 51–52.

21. First Baptist Church, Hamilton, N.Y., Record Book, 1857–1892, 6, 7 March 1858; Clement, notes on Douglas.

22. Clement, "Jonathan Goble," 183; Alexander Beebee obituary in *Madison County Herald*, February 1897, Beebee vertical file in the American Baptist-Samuel Colgate Historical Library.

23. Nitobe, *United States and Japan,* 158.

24. *Friend* 9 (1 March 1860): 22.

25. *American Baptist,* 8 November 1859, copied from the *New York Evening Express.*

26. *American Baptist,* 8 November 1859.

27. *American Baptist,* 8 November 1859.

28. Specimens of Manjiro's and Heco's English are given in Miyoshi, *As We Saw Them,* 12.

29. *American Baptist,* 8 November 1859.

30. *Friend* 9 (1 March 1860): 22; Edwin Munsell Bliss, ed., *The Encyclopædia of Missions: Descriptive, Historical, Biographical, Statistical,* vol. 2 (New York, 1891), s.v. "Seamen, Missions to."

31. *New York Times,* 5, 6 November 1859.

32. *Hutchings' California Magazine* 3, no. 8 (February 1859); Charles Wolcott Brooks, "Report of Japanese Vessels wrecked in the North Pacific Ocean, from the Earliest Records to the Present Time," *Proceedings of the California Academy of Sciences* 6 (1875): 56.

33. Goble to J. Philips, 4 December 1859, *American Baptist,* 7 February 1860.

34. Murakami, "Kurobune no Nihonjin suifu," 16–17; Haruna, *Hyōryū,* 227.

35. *Daily Alta California,* 2, 3 December 1859, 21 January 1860; *New American Cyclopaedia,* v. 14, 318–19; Byington, *History of San Francisco,* 287.

36. *Daily Alta California,* 11 December 1859, 8, 9 January, 1 February 1860.

37. *Daily Alta California,* 26, 12, 25 January 1860; *Polynesian,* 25 February 1860.

38. *Daily Alta California,* 24 January 1860; Heco, *Narrative of a Japanese,* 1:235–36, 241.

39. Goble to N. Brown, 18 January 1860, *American Baptist,* 6 March 1860.

40. *Polynesian,* 25 February 1860; Goble to Brown, 16, 22 February 1860, *American Baptist,* 17 April 1860.

41. *Friend* 9 (1 March 1860): 22–23; *Missionary Album,* 76–77, Hawaiian Mission Children's Society Library, Honolulu.

42. *Friend* 9 (7 July 1860): 51.

43. *American Baptist,* 21 February 1860; Miyoshi, *As We Saw Them,* 39, 59.

44. Bradford Smith, *Yankees in Paradise: The New England Impact on Hawaii* (New York: J. B. Lippincott, 1956), 265–66.

45. *Polynesian,* 3 March 1860.

46. Yukichi Fukuzawa, *The Autobiography of Fukuzawa Yukichi,* tran. Eiichi Kiyooka (Tokyo: Hokuseido Press, 1934), 127–28.

47. *Friend* 9 (1 March 1860): 21.

48. *Friend* 9 (1 March 1860): 20.

49. *Polynesian,* 25 February 1860; *Friend* 9 (1 April 1860): 32.

Chapter 6. Protection under the Flag

1. J. Goble to N. Brown, 25 April 1860, *American Baptist,* 10 July 1860.
2. Goble to W. Newton, [July 1860], *American Baptist,* 11 December 1860. The population of Kanagawa in an 1843 census was 5,793 (Yazaki, *Social Change,* 136).
3. *American Baptist,* 22 May 1860.
4. J. C. Hepburn to Walter Lowrie, 14 May 1860, Presbyterian Church in the U.S.A., Board of Foreign Missions, Missions Correspondence and Reports, Microfilm Series, Japan, Presbyterian Historical Society, Philadelphia.
5. S. R. Brown to D. E. Bartlett, 14 April 1860, W. E. Griffis Collection, Rutgers University.
6. Goble to N. Brown, 7 April 1860, *American Baptist,* 24 July 1860; Haruna, *Hyōryū,* 228.
7. Goble to N. Brown, 25 April 1860, *American Baptist,* 10 July 1860.
8. Kawashima, *Jonasan Goburu kenkyū,* 87.
9. Donald R. Bernard, *The Life and Times of John Manjiro* (New York: McGraw-Hill, 1992), 203, 206; Francis Hall journal, entry of 29 October 1860, in F. G. Notehelfer, ed., *Japan through American Eyes: The Journal of Francis Hall, Kanagawa and Yokohama, 1859–1866* (Princeton, N.J.: Princeton University Press, 1992), 256.
10. Alcock, *Capital of the Tycoon,* 1:280; Black, *Young Japan,* 1:39, 42–43; Hall journal, 26 February 1860, in Notehelfer, *Japan through American Eyes,* 129–30; Robert Fortune, *Yedo and Peking: A Narrative of a Journey to the Capitals of Japan and China* (London, 1863), 40.
11. Alcock, *Capital of the Tycoon,* 1:347–53.
12. Alcock to Lord J. Russell, 21 February 1860, in *British Parliamentary Papers, Japan, 1, Reports, returns, and correspondence respecting Japan 1856–64,* Irish University Press Area Studies Series (Shannon: Irish University Press, 1971), 187.
13. Alcock to Lord J. Russell, 21 February 1860, in *British Parliamentary Papers,* 187; Alcock, *Capital of the Tycoon,* 1:332; Hall journal, 30 January 1860, in Notehelfer, *Japan through American Eyes,* 115.
14. Hall journal, 30 January 1860, in Notehelfer, *Japan through American Eyes,* 115; Alcock, *Capital of the Tycoon,* 1:331–36; Black, *Young Japan,* 1: 46; Heco, *Narrative of a Japanese,* 1: 236–37.
15. Hall journal, 22 January 1861, in Notehelfer, *Japan through American Eyes,* 297; Alcock, *Capital of the Tycoon,* 2:47. The *jōi* movement was active since the 1850s; the *sonnō jōi* movement ("honor the emperor and expel the barbarians") started about 1861 and was very strong by 1863.
16. Heco, *Narrative of a Japanese,* 1:278; Robert H. Pruyn to Secretary of State Seward, 7 January 1862, U.S. Consular despatches, National Archives.
17. Eliza Goble to Mrs. N. Brown, n.d., *American Baptist,* 4 September 1860.
18. *American Baptist,* 10 July 1860.
19. *Friend* 9 (1 March 1860): 20.
20. Satow, *Diplomat in Japan,* 57.
21. John L. Nevius to his mother, 3 July 1860, quoted in Helen S. Coan Nevius, *The Life of John Livingston Nevius* (New York, 1895), 198.
22. Hall journal, 3 May 1860, in Notehelfer, *Japan through American Eyes,* 162.
23. *New York Times,* 8 December 1870.
24. Alcock, *Capital of the Tycoon,* 1:83.

25. Hall journal, 30 May 1860, in Notehelfer, *Japan through American Eyes,* 177; William Elliot Griffis, *Hepburn of Japan* (Philadelphia: Westminister Press, 1913), 105.

26. Hepburn to Lowrie, 5 June 1860; Presbyterian Historical Society; Hall journal, 6 June, 31 August 1860, 18 January 1861, in Notehelfer, *Japan through American Eyes,* 180, 217, 295; Nevius, *Our Life in China,* 258–59, 272.

27. Hall journal, 28 August 1860, in Notehelfer, *Japan through American Eyes,* 216.

28. George Smith, *Ten Weeks in Japan* (London, 1861), 413; Goble to N. Brown, 14 September 1860, *American Baptist,* 8 January 1861; William Elliot Griffis, *A Maker of the New Orient: Samuel Robbins Brown* (New York: Fleming H. Revell Co., 1902), 277.

29. Fortune, *Yedo and Peking,* 52.

30. Griffis, *Hepburn of Japan,* 118–19.

31. Hall journal, 1, 2, 19 June 1860, in Notehelfer, *Japan through American Eyes*, 178–79, 185.

32. Hepburn to Lowrie, 22 November 1859, Presbyterian Historical Society.

33. Alcock, *Capital of the Tycoon,* 1:124.

34. Hall journal, 7 November, 7 December 1859, in Notehelfer, *Japan through American Eyes*, 74, 84; Hepburn to Lowrie, 18 October 1860, Presbyterian Historical Society.

35. Alcock, *Capital of the Tycoon,* 2:10–11.

36. Goble to Brown, May 25, 1860, *American Baptist,* 21 August 1860.

37. Hepburn to Lowrie, 12 June 1860, Presbyterian Historical Society; J. B. Hartwell, letter, *Commission* 5 (February 1861): 233–34; Goble to N. Brown, 14 September 1860, *American Baptist,* 8 January 1861.

38. Jonathan Goble, *The Triumph of Faith* (Yokohama, 1882), 4.

39. Hall journal, 5 August 1860, in Notehelfer, *Japan through American Eyes*, 208; Satow, *Diplomat in Japan,* 50.

40. McCartee, *Missionary Pioneer in the Far East,* 150; James H. Ballagh to Philip Peltz, 3 January 1862, Reformed Church in America, Japan Mission correspondence, Gardner A. Sage Library, New Brunswick Theological Seminary, New Brunswick, N.J. (afterwards cited as Sage Library).

41. Hall journal, 21 May 1861, 11 June, 15 June 1860, in Notehelfer, *Japan through American Eyes,* 339, 182–83.

42. Brown to Peltz, 19 December 1860, Sage Library.

43. Brown to Peltz, 23 November 1860, Sage Library.

44. Hall journal, 22 July, 14 October 1860, in Notehelfer, *Japan through American Eyes*, 205, 254–55.

45. Hall journal, 29 August 1860, in Notehelfer, *Japan through American Eyes,* 216.

46. Heco, *Narrative of a Japanese,* 1:240.

47. Heco, *Narrative of a Japanese,* 1:191–92.

Chapter 7. Nurse for the Children

1. Margaret Ballagh, *Glimpses of Old Japan,* 123.

2. James H. Ballagh to T. Ferris, 25 January 1868, Sage Library.

3. M. Leila Winn, "Dr. Ballagh of Japan," *Christian Intelligencer,* 28 April 1920; J. H. Ballagh, "Reminiscences," in *Biographical Sketches Read at The Council of Missions 1909.*

4. J. H. Ballagh to Peltz, 20 February 1861, 3 January 1862, Sage Library; Ozawa Saburō, *Bakumatsu Meiji Yasokyōshi kenkyū* (Studies in Christian history in the closing years of the Tokugawa era and in the Meiji era) (Tokyo: Nihon Kirisuto Kyōdan, 1973), 261.

5. M. Ballagh, *Glimpses of Old Japan*, 20, 34, 42, 58.

6. M. Ballagh, *Glimpses of Old Japan*, 75–76.

7. M. Ballagh, *Glimpses of Old Japan*, 75–76.

8. M. Ballagh, *Glimpses of Old Japan*, 58–59. "I-ro-ha" *(iroha)* is the Japanese syllabary (alphabet).

9. M. Ballagh, *Glimpses of Old Japan*, 76–77, 81–82.

10. J. H. Ballagh to Peltz, 31 December 1862, Sage Library; M. Ballagh, *Glimpses of Old Japan*, 97–98.

11. J. H. Ballagh to Peltz, 31 December 1862; D. B. Simmons to Peltz, 31 October 1862, Sage Library.

12. J. H. Ballagh to Peltz, 9 December 1861, S. R. Brown to Peltz, 2 March 1863, Sage Library; First Baptist Church, Hamilton, N.Y., Record Book, 1857-1892.

13. M. Ballagh, *Glimpses of Old Japan*, 37.

14. Alcock, *Capital of the Tycoon*, 1:320–23.

15. Robert H. Pruyn to Secretary of State William C. Seward, 26 May 1863, National Archives; Pruyn to Edward St. John Neale, 9 June 1863, in *British Parliamentary Papers*, 74.

16. Johnson, *Far China Station* 114–20; Griffis, *Maker of the New Orient*, 189. The *Alabama* was later sunk off the coast of France by another American warship.

17. Black, *Young Japan*, 1:193; M. Ballagh, *Glimpses of Old Japan*, 105; Hall journal, 31 May, 1 June 1863, in Notehelfer, *Japan through American Eyes*, 479–80.

18. M. Ballagh, *Glimpses of Old Japan*, 106–7.

19. Alcock, *Capital of the Tycoon*, 1:122.

20. J. H. Ballagh to Peltz, 28 August 1863, Sage Library; Griffis, *Maker of the New Orient*, 174–75, 182.

21. Conrad Totman, *The Collapse of the Tokugawa Bakufu 1862–1868* (Honolulu: University Press of Hawaii, 1980), 69, 72; Satow, *Diplomat in Japan*, 80.

22. Heco, *Narrative of a Japanese*, 1:332–33.

23. Quoted in Hugh Cortazzi, *Victorians in Japan: In and around the Treaty Ports* (London: Athlone Press, 1987), 69; Iwata Masakata, *Ōkubo Toshimichi: The Bismarck of Japan* (Berkeley: University of California Press, 1964), 64; M. Ballagh, *Glimpses of Old Japan*, 107–8; Parker, *Jonathan Goble of Japan*, 115–16.

24. J. H. Ballagh to Peltz, 28 August 1863; Hall journal, 30 November 1863, in Notehelfer, *Japan through American Eyes*, 515.

25. J. H. Ballagh to Peltz, 8 January 1864, Sage Library; Pruyn to the Gorōjū, 14, 19 December 1863, U. S. consular correspondence, National Archives; Griffis, *Maker of the New Orient*, 188–89.

26. J. H. Ballagh to Peltz, 8 January 1864, Sage Library.

27. M. Ballagh, *Glimpses of Old Japan*, 108–9.

28. Hall journal, 18 April 1864, in Notehelfer, *Japan through American Eyes*, 535.

29. Cary, *History*, 2:56.

30. M. Ballagh, *Glimpses of Old Japan*, 124–25.

31. Cary, *History*, 2:56–62.

32. *Christian Intelligencer*, 2 August 1866; J. H. Ballagh to Ferris, 4 December 1867, Sage Library; Griffis, *Hepburn of Japan*, 103.

33. M. Ballagh, *Glimpses of Old Japan*, 22; *Daily Alta California*, 27, 29 April 1866.

34. J. H. Ballagh to Ferris, 4 December 1867, Sage Library.

35. *Daily Alta California*, 19 May 1866.

36. D. L. Kinnear to author, 12 December 1990.

37. James William Smith, Journal, entry of June 17–19, 1866, Mission Houses Museum Library, Honolulu; *Pacific Commercial Advertiser*, 23 June 1866; J. H. Ballagh, letter, 7 August 1866, *Christian Intelligencer* 37, no. 44 (1 November 1866).

38. J. H. Ballagh to Ferris, 25 January 1868, Sage Library.

39. Reformed Church in America, *Annual Report, 1869*, 43; Charles W. Turner, ed., *The Diary of Henry Boswell Jones of Brownsburg (1842–1871)* (Verona, Va.: McClure Press, 1979), 95, 97; *Far East*, vol. 7, no. 11 (31 August 1875): 38; *Japan Weekly Mail*, 26 November 1870, 573; J. H. Ballagh to Ferris, 22 December 1870, Sage Library.

40. *Pacific Commercial Advertiser*, 27 June 1868; Ernest K. Wakukawa, *A History of the Japanese People in Hawaii* (Honolulu: Toyo Shoin, 1938), 18, 28–29, 40; Hilary Conroy, *The Japanese Frontier in Hawaii, 1868–1898* (Berkeley: University of California Press, 1953), 15–29. The number 148 does not include a man who died on the *Scioto* en route to Honolulu.

41. Conroy, *Japanese Frontier in Hawaii*, 28; Ogasa, "Kurobune ni notta Hiroshimajin," part 5, no. 6 (10 April 1994).

42. Ogasa, "Kurobune ni notta Hiroshimajin," part 5, no. 6 (10 April 1994).

Chapter 8. Rice Cakes and the Fatted Duck

1. Clark, *Life and Adventure*, 41.

2. E. W. Clark, letter, undated, *Albany Evening Journal*, 20 January 1872, and *New York Evangelist*, 7 March 1872.

3. Edward R. Beauchamp, *An American Teacher in Early Meiji Japan* (Honolulu: University Press of Hawaii, 1976), 16.

4. *National Cyclopaedia of American Biography*, s.v. "Clark, Rufus Wheelwright" (10:359), "Clark, Thomas March" (1:445).

5. Clark, *Life and Adventure;* Nitobe, *United States and Japan,* 145. Clark's book was translated by Iida Hiroshi as *Nihon Taizai Ki* and published by Kodansha in 1967.

6. E. Warren Clark, *Katz Awa: The Bismarck of Japan* (New York: B. F. Buck & Co., 1904), 32.

7. *Kadokawa Nihon Chimei Daijiten* (Kadokawa encyclopedia of Japanese geography) (Tokyo: Kadokawa shoten, 1990), 22:1033.

8. Clark, letter, 5 June 1873, *New York Evangelist,* 31 July 1872; Clark, letter, 9 October 1872, *New York Evangelist,* 1 May 1873; Clark, *Katz Awa,* 31; A. Hamish Ion, "Edward Warren Clark and the Formation of the Shizuoka and Koishikawa Christian Bands (1871–1879)," in Edward R. Beauchamp and Akira Iriye, eds., *Foreign Employees in Nineteenth-Century Japan* (Boulder: Westview Press, 1990), 174; *Shizuoka*, no. 704 (1 January 1985), 3. Gakumonjo in a sense was a consolidation of Shōheikō, a school of Confucian studies in Tokyo, Kaiseijo, a school of Western learning in Tokyo, and the School of Foreign Languages in Yokohama. Among the stellar teachers were Mukōyama Kōson, a Chinese scholar who had visited France in 1866 and later had given Sumpu its new name of Shizuoka; Katō Hiroyuki, the first Japanese to specialize in German studies and later

president of Tokyo University; Tsuda Mamichi, an expert in law who had studied in Holland at the University of Leiden; and Nakamura Masanao, introduced in the text below.

9. Clark, letter, n.d., *Albany Evening Journal,* 20 January 1872, and *New York Evangelist,* 7 March 1872. The other two women on the Mission Home staff were Mrs. Louise H. Pierson, like Pruyn a widow, and Miss Julia Crosby.

10. Clark, letter, n.d., *Albany Evening Journal,* 20 January 1872, and *New York Evangelist,* 7 March 1872. See also Louise Henrietta Pierson, *A Quarter of a Century in the Island Empire or the Progress of a Mission in Japan* (Tokyo: Methodist Publishing House, 1899), 17.

11. E. Papinot, *Historical and Geographical Dictionary of Japan* (1910; reprint, with an introduction by Terence Barrow, Tokyo: Charles E. Tuttle Co., 1972), 482–83; Nihon rekishi gakkai, comp., *Meiji ishin jimmei jiten* (Biographical dictionary of the Meiji Restoration) (Tokyo: Yoshikawa Kōbunkan, 1981), 181; Clark, letter, August 1873, *New York Evangelist,* 23 October 1873.

12. Clark, *Katz Awa,* 8, 66.

13. Clark to W. E. Griffis, 17, 26 October (later postscript), 24 November 1871, W. E. Griffis Collection, Rutgers University; A. Hamish Ion, "Edward Warren Clark and Early Meiji Japan: A Case Study of Cultural Contact," *Modern Asian Studies* 11, no. 4 (1977): 572. All letters to or from William E. Griffis cited in these notes are found in the Griffis Collection unless otherwise noted.

14. Clark, *Life and Adventure,* 14; Clark to W. E. Griffis, 24 November 1871; Jerry K. Fisher, "Nakamura Keiu: The Evangelical Ethic in Japan," in *Religious Ferment in Asia,* ed. Robert J. Miller (Lawrence: University Press of Kansas, 1974), 41–42.

15. Clark to W. E. Griffis, 27 November 1871; Mary Pruyn, letter, 16 December 1871, *Albany Evening Journal,* 9 February 1872; Clark, letter, 22 November 1871, *Albany Evening Journal,* 3 February 1872, and *New York Evangelist,* 7 March 1872.

16. Clark, letter, November 1871, *New York Evangelist,* 7 March 1872; Clark to W. E. Griffis, 17 October 1871.

17. Kodera Atsushi, "Nami no manimani: Kikokugo no Samu Patchi" (At the mercy of the waves: Sam Patch after his return to Japan), *Shimin gurafu Yokohama,* special number (1 November 1978): 38.

18. J. H. Ballagh to Ferris, 14 March 1871, Sage Library; W. E. Griffis to Ferris, 18 January 1871, Sage Library.

19. J. H. Ballagh to Ferris, 20 December 1871, Sage Library.

20. Parker, *Jonathan Goble of Japan,* 160–63.

21. W. E. Griffis to Sisters, 29 July 1873; Isobe Hirodaira. *E. W. Kurāku to Shizuoka Gakumonjo* (published by the author, 1996), 12; budget statement in Japan Mission, Letters, vol. 44, p. 99, Sage Library.

22. Clark, letter, 22 November 1871, *Albany Evening Journal,* 3 February 1872; Clark to W. E. Griffis, 26 October 1871 (postscript written later); Clark, letter, 21 November 1871, *Albany Evening Journal,* 27 January 1872.

23. Beauchamp, *American Teacher in Japan,* 30–31.

24. Clark, letter, 18 July 1873, *New York Evangelist,* 11 September 1873.

25. Clark to Maggie Griffis, 5 February 1872; Clark, *Life and Adventure,* 27; W. E. Griffis, *Yokohama Guide, 1874,* 7.

26. Satow, *Diplomat in Japan,* 223; Clark, *Life and Adventure,* 27; Clark, letter, 21 January 1873, *New York Evangelist,* 10 April 1873.

27. Shizuoka Shiyakusho, ed., *Shizuoka shishi: Sōmokuji nenpyō sakuin* (History of Shizuoka City: Chronological table and index) (Shizuoka: City office, n.d.), 614.

28. Clark, letter, 17 December 1871, *New York Evangelist*, 22 February 1872; Clark, *Life and Adventure*, 78.

29. Clark, letter, 17 December 1871, *New York Evangelist*, 22 February 1872.

30. Ibid., Clark, *Life and Adventure*, 51.

31. Ground plan of his temple home drawn by Clark. Edith (Mrs. Jack) Knox, a granddaughter of Clark, kindly showed me the plan at her Nashville home in April 1996 and allowed me to photograph it.

32. Griffis, *Mikado's Empire*, 547; Clark, *Life and Adventure*, 40. Shimojō could be a surname or given name, but he probably was the interpreter Griffis called Yoshi, which would make Shimojō his surname. W. E. Griffis to his sister Maggie, 4 February 1872.

33. Clark, letter, 3 August 1872, *New York Evangelist*, 14 November 1872.

34. Clark, letter, 17 December 1871, *New York Evangelist*, 22 February 1872, and *Albany Evening Journal*, 24 February 1872.

35. Clark, letter, 16 May 1872, *New York Evangelist*, 1 August 1872; Mason, *Etchings from Two Lands*, 118.

36. Clark, letter, 21 November 1871, *New York Evangelist*, 7 March 1872.

37. Clark, letter, 9 October 1872, *New York Evangelist*, 1 May 1873.

38. Clark, letter, 9 February 1872, *New York Evangelist*, 18 April 1872, and *Albany Evening Journal*, 22 April 1872; Clark, letter, 18 March 1872, *New York Evangelist*, 30 May 1872, and *Albany Evening Journal*, 1 June 1872; Clark, letter, 15 June 1872, *New York Evangelist*, 12 September 1872.

39. Clark, letter, 13 January 1872, *New York Evangelist*, 14 March 1872.

40. *Shizuoka*, no. 704 (1 January 1985), 4.

41. Clark, letter, 9 October 1872, *New York Evangelist*, 1 May 1873; Clark, *Katz Awa*, 31.

42. Clark, letter, 15 January 1872, *Albany Evening Journal*, 16 March 1872; Clark to W. E. Griffis, 18 March 1873; Clark, *Life and Adventure*, 50.

43. Clark, letter, 4 June 1872, *New York Evangelist*, 15 August 1872; Clark, *Life and Adventure*, 48.

44. Clark, letter, 16 June 1872, 19 August 1874, *New York Evangelist*, 10 October 1872, 8 April 1875.

45. Griffis, Fukui Journal 1871–77, 31 January 1872; W. E. Griffis to "Dear Ones at Home," 20 January 1872.

46. Clark to M. Griffis, 5 February 1872, edited and published as "A Happy Meeting in Japan," *New York Evangelist*, 9 May 1872; Clark, letter, 16 May 1872, *New York Evangelist*, 1 August 1872; W. E. Griffis, Travel Journal, 1873, 4 January 1873, Griffis Collection, box 7, item 12 (microfilm reel 22); Clark, letter, 1 January 1873, *New York Evangelist*, 20 March 1873. On Hattori, see Nihon Rekishi Gakkai, *Meiji ishin jinmei jiten*, 787–78.

47. Clark to Maggie Griffis, 5 February 1872.

48. W. E. Griffis to Maggie, 4 February 1872; Griffis, *Mikado's Empire*, 548.

49. Clark, letter, 9 February 1872, *New York Evangelist*, 18 April 1872, and *Albany Evening Journal*, 22 April 1872.

50. Clark, letter, 9 February 1872, *Albany Evening Journal*, 22 April 1872, and *New York Evangelist*, 18 April 1872.

51. Clark, letter, 9 February 1872, *New York Evangelist,* 18 April 1872, and *Albany Evening Journal,* 22 April 1872; Clark, letter, 4 June 1872, *New York Evangelist,* 15 August 1872; Clark, *Katz Awa,* 19–20.

52. Clark, letter, 12 April 1872, *New York Evangelist,* 27 June 1872; Clark, letter, 16 September 1872, *New York Evangelist,* 14 November 1872.

53. Clark, letter, 16 May 1872, *New York Evangelist,* 1 August 1872.

54. Clark, letter, 16 June 1872, *New York Evangelist,* 10 October 1872; Clark, letter, 16 September 1872, *New York Evangelist,* 14 November 1872.

55. Clark to W. E. Griffis, 26 October 1872; Takahashi Masao, *Nakamura Keiu* (Tokyo: Yoshikawa Kōbunkan, 1966), 115.

56. Clark, letter, 3 August 1872, *New York Evangelist,* 14 November 1872; Clark, letter, 15 October 1872, *New York Evangelist,* 12 December 1872. See also Margaret Clark Griffis Diary, 1 March 1871–8 May 1874, p. 93, Griffis Collection, Rutgers University, box 119, folder 6 (microfilm reel 58).

57. Clark to W. E. Griffis, 5 June 1872.

58. J. H. Ballagh, letter, 2 September 1873, *New York Evangelist,* 6 November 1873.

59. Ibid.; Isobe, *E. W. Kurāku,* 30.

60. Clark, letter, 16 December 1872, *New York Evangelist,* 6 February 1873, and *Albany Evening Journal,* 8 February 1873.

61. Clark, letter, March 1873, *New York Evangelist,* 26 June 1873; Clark, *Katz Awa,* 13; Clark, *Life and Adventure,* 58..

62. Clark, letter, 18 December 1872, *New York Evangelist,* 27 February 1873, and *Albany Evening Journal,* 1 March 1873.

63. J. H. Ballagh, letter, 2 September 1873, *New York Evangelist,* 6 November 1873; Clark, *Life and Adventure,* 71.

64. Clark, letter, 18 December 1872, *New York Evangelist,* 27 February 1873.

65. Clark, letter, 18 March 1872, *New York Evangelist,* 30 May 1872, and *Albany Evening Journal,* 1 June 1872; Clark, letter, 1 January 1873, *New York Evangelist,* 20 March 1873, and *Albany Evening Journal,* 22 March 1873.

66. Clark, letter, 1 January 1873, *New York Evangelist,* 20 March 1873, and *Albany Evening Journal,* 22 March 1873.

67. Clark, letter, 1 January 1873, *New York Evangelist,* 20 March 1873, and *Albany Evening Journal,* 22 March 1873.

68. Clark, *Life and Adventure,* 61.

69. Griffis, Fukui Journal 1871–77, 3 January 1873; Griffis, Travel Journal, 1873, 3, 4 January 1873.

70. Griffis, Fukui Journal 1871–77, 4, 5 January 1873; Griffis, Travel Journal, 1873, 4, 5 January 1873.

71. Clark, letter, 21 January 1873, *New York Evangelist,* 10 April 1873; W. E. Griffis to Martha, 19 January 1873; Sukeo Kitasawa, *The Life of Dr. Nitobe* (Tokyo: Hokuseido Press, 1953), 9; Shigehisa Tokutarō, *Oyatoi gaikokujin: kyōiku, shūkyō* (Foreign employees: education, religion), Oyatoi gaikokujin, no. 5 (Tokyo: Kashima kenkyū shuppankai, 1968), 26. After transferring to Tokyo English School, Marion Scott taught English Bible to Uchimura Kanzō and Nitobe Inazō, two of Japan's most influential Christians. Later he was the longtime principal of what is now McKinley High School in Honolulu.

72. Mary Pruyn, letter, 9 May 1873, *New York Evangelist,* 10 July 1873; Mrs. Mary Pruyn, *Grandmamma's Letters from* Japan (Boston, 1877), 126–28. See also Isabella L. Bird, *Unbeaten Tracks in Japan* (Tokyo: Charles E. Tuttle Co., 1973).

73. Pruyn, letter, 9 May 1873, *New York Evangelist,* 10 July 1873.

Chapter 9. Faithful in Life, Peaceful in Death

1. Clark, *Life and Adventure,* 231, 233.

2. Clark to W. E. Griffis, 21 April 1873; Clark to W. E. Griffis, n.d.; Clark, letter, 26 May 1873, *New York Evangelist,* 14 August 1873.

3. Clark, letter, 26 May 1873, *New York Evangelist,* 14 August 1873.

4. Kawashima, *Jonasan Gōburu kenkyū,* 83; Clark, *Katz Awa,* 17.

5. Clark to W. E. Griffis, 1 February 1873.

6. Clark, letter, 26 May 1873, *New York Evangelist,* 14 August 1873.

7. Clark, letter, 26 May 1873, *New York Evangelist,* 14 August 1873; Clark to W. E. Griffis, 26 September 1873.

8. Margaret Griffis Diary, 1871–74, 195–96; W. E. Griffis, Fukui Journal 1871–77, 18–22 July 1873.

9. W. E. Griffis to sisters, 29 July 1873.

10. Clark, letter, *New York Evangelist,* 12 June 1873; Clark, *Life and Adventure,* 86.

11. Clark, letter, 16 December 1873, *New York Evangelist,* 12 March 1874.

12. Clark, letter, 3 July 1873, *New York Evangelist,* 2 October 1873.

13. Clark to W. E. Griffis, 7 October 1873.

14. Clark to W. E. Griffis, 21 April 1872; Clark, *Katz Awa,* 16; Clark, letter, 5 June 1873, *New York Evangelist,* 31 July 1873.

15. Clark, letter, 8 September 1873, *New York Evangelist,* 4 December 1873; Ballagh to Ferris, 6 September 1873, Sage Library.

16. J. H. Ballagh, letter, 3 September 1873, *New York Evangelist,* 6 November 1873; Clark to W. E. Griffis, 22 September 1873. On Ichabod, "alas for the glory,"see 1 Samuel 4:19–22.

17. Clark to W. E. Griffis, 28 October 1873; Clark, letter, [fall 1873], incomplete newspaper clipping owned by Mrs. Jack Knox; A. Hamish Ion, *The Cross and the Rising Sun: The Canadian Protestant Missionary Movement in the Japanese Empire, 1872–1931* (Waterloo, Ontario: Wilfrid Laurier University Press, 1990), 39, 52. On Loomis, see Clara D. Loomis, *Henry Loomis: Friend of the East* (New York: Revell, 1923), 25, 45. On Cochran, see *Dictionary of Canadian Biography,* vol. 13 (Toronto: University of Toronto Press, 1994), 206–7.

18. Clark, letters, 16 December 1873, 24 April 1874, *New York Evangelist,* 12 March, 30 July 1874.

19. Brooks, "Report of Japanese Vessels," 51, 65.

20. W. E. Griffis, Fukui Journal 1871–1877, 24 December 1873; M. Griffis Diary, 1871–74, 230; M. Griffis to Sisters (Mary, Martha), 8 January 1874, Griffis Collection.

21. W. E. Griffis to M. Griffis, 26 February 1872; W. E. Griffis to Sisters, 9 September 1872; Usui Chizuko, "Margaret C. Griffis and the Education of Women in Early Meiji Japan," in Beauchamp and Iriye, *Foreign Employees in Japan,* 217.

22. W. E. Griffis to Martha, 19 January 1873, Griffis Collection; M. Griffis Diary, 1871–74, 87, 186; Beauchamp, *American Teacher in Japan,* 95, 108.

23. Ogasa, "Kurobune ni notta Hiroshimajin," part 6, no. 4 (21 April 1994).

24. Clark, *Life and Adventure,* 147.

25. Clark, *Life and Adventure,* 152–53.

26. Black, *Young Japan,* 2:412.

27. M. Griffis to Sisters, 17 January 1874, Griffis Collection; M. Griffis Diary, 1871–74, 236–37; W. E. Griffis, Fukui Journal 1871–1877, 25 January 1874.

28. M. Griffis to Sisters, 2 May 1874, Griffis Collection.

29. Clark, letter, 20 March 1874, *New York Evangelist,* 11 June 1874; Clark, *Life and Adventure,* 163; Beauchamp, *American Teacher in Japan,* 112.

30. Clark, letter, 20 March 1874, *New York Evangelist,* 11 June 1874.

31. C. R. Boxer, *The Christian Century in Japan 1549–1650* (Berkeley: University of California Press, 1951), 391–92; Clark to W. E. Griffis, 18 March 1873; Clark, letter, 24 April 1874, *New York Evangelist,* 9 July 1874; Clark, *Life and Adventure,* 144; Takahashi, *Nakamura Keiu,* 128, 132–33. Other missionaries who taught in Nakamura's school were T. P. Poate, C. S. Eby, David Thompson, and Mrs. L. H. Pierson.

32. Clark, letter, 24 April 1874, *New York Evangelist,* 9 July 1874; W. E. Griffis, Fukui Journal, 11 April 1874.

33. M. Griffis Diary, 1871–74, 151; W. E. Griffis, Fukui Journal 1871–1877, 14 February, 7, 21 March, 21 May, 9 July 1874; Griffis, *Maker of the New Orient,* 261; Clark, letter, 21 May 1874, *New York Evangelist,* 30 July 1874; Beauchamp, *American Teacher in Japan,* 95, 570; Clark, letter, 21 February 1874, *New York Evangelist,* 23 April 1874; Clark, *Life and Adventure,* 139. Hatakeyama had used the name Sugiwara Kōzō while in the United States.

34. Griffis, *Mikado's Empire,* 571.

35. Clark, letter, 21 April 1874, *New York Evangelist,* 18 June 1874; Clark, *Life and Adventure,* 142; Masakata Iwata, *Ōkubo Toshimichi: The Bismarck of Japan* (Berkeley: University of California Press, 1964), 182–83; Griffis, *Mikado's Empire,* 575. For the names of those executed and listings of other punishments meted out, see W. E. Griffis, Fukui Journal 1871–1877, 60–61.

36. Clark, letters, 22 March 1873, 24 April 1874, *New York Evangelist,* 26 June 1873, 30 July 1874; Clark, *Life and Adventure,* 83–84; Clark, *Katz Awa,* 64.

37. Clark, letter, 19 August 1874, *New York Evangelist,* 8 April 1875.

38. Clark, letters, 20 March, 19 August 1874, n.d., *New York Evangelist,* 14 May 1874, 8 April, 25 February 1875; *Shizuoka,* no. 704 (1 January 1985), 7.

39. Clark, letter, 19 August 1874, *New York Evangelist,* 8 April 1875; Ion, "Edward Warren Clark," 178–82; John W. Krummel, ed., *A Biographical Dictionary of Methodist Missionaries to Japan: 1873–1993* (Tokyo: Kyo Bun Kwan, 1996), 163.

40. Clark, *Life and Adventure,* 231; Kawashima, *Jonasan Gōburu kenkyū,* 92–93; *Chōya Shimbun,* October 15, 1874; Kawashima to author, 10 December 1994. Black, *Young Japan,* 2:411. According to *Shu no ashiato,* no. 25 (26 November 2000), the hospital's address was Atago-chō. 2-chōme, 8-banchi (now Nishi Shimbashi 3-chōme).

41. Clark, *Life and Adventure,* 231; Margaret Clark Griffis Journal, 10 May 1874–31 October 1905, 18 May 1874, Griffis Collection, Rutgers University, box 119, folder 7 (microfilm reel 59); Griffis, *Mikado's Empire,* 548; *Sekai daihyakkajiten* (World encyclopedia), 1955 ed., s.v. "*kakke.*"

42. Kodansha, *Encyclopedia of Japan,* s.v. "Takagi Kenkan."

43. *Nisshin shinjishi*, no. 54 (7 July 1873), 2, quoted in Ozawa, *Bakumatsu Meiji Yasokyōshi kenkyū*, 57; Hugh Cortazzi, *Dr. Willis in Japan, 1862–1877: British medical pioneer* (London: Athlone Press, 1985), 195.

44. Essays titled "Kakke," by Harafuchi, Matsui, Sakiki, et al., Griffis Collection; Griffis, *Mikado's Empire*, 570.

45. Clark, letter, 26 May 1873, *New York Evangelist*, 14 August 1873; Clark, *Life and Adventure*, 233.

46. W. E. Griffis, Fukui Journal 1871–1877, 24 June, 3 July 1874.

47. Mason, *Etchings from Two Lands*, 132.

48. W. E. Griffis, Fukui Journal 1871–1877, 7 March 1874; Clara Arthur to J. H. Murdock, 15 June 1874, American Baptist Historical Library, Atlanta, Ga.; Kawashima, *Jonasan Gōburu kenkyū*, 82. The Arthurs' address was 12 Takegawa-chō (mistakenly called Tokugawa-chō in some sources); it is now Ginza 7-chōme).

49. J. H. Arthur, letter, 9 August 1874, *Baptist Missionary Magazine*, November 1874, 395; Clara Arthur to J. N. Murdock, 15 June 1874; Mason, *Etchings from Two Lands*, 90.

50. Clark, *Life and Adventure*, 232; Mason, *Etchings from Two Lands*, 133; Harold S. Williams, *Shades of the Past or Indiscreet Tales of Japan* (Tokyo: Charles E. Tuttle Co., 1959), 166–67; Basil Hall Chamberlain, *Things Japanese* (Tokyo: Charles E. Tuttle Co., 1971), 108.

51. Clark, *Life and Adventure*, 232–33.

52. Frank Cary, *Side Excursions in History* (1934), 165.

53. *Chōya shimbun*, 15 October 1874.

54. A reproduction of the temple register appears in *Shu no ashiato*, no. 3 (1 March 1979).

55. Clark, *Life and Adventure*, 233–34.

56. John Jas. Lewis, "Sundown to Palestine"; *Far East* 6 (30 September 1874): 69.

57. Georg Schurhammer, *Francis Xavier, His Life, His Times*, trans. M. Joseph Costelloe, 4 vols. (Rome: Jesuit Historical Institute, 1973–82), 4:129–30; Stephen Neill, *A History of Christian Missions* (Baltimore: Penguin Books, 1964), 154.

58. Hikozo, *Floating on the Pacific Ocean*, 63.

Epilogue

1. Clark, *Life and Adventure*, 238.

2. Kawashima, *Jonasan Gōburu kenkyū*, 87-88. Translation by the author. I am further indebted to Okayasu Takao for his transcription.

3. Kawashima, *Jonasan Gōburu kenkyū*, 88-89; Kawashima Daijirō, *Jonasan Gōburu yaku "Matai fukuinsho" no kenkyū* (Study of Jonathan Goble's translation of the Gospel of Matthew) (Tokyo: Akashi shoten, 1993), 33-46.

4. Kawashima to author, 3 December 1985; Kimura Ki, comp. and ed., *Japanese Literature; Manners and Customs in the Meiji-Taisho Era*, trans. and adapt. by Philip Yampolsky (Tokyo: Obunsha, 1957), 126-28; *Kodansha Encyclopedia of Japan*, s.v. "Nakamura Masanao."

Bibliography

Albany Evening Journal, 1872–73.

Altrocchi, Julia Cooley. "Paradox Town: San Francisco in 1871." *California Historical Society Quarterly* 28 (1949): 31–46

American Baptist, 1855–60.

American Baptist Memorial, April 1856.

Alta California, 1851–52, 1854, 1860–61, 1866.

Alcock, Sir Rutherford. *The Capital of the Tycoon: A Narrative of a Three Years' Residence in Japan.* 2 vols. 1863. Reprint, New York: Greenwood Press, 1969.

Ballagh, James H. "Empire-Builders of the New Japan." *Japan Gazette Yokohama Semi-Centennial, 1859–1909.* Yokohama, 1909.

———. Letters, 1861–72. Reformed Church in America, Japan Mission correspondence, Gardner A. Sage Library, New Brunswick Theological Seminary, New Brunswick, N.J.

———. "Reminiscences." In *Biographical Sketches Read at The Council of Missions 1909.*

Ballagh, Margaret Tate Kinnear. *Glimpses of Old Japan, 1861–1866.* Tokyo: Methodist Publishing House, 1908.

Baptist Family Magazine, May 1858.

Bara-Makarupin senkyō kinenshi hakkan henshū iinkai (Committee for editing and publishing a memorial history of Ballagh-McAlpine evangelism in Japan). *Nihon dendō hyakunenshi* (Centennial history of evangelism in Japan). Nagoya, 1978.

Bauer, K. Jack. *The New American State Papers, Naval Affairs.* Vol. 7, Personnel. Wilmington, Del.: Scholarly Resources, 1981.

Beasley, W. G. *Great Britain and the Opening of Japan, 1834–1858.* London: Luzac & Co., 1951.

———. *The Meiji Restoration.* Stanford, Calif.: Stanford University Press, 1972.

Beauchamp, Edward R. *An American Teacher in Early Meiji Japan.* Asian Studies at Hawaii, No. 17. Honolulu: University Press of Hawaii, 1976.

Bennett, Tony, and Sebastian Dobson. "The Sentaro Daguerreotype: A New Episode in Japanese Photo-History Discovered." Internet, www.old-japan.co.uk/Sentaro.article.html. Based on article in *PhotoHistorian: Quarterly of the Historical Group of the Royal Photographic Society* 116 (summer 1997).

Bernard, Donald R. *The Life and Times of John Manjiro.* New York: McGraw-Hill, 1992.

Bingham, Hiram. *A Residence of Twenty-One Years in the Sandwich Islands,* 3d ed. Hartford, Conn., 1849.

Bird, Isabella L. *Unbeaten Tracks in Japan.* 1880. Reprint. Tokyo: Charles E. Tuttle Co., 1973.

Bliss, Edwin Munsell, ed. *The Encyclopædia of Missions: Descriptive, Historical, Biographical, Statistical.* Vol. 2. New York, 1891.

Black, John R. *Young Japan: Yokohama and Yedo 1858–79.* 2 vols. 1883. Reprint, Tokyo: Oxford University Press, 1968.

Boxer, C. R. *The Christian Century in Japan 1549–1650*. Berkeley: University of California Press, 1951.

British Parliamentary Papers, Japan, 1. Reports, returns, and correspondence respecting Japan 1856–64. Irish University Press Area Studies Series. Shannon: Irish University Press, 1971.

Brooks, Charles Wolcott. "Report of Japanese Vessels Wrecked in the North Pacific Ocean, from the Earliest Records to the Present Time." *Proceedings of the California Academy of Sciences* 6 (1875): 50–66.

Burks, Ardath W., ed. *The Modernizers: Overseas Students, Foreign Employees, and Meiji Japan.* Boulder, Col.: Westview Press, 1985.

Canney, Donald L. *Frigates, Sloops, and Gunboats, 1815–1885*. Vol. 1 of *The Old Steam Navy*. Annapolis: Naval Institute Press, 1990.

———. *U.S. Coast Guard and Revenue Cutters, 1790–1935*. Annapolis: Naval Institute Press, 1995.

Cary, Frank. *Side Excursions in History*. 1934. Compilation of articles first published in the *Japan Chronicle*.

Cary, Otis. *A History of Christianity in Japan: Roman Catholic, Greek Orthodox, and Protestant Missions*. 2 vols. 1909. Reprint (2 vol. in 1). Tokyo: Charles E. Tuttle Co., 1976.

Catalogue of the Officers and Students of Madison University. Hamilton, N.Y., 1855–59.

Chamberlain, Basil Hall. *Things Japanese*. Tokyo: Charles E. Tuttle Co., 1971.

Chandler, Katherine H. "San Francisco at Statehood." Internet, www.sfmuseum.org/hist5/oldsf.html.

Chikamori Haruyoshi. *Kurisuchan Josefu Hiko*. Tōkyō: Amurita Shobō, 1985.

———. *Josefu=Hiko*. Edited by Japan Historical Society. Tokyo: Yoshikawa Kōbunkan, 1963.

Clark, E. Warren. *Katz Awa, "The Bismarck of Japan" or the Story of a Noble Life*. New York: B. F. Buck & Co., 1904.

———. Letters. *Albany Evening Journal*, 1872–73. *New York Evangelist*, 1872–75.

———. *Life and Adventure in Japan*. New York: American Tract Society, 1878.

Clement, Ernest W. "Jonathan Goble and his Japanese Protégé." *Japan Evangelist* 20 (April 1913): 181–85. A shortened version appears in *Standard* 60 (8 March 1913): 801–3.

Coan, Titus. *Life in Hawaii: An Autobiographic Sketch of Mission Life and Labors (1835–1881)*. New York, 1882.

Conroy, Hilary. *The Japanese Frontier in Hawaii, 1868–1898*. University of California Publications in History, vol. 46. Berkeley: University of California Press, 1953.

Cortazzi, Hugh. *Victorians in Japan: In and around the Treaty Ports*. London: Athlone Press, 1987.

Dice, Walter F. "The History of New Providence Church." *Proceedings of the Rockbridge Historical Society*. Vol. 1, 1937–1941. Lexington, Va.

Diehl, George West. *The Brick Church on Timber Ridge*. Verona, Va., 1975.

Dictionary of American Naval Fighting Ships. Vol. 6. Washington, D.C.: Naval History Division, Department of the Navy, 1976.

Dictionary of Canadian Biography. Vol. 13. Toronto: University of Toronto Press, 1994.

Dunn, Charles J. *Everyday Life in Traditional Japan*. Tokyo: Charles E. Tuttle Co., 1972.

Ebisawa, Arimichi. *Nihon no seisho: seisho wayaku no rekishi* (The Japanese Bible: History of Japanese translations). Tōkyō: Nihon Kirisuto Kyōdan Shuppankyoku, 1981.

Eden, Charles H. *Japan Historical and Descriptive.* London, 1877.

Elison, George. *Deus Destroyed: The Image of Christianity in Early Modern Japan.* Cambridge, Mass.: Harvard University Press, 1973.

The First Half Century of Madison University (1819–1869). Hamilton, N.Y., 1872.

Fisher, Jerry K. "Nakamura Keiu: The Evangelical Ethic in Japan." In *Religious Ferment in Asia,* edited by Robert J. Miller. Lawrence: University Press of Kansas, 1974.

Fortune, Robert. *Yedo and Peking: A Narrative of a Journey to the Capitals of Japan and China.* London, 1863.

Friend (Honolulu), 1852–68.

Fukuzawa Yukichi. *The Autobiography of Fukuzawa Yukichi.* Translated by Eiichi Kiyooka. Tokyo: Hokuseido Press, 1934.

Goble, Jonathan. "The Baptist Mission in Japan." *Freeman* (London), 2 August 1872, 377–78.

———. Letters. *American Baptist,* 1860.

———. *The Triumph of Faith.* Yokohama, 1882.

Graff, Henry F., ed. *Bluejackets with Perry in Japan: A day-by-day account kept by Master's Mate John R. C. Lewis and Cabin Boy William B. Allen.* New York: New York Public Library, 1952.

Greene, Daniel Crosby. "The Japanese Version of the New Testament." *Japan Evangelist* 13 (August 1906).

Griffis, Margaret Clark. Correspondence, diaries, and journal. W. E. Griffis Collection, Rutgers University.

Griffis, William Elliot. Correspondence, journals, and other manuscripts. W. E. Griffis Collection, Rutgers University.

———. *Hepburn of Japan.* Philadelphia: Westminster Press, 1913.

———. *A Maker of the New Orient: Samuel Robbins Brown.* New York: Fleming H. Revell Co., 1902.

———. *Matthew Calbraith Perry: A Typical American Naval Officer.* Boston, 1887.

———. *The Mikado's Empire.* 9th ed. New York: Harper & Brothers, 1900.

———. *Yokohama Guide, 1874.* Copy in Yokohama Archives of History.

Gustaitis, Joseph. "There's No Mistake in Sam Patch." *American History Illustrated* 25 (January / February 1991): 38–39, 74.

Hall, Ivan Hall. *Mori Arinori.* Cambridge: Harvard University Press, 1973.

Hartwell, J. B. Letter. *Commission* 5 (February 1861): 233–34.

Haruna Akira. *Hyōryū: Josefu Hiko to nakamatachi* (Drifting: Joseph Heco and his companions). Tōkyō: Kadokawa Shoten, 1982.

Heco, Joseph. *The Narrative of a Japanese.* 2 vols. Edited by James Murdoch. Yokohama, [1892]. Reprint. 2 vols. in 1. San Francisco: American-Japanese Publishing Association, n.d.

Hikozo [Joseph Heco]. *Floating on the Pacific Ocean.* Translated by Tosh Motofuji. Los Angeles: Glen Dawson, 1955. Originally published as *Hyōryūki,* 1863.

Humanity above Nation: The Impact of Manjiro and Heco on America and Japan. Honolulu: Joseph Heco Society of Hawaii and Japanese Cultural Center of Hawaii, 1995.

Illustrated News (London), 22 January 1853.
Inoue Tomoyoshi, Higashine Buichi, and Nakajima Yoshine. *Dotō o koeta otokotachi: Hyōryū shiryō kenkyū* (Men who overcame the raging sea: Studies of historical materials on sea drifting). Harima, Hyōgo Prefecture: Harima Education Committee, Town of Harima, 1997.
Ion, A. Hamish. *The Cross and the Rising Sun: The Canadian Protestant Missionary Movement in the Japanese Empire, 1872–1931.* Waterloo, Ontario: Wilfrid Laurier University Press, 1990.
———. "Edward Warren Clark and Early Meiji Japan: A Case Study of Cultural Contact." *Modern Asian Studies* 11, no. 4 (1977): 557–72.
———. "Edward Warren Clark and the Formation of the Shizuoka and Koishikawa Christian Bands (1871–1879)." In Edward R. Beauchamp and Akira Iriye, eds., *Foreign Employees in Nineteenth-Century Japan.* Boulder: Westview Press, 1990.
Isobe Hirodaira. *E. W. Kurāku to Shizuoka Gakumonjo.* Published by the author, 1996.
Iwata, Masakata. *Ōkubo Toshimichi: The Bismarck of Japan.* Berkeley: University of California Press, 1964.

Japan National Tourist Organization. *The New Official Guide: Japan.* Tokyo: Japan Travel Bureau, 1975.
Japan Queries & Answers, 6 May 1956, 6–8.
Johnson, Robert Erwin. *Far China Station: The U.S. Navy in Asian Waters, 1800–1898.* Annapolis: Naval Institute Press, 1979.
Jones, H. L. *Live Machines: Hired Foreigners and Meiji Japan.* Vancouver: University of British Columbia Press, 1980.
Josefu Hiko Kinenkaishi (Journal of the Joseph Heco Society). 1977, 1990, 1996.

Kadokawa Kiyoshi and Ōshiba Kō. *Nihongo seisho honyaku shi* (History of Japanese Bible translations). Tōkyō: Shinkyō Shuppansha, 1983.
Kaneko, Hisakazu. *Manjirō, the Man Who Discovered America.* Tokyo: Hokuseido Press, 1954.
Kadokawa Nihon Chimei Daijiten (Kadokawa encyclopedia of Japanese geography). Vol. 22. Tōkyō: Kadokawa shoten, 1990.
Kawashima Daijirō. Correspondence with author, 1978–98.
———. "Gōburu to Samupachi" (Goble and Sam Patch). *Genryū,* no. 4 (3 September 1983): 55–71.
———. *Jonasan Gōburu kenkyū* (Jonathan Goble studies). Tōkyō: Shinkyō Shuppansha, 1988.
———. *Jonasan Gōburu yaku "Matai fukuinsho" no kenkyū* (Study of Jonathan Goble's translation of the Gospel of Matthew). Tōkyō: Akashi shoten, 1993.
———. "Sentarō no hyōka ni tsuite" (Concerning an appraisal of Sentarō). *Tō no hikari,* no. 285 (February 1983): 1–2.
Kimura Ki, comp. and ed. *Japanese Literature; Manners and Customs in the Meiji-Taisho Era.* Translated and adapted by Philip Yampolsky. Tokyo: Obunsha, 1957.
Kitasawa Sukeo. *The Life of Dr. Nitobe.* Tokyo: Hokuseido Press, 1953.

Kobayashi Motoki. "Diversity from 'Double Desire': Why are there so many Japanese family names?" *East* 35, no. 6 (March/April 2000): 48–51.

Kodansha Encyclopedia of Japan. 9 vols. 1983.

Kodera Atsushi. "Nami no manimani: Kikokugo no Samu Patchi" (At the mercy of the waves: Sam Patch after his return to Japan). *Shimin gurafu Yokohama,* special number (1 November 1978): 37–40.

Kohl, Stephen W. "Strangers in a Strange Land: Japanese Castaways and the Opening of Japan." *Pacific Northwest Quarterly* 73 (1982): 20–28.

Kōhō Shizuoka, no. 704 (1 January 1985).

Krummel, John W., ed. *A Biographical Dictionary of Methodist Missionaries to Japan: 1873–1993.* Tokyo: Kyo Bun Kwan, 1996.

Kuykendall, Ralph S. *The Earliest Japanese Labor Immigration to Hawaii.* 1935.

Kuykendall, Ralph S., and A. Grove Day. *Hawaii: A History.* New York: Prentice-Hall, 1948.

Lewis, John Jas. "Sundown to Palestine." *Democratic Republican* (Hamilton, N.Y.), 7 January 1875.

Lind, A. W. *Hawaii's Japanese: An Experiment in Democracy.* Princeton, N.J.: Princeton University Press, 1946.

Loomis, Clara D. *Henry Loomis: Friend of the East.* New York: Fleming H. Revell, 1923.

Lutz, Jessie G. "Karl F. A. Gützlaff: Missionary Entrepreneur." In *Christianity in China: Early Protestant Missionary Writings.* Cambridge: Committee on American-East Asian Relations of the Department of History in collaboration with the Council on East Asian Studies / Harvard University, 1985.

Madison University Student Register, 1818–1856. Colgate University Archives.

Mason, Clara Arthur. *Etchings from Two Lands.* Boston, 1886.

McAlpine, James A. "The Rev. James Hamilton Ballagh, D.D." *Japan Christian Quarterly* 21 (April 1955): 168–70.

McCartee, D. B. *A Missionary Pioneer in the Far East: A Memorial of Divie Bethune McCartee.* Edited by Robert E. Speer. New York: Fleming H. Revell Co., 1922.

McClellan, Edwin North. "Sam Patch." *Honolulu Advertiser,* 28 May 1926.

Miller, Stuart Creighton. "Ends and Means: Missionary Justification of Force in Nineteenth Century China." In *The Missionary Enterprise in China and America,* edited by John K. Fairbank. Cambridge: Harvard University Press, 1974.

Minutes of the Fiftieth Anniversary of the Madison Baptist Association held in Cazenovia, Madison County, New York, September 8 & 9, 1858. Cazenovia, N.Y., 1858.

Missionary Album. Available in Hawaiian Mission Children's Society Library, Honolulu.

Miyachi Yasunobu. *Sentarō.* Tōkyō: Kyōkai Shimpōsha, 1982.

Miyoshi, Masao. *As We Saw Them: The First Japanese Embassy to the United States (1860).* Berkeley: University of California Press, 1979.

Mizugaki Kiyoshi. *One Hundred Years of Evangelism in Japan.* Translated by J. A. McAlpine. Columbus, Ga.: Quill Publications, 1986.

Morison, Samuel Elliot. *"Old Bruin": Commodore Matthew C. Perry 1794–1858.* Boston: Little, Brown, and Co., 1967.

Morris, J. *Makers of Japan.* London: Methuen & Co., 1906.

Morton, Oren F. *A History of Rockbridge County, Virginia*. 1920. Reprint, Baltimore: Regional Publishing Co., 1973.

Mukōyama Hiro. "Names and Lineages in Japan." Part 1. *East* 13 (November 1977): 8–12.

Murakami Mitsugi. "Kurobune no Nihonjin suifu" (Japanese sailor on a black ship). *Kaiji shi kenkyū* (Studies in maritime history). No. 7 (March 1982), 12–27. Expanded version of "Kurobune no Nihonjin suifu," *Shimin gurafu Yokohama*, special issue 1978, 34–36.

———. "Nichibei gaikō shijō ni arawareta Geiyo shojima no hyōryū sen'in" (Shipwrecked sailors from the islands of Aki and Iyo provinces as seen in the history of Japan-America diplomatic relations). *Kaiji shi kenkyū* (Studies in maritime history). No. 4 (March 1972).

Neill, Stephen. *A History of Christian Missions*. Baltimore: Penguin Books, 1964.

Nevius, Helen S. Coan. *The Life of John Livingston Nevius*. New York, 1895.

———. *Our Life in China*. New York, 1876.

Newcomb, Harvey. *A Cyclopedia of Missions; Containing a Comprehensive View of Missionary Operations throughout the World*, rev. ed. New York, 1855.

The New York Baptist Annual. 1873, 1894, 1915.

New York Daily Tribune, 1855.

New York Evangelist, 1872–75.

New York Times, 1859, 1866.

Nihon Baputesuto senkyō 100nen shi (Centennial history of Japan Baptist missions). Tokyo: Nihon Baputesuto Dōmei, 1973.

Nihon Kirisutokyō rekishi daijiten (Dictionary of Japanese Christian history). Tōkyō: Kyōbunkan, 1988.

Nihon rekishi gakkai, comp. *Meiji ishin jimmei jiten* (Biographical dictionary of the Meiji Restoration). Tōkyō: Yoshikawa Kōbunkan, 1981.

Nitobe, Inazō. *The Intercourse between the United States and Japan: An Historical Sketch*. 1891. Reprint, Wilmington, Del.: Scholarly Resources, 1973.

Notehelfer, F. G. *American Samurai: Captain L. L. Janes and Japan*. Princeton, N.J.: Princeton University Press, 1985.

———, ed. *Japan through American Eyes: The Journal of Francis Hall, Kanagawa and Yokohama, 1859–1866*. Princeton, N.J.: Princeton University Press, 1992.

Numajiri Tōru. "Baputesuto dee ni omou" (Thoughts on Baptist Day). *Baputesuto Kyōhō*, no. 271 (1 February 1983): 1.

Ogasa Yoshinori, "Kurobune ni notta Hiroshimajin" (Hiroshiman on a black ship), series of 44 articles in *Chūgoku shimbun*, 31 January–30 April 1994.

Okihiro, Gary Y. *Cane Fires: The Anti-Japanese Movement in Hawaii, 1865–1945*. Philadelphia: Temple University Press, 1991.

Ozawa Saburō. *Bakumatsu Meiji Yasokyōshi kenkyū* (Studies in Christian history in the closing years of the Tokugawa era and in the Meiji era). Tōkyō: Nihon Kirisuto Kyōdan, 1973.

———. *Nihon Purotesutanto Shi Kenkyū* (Studies in Japanese Protestant history). Tōkyō: Tōkyō Daigaku Shuppankai, 1964.

Pacific Commercial Advertiser, 1860–68.

Papinot, E. *Historical and Geographical Dictionary of Japan*. 1910. Reprint, with an introduction by Terence Barrow, Tokyo: Charles E. Tuttle Co., 1972.

Parker, F. Calvin. *Jonathan Goble of Japan: Marine, Missionary, Maverick*. Lanham, Md.: University Press of America, 1990.

Parker, Jenny Marsh. *Rochester: A Story Historical*. Rochester, 1884.

Paske-Smith, M. *Western Barbarians in Japan and Formosa in Tokugawa Days, 1603–1868*. 1930. Reprint, New York: Paragon Book Reprint, 1968.

———, ed. *Japanese Traditions of Christianity*. Kōbe: J. L. Thompson & Co., 1930.

Pedlar, Neil. *The Imported Pioneers: Westerners Who Helped Build Modern Japan*. New York: St. Martin's Press, 1990.

Perry, Matthew C. *The Japan Expedition, 1852–54: The Personal Journal of Commodore Matthew C. Perry*. Washington: Smithsonian Institution, 1968.

———. *Narrative of the Expedition of an American Squadron to the China Seas and Japan, Performed in the Years 1852, 1853, and 1854, under the Command of Commodore M. C. Perry, United States Navy, by Order of the Government of the United States*. Compiled by Francis L. Hawks. Washington: Beverley Tucker, Senate Printer, 1856. New York: D. Appleton & Co., 1856.

Pierson, Louise Henrietta. *A Quarter of a Century in the Island Empire or the Progress of a Mission in Japan*. Tokyo: Methodist Publishing House, 1899.

Plummer, Katherine. *The Shogun's Reluctant Ambassadors: Sea Drifters*. Tokyo: Lotus Press, 1984.

Pollay, F. C. "Japan in 1852." Unidentified newspaper clipping, 1904, transcribed by Herbert A. Wisbey Jr. *Crooked Lake Review*, no. 27 (June 1990).

Polynesian (Honolulu), 1852–60.

Pruyn, Mary. *Grandmamma's Letters from Japan*. Boston, 1877.

Rasmussen, Lewis J. *Railway Passenger Lists of Overland Trains to San Francisco and the West*. Vol. 1. Colma, Calif.: San Franscisco Historic Records, 1966.

Reformed Church in America. *Annual Report*. 1868–73.

Reischauer, Edwin O., and Albert M. Craig. *Japan: Tradition and Transformation*. Tokyo: Charles E. Tuttle Co., 1978.

Rosenberg-Naparsteck, Ruth. "The Real Simon Pure Sam Patch." *Rochester History* 52 (summer 1991): 1–23.

Satow, Sir Ernest. *A Diplomat in Japan*. 1921. Reprint, Tokyo: Oxford University Press, 1968.

Scientific American, 1851.

Schneider, Bernardin. "Japan's Encounter with the Bible." *Japan Christian Quarterly* 48 (spring 1982): 69–78.

Schurhammer, Georg. *Francis Xavier, His Life, His Times*. Translated by M. Joseph Costelloe. 4 vols. Rome: Jesuit Historical Institute, 1973–82.

Seat, Keith, ed. "Jonathan Goble's Book." *Transactions of the Asiatic Society of Japan*. 3d ser., 16 (1981): 109–52.

Sewall, John S. "With Perry in Japan." *Century Magazine* 70 (1905): 349–60.

Shigehisa Tokutarō. *Oyatoi gaikokujin: kyōiku, shūkyō* (Foreign employees: education, religion). Oyatoi gaikokujin, no. 5. Tōkyō: Kashima kenkyū shuppankai, 1968.

Shimin Gurafu Yokohama (Yokohama citizens' graphic), 1978–80.

Shizuoka. No. 704, 1 January 1985. Publication of Shizuoka City.

Shizuoka Shiyakusho, ed. *Shizuoka shishi: Sōmokuji nenpyō sakuin* (History of Shizuoka City: Chronological table and index). Shizuoka: City office, n.d.

Shu no ashiato (The Lord's footprints). Nos. 1–25, 1979–2000. Articles on Sam Patch published irregularly by Miyachi Yasunobu.

Smith, Bradford. *Yankees in Paradise: The New England Impact on Hawaii.* New York: J. B. Lippincott, 1956.

Smith, George. *Ten Weeks in Japan.* London, 1861.

Smith, James William. Journal, 26 April 1866–3 December 1879. Mission Houses Museum Library, Honolulu.

Spalding, J. W. *The Japan Expedition: Japan and Around the World.* New York, 1855.

Speiden, William Jr. Journal of a Cruise in the U.S. Steam Frigate Mississippi. Manuscript journal in 2 vols., 9 March 1852 to 16 January 1855. Naval Historical Foundation, Washington, D.C. Issued in microfilm by Scholarly Resources, Wilmington, Del.

Sugimoto, Etsu Inagaki. *A Daughter of the Samurai.* 1926. Reprint, Tokyo: Charles E. Tuttle Co., 1966.

Sugimoto, Masayoshi, and David L. Swain. *Science and Culture in Traditional Japan, A.D. 600–1854.* Cambridge, Mass.: MIT Press, 1978.

Takahashi Masao. *Nakamura Keiu.* Edited by Nihon Rekishi Gakkai. Tōkyō: Yoshikawa Kōbunkan, 1966.

Taylor, Bayard. *A Visit to India, China, and Japan, in the Year 1853.* New York, 1855.

Thirty-Sixth Annual Meeting of the Baptist Convention of the State of Michigan, 1871. Detroit, 1872.

Thompson, David. *Funeral Sermon Preached for Mrs. Margaret T. K. Ballagh.* Yokohama, 1909.

Totman, Conrad. *The Collapse of the Tokugawa Bakufu 1862–1868.* Honolulu: University Press of Hawaii, 1980.

Turner, Charles W., ed. *The Diary of Henry Boswell Jones of Brownsburg (1842–1871).* Verona, Va.: McClure Press, 1979.

Uchimura Kanzō. *How I Became a Christian: Out of My Diary.* Tokyo: Keiseisha, 1918.

Van Zandt, Howard F. *Pioneer American Merchants in Japan.* Tokyo: Lotus Press, 1980.

Wakukawa, Ernest K. *A History of the Japanese People in Hawaii.* Honolulu: Toyo Shoin, 1938.

Walworth, Arthur. *Black Ships off Japan: The Story of Commodore Perry's Expedition.* 1946. Reprint, Hamden, Conn.: Archon Books, 1966.

Warriner, Emily V. *Voyager to Destiny.* New York: Bobbs-Merrill Co., 1956.

Wildes, Harry Emerson. *Aliens in the East: A New History of Japan's Foreign Intercourse.* Philadelphia: University of Pennsylvania Press, 1937.

———. "The Kuroshiwo's Toll." *Transactions of the Asiatic Society of Japan.* 2d ser., vol. 17 (1938): 211–33.

Wiley, Peter Booth, with Ichiro Korogi. *Yankees in the Land of the Gods: Commodore Perry and the Opening of Japan.* New York: Penguin Books, 1991.

Williams, Frederick Wells. *The Life and Letters of Samuel Wells Williams, LLD.: Missionary, Diplomatist, Sinologue.* New York, 1889.

Williams, Harold S. *Foreigners in Mikadoland.* Tokyo: Charles E. Tuttle Co., 1963.

———. *Shades of the Past or Indiscreet Tales of Japan.* Tokyo: Charles E. Tuttle Co., 1959.

———. *Tales of the Foreign Settlements in Japan.* Tokyo: Charles E. Tuttle Co., 1958.

Williams, Howard D. *A History of Colgate University 1819–1969.* New York: Van Nostrand Reinhold Co., 1969.

Williams, S. Wells. "A Journal of the Perry Expedition to Japan (1853–1854)." Edited by F. W. Williams. *Transactions of the Asiatic Society of Japan.* Vol. 37, part 2 (1910): 1–259.

———. "Narrative of a voyage of the ship Morrison, captain D. Ingersoll, to Lewchew and Japan, in the months of July and August, 1837." Parts 1, 2. *Chinese Repository* 6 (1837): 209–29, 353–80.

Winn, M. Leila. "Dr. Ballagh of Japan." *Christian Intelligencer,* 28 April 1920.

Yanagawa, Masakiyo Kanesaburo. *The First Japanese Mission to America (1860): Being a Diary Kept by a Member of the Embassy.* Translated by Jun'ichi Fukuyama and Roderick H. Jackson. Edited by M. G. Mori. 1938. Reprint, Wilmington, Del.: Scholarly Resources, 1973.

Yamaguchi, H. S. K., et al. *We Japanese.* Combined edition of 3 books. Miyanoshita: Fujiya Hotel, ca. 1951.

Yazaki Takeo. *Social Change and the City in Japan: From earliest times through the Industrial Revolution.* Translated by David L. Swain. Tokyo: Japan Publications, 1968.

Yokohama omoide no arubamu (Yokohama album of reminiscences). Yokohama City, 1979.

Yonekura, Isamu. "Manjiro: the Remarkable Life of a Fisherman's Son." *East* 12, No. 4 (May 1976): 9–21.

Index

Page numbers in italics refer to illustrations

LaVergne, TN USA
25 February 2010
174144LV00001B/119/P